M000250426

NOT
WITHOUT
SCARS...

The Inspiring Life Journey of Mark C. Olds
As told to Christopher Broussard

An exciting new book capturing the life of Mark C. Olds
and unfolding a message of hope

NOT WITHOUT SCARS

Not Without Scars is a dramatic and heartening story that can educate and encourage anyone interested in the redemption of human beings, particularly young African American men who are walking the wayward path. It is proof that no life is beyond saving and in a time when many young men aspire to become the "gansta" that Mark Olds was, a refreshing sign of hope.

As this stirring tale unfolds, the reader will also receive an invaluable history lesson. Olds' life journey takes us through the infamous sharecropping system that enslaved many Blacks, including his family; the dysfunctional subculture created by Black Southerners whose migration up North left them disenfranchised; the militant period of the 1960's; the disturbing and perverse culture of prison; and even the birth of the hip-hop culture that now dominates the lives of America's youth.

This book has something for everyone: Black and White, young and old, rich and poor, Christian and non-Christian. Compelling and inspirational, historical and spiritual, *Not Without Scars* is an American success story.

Wardrobe selection by Brittney Ragin
Cover design by Tim Litton, Motion Media Group, 5368 Central College Road, Westerville, Ohio 43081
Front cover and back cover photographs by Barvern Pillow
Front cover background photos, family archives

MCO Media Group, Inc.
3798 Northwood Road
University Heights, Ohio 44118
Tel. 216-932-9949
Fax 216-932-9965
www.mcomediagroupinc.com

ISBN 0-9701337-0-7

ACKNOWLEDGEMENTS

No work such as this could be completed without the great contributions of several dedicated individuals, and I would like to give my sincerest thanks to all of those who played a part in transforming Not Without Scars from an idea into a reality. Extra special thanks goes to Shakeenah Bari-Harold, who transcribed a seemingly endless number of taped interviews; Reverend Dr. Harold Carter, Ernest Holsendolph, Howard Lyles, Miriama Whyte, Donna Whyte, Beverly Gaffney and Liz Presley-Fields, each of whom read early drafts and offered invaluable critiques; and Kathleen McElroy, who put on the finishing touches with her deft editing. I also want to thank Reverend Dr. Otis Moss, Reverend Milton Brown, Jack Best, Jasper Ormond and Willie and Douglas Olds for sharing many of their experiences and recollections of Mark C. Olds with me. I must thank my wonderful wife, Crystal Broussard, M.D., and my lovely twin daughters, Alexis and Noelle, for allowing "honey" and "daddy" to work overtime on this project. One of my greatest joys was sprinting upstairs and into the bedroom to show the completed version to you "Bay." Above all, I want to thank my Lord and Savior Jesus Christ for blessing and equipping me with the ability and the discipline to write this book in a way that will glorify Him and introduce one of his remarkable disciples to the world.

Published By:

MCO MEDIA GROUP, INC.
3798 NORTHWOOD ROAD
UNIVERSITY HEIGHTS, OHIO 44118
TEL. 216-932-9949
FAX 216-932-9965
www.mcomediagroupinc.com

DEDICATION

To the memory of

**Willie Grey Olds
And
Ida Mae Olds**

TABLE OF CONTENTS

Not Without Scars

*The Inspiring Life Journey of
Mark C. Olds
as told to Christopher Broussard*

PREFACE

*N*ot Without Scars - The Inspiring Life Journey of Mark C. Olds tells an intense and miraculous story in a way that makes it impossible for the reader to put down. Early on, Mark Olds, the son of sharecroppers in Farmville, North Carolina, raises the relevant question as to why a friend of his, Edwin, dies tragically in an automobile accident and yet he lives. Edwin, nicknamed "Smooth" by Mark, was about the good things in life. He graduated from North Carolina A&T State University and entered the Air Force. One weekend, on his way home from the military, a disastrous automobile accident took Edwin's life. The young Olds made the statement, "I wonder why he died despite following all the rules, and why I lived despite breaking them." It is this tension that runs throughout the book and makes it so compelling.

Mark Olds opens his life to us and lets us see him in all of his rebellion. We see his brief stints in college and his obsession with being the biggest and baddest drug pusher on the East Coast, with a dream of going international. We see his compulsion for gambling and witness him in his role as the vicious "Bronx Star," a hyper-violent character who was quick to take down anyone who crossed his path. Eventually, his defiant behavior caught up with him, and he landed in the Lewisburg (Pa.) Federal Penitentiary, one of the most ferocious prisons in America.

This is where I come in. While serving time as an inmate in Lewisburg, Mark heard our Sunday night New Shiloh Radio Ministry, which was beamed out of Baltimore, Maryland for one hour over WBAL Radio 11. God used this ministry to have a deep and abiding impact upon Mark's life. Mark quickly contacted our church, and we began a ministry in Lewisburg Penitentiary. Some years later, we were able to license and ordain Mark into gospel ministry, even setting apart a church he founded in the prison, The Solid Rock Baptist Church. To our knowledge, this is the only Christian Church ever founded by an inmate in a Federal Prison.

In the providence of God, Mark Olds, now a preacher of the gospel, was paroled from Lewisburg and granted his freedom. He has ministered at New Shiloh several times since then and has given evidence of rigorous study and focus in God's Word. I consider the Reverend Mark Olds a true friend whose amazing life story, yet unfolding, will provide the reader with a deeper sense of God's grace to forgive even the most wretched life and to transform that life into a model of servanthood in the work of redemption.

Thank you, Mark Olds, for making your life's story available to us. It can only encourage all of us to never give up on anyone. If change can occur in the life of one so completely rebellious and out of control, surely it can happen for all of God's people. Our God is no respecter of persons. This is the new spiritual resolve I have received from reading such a profoundly moving book.

Dr. Harold A. Carter Sr.
Pastor, New Shiloh Baptist Church
Baltimore, Maryland
March 3, 2000

FOREWORD

The contents of this book emerged out of a real life experience with an unidentifiable force. This force presents itself, manifests itself, and in the process, delivers a spiritual blessing that only God can identify. Praise Him! Truly, eye hath not seen, nor ear heard, neither have entered into the heart of the writer what God has in store for Mark Olds. It was my privilege to witness and in part, mentor Mark in his miraculous transformation. That is why it is an honor to write the foreword to this redemptive book.

In the early stages of my relationship with Mark, the "Why" question and thought was raised. Why leave 1,200 inmates to whom I had hands-on access and travel over 300 miles at my own expense to mentor and fellowship with one inmate? Having never seen or heard of Mark Olds before, this was a mystery even to me. I later realized that it was necessary to enter his domain, surrounded by the strict bureaucratic position of the U.S. Federal Bureau of Prisons, to gain his confidence and trust. He accepted my contribution and I have confidence in his ability to make a distinctive contribution to society. His ownership of perception, creativity and a maturity birthed in real-life experiences will lead him to be a productive contributor to humanity.

As we move into this New Millennium, this work can be used to gain much needed insight into the thoughts, fears, motives, and finally, the possibilities and promises, of the legions of young African-American men who, like the young Mark, are at risk of wasting the unique talents and gifts that God has given them. The miracle of redemption, as played out in this writing, describes liberation and deliverance from human-caused states of oppression; liberation that can only derive from God, the creator and sustainer of life. Prayerfully, this product, which speaks for itself in these contemporary times, will help to positively shape and develop the present and oncoming generations.

Once again, it is a personal privilege to share this insightful release. I praise God and congratulate the author and the publisher for their efforts in making this must-read publication a part of our library. To God be the glory!

Howard N. Lyles
Retired Warden, Maryland Division of Correction
1958-1988

INTRODUCTION

It was a miracle that I was even there. Me, a convicted felon - a man who had sold drugs, robbed banks, committed murder - on stage with the most powerful woman in the world. I wonder if Hillary Rodham Clinton, the First Lady of the United States, knew that she was being introduced to the most influential ministers in Cleveland, Ohio by someone who had spent one-third of his life in prison. She could not have known. Besides, even if my background had not bothered her, it certainly would have bothered the group of secret service agents that arrived at Olivet Institutional Baptist Church a week before Mrs. Clinton was scheduled to speak. Privileged, or perhaps burdened, with the responsibility of protecting the President's wife, they had combed every crack, crease and crevice of the church, taking note of all possible entries and exits to the building. The fact that Mrs. Clinton's audience of 300 people would be filled with decidedly partisan preachers and politicians did not stop this team of eight agents from running thorough, computerized background checks on anyone who might be in the vicinity of Olivet on October 31, 1996.

Which brings me back to me. I am not proud of my past but since I have truly experienced redemption, I am not ashamed to speak about it either. I have undergone about as much of a reformation as is possible, so much so that, while 25 years ago I would have gone to church only on Easter and on Mother's Day, on this October morning I was serving as the assistant to the pastor at Olivet, one of the most influential African-American churches in Cleveland. The pastor of Olivet, Reverend Dr. Otis Moss Jr., was in Martin Luther King's inner circle during the Civil Rights movement and in 1993 was honored as one of America's 15 greatest Black preachers by Ebony Magazine. His ministry has taken him to Israel, Japan, South Africa and South Korea as well as into the confidences of Presidents Jimmy Carter and Bill Clinton. In 1994, Reverend Moss accompanied President Clinton to the signing of the Peace Treaty between Israel and Jordan. Two years earlier, he had championed Clinton's presidential campaign in Cleveland, which is why Hillary Clinton was speaking at Olivet the week before the 1996 election.

Though we work well together, Reverend Moss and I are quite different. Taking a more traditional route, he began preparing himself early for a life in the ministry, earning bachelor's and master's degrees from Morehouse College and a doctorate from United Theological Seminary. I, on the other hand, grew up in the "sticks and the streets." Born and raised in rural North Carolina, I migrated to New York City as a teenager and there became what my brother Willie called "one of the most ruthless people" he has ever known. It was not until my fourth stint behind bars that I turned my life around, finally deciding to work toward being an asset rather than a detriment to society.

As one might imagine, I was in the distinct minority on that Halloween morning in 1996. Most of the men and women whom Mrs. Clinton addressed had more conventional backgrounds and many were notably accomplished in public service. Among those sitting on the dais or addressing the audience were Michael White, the African-American mayor who has overseen what many laud as the renaissance of downtown Cleveland; Congressman Louis Stokes, whose brother Carl won Cleveland's mayoral race in 1967 to become the first African-American mayor of a major American city; and the Reverend Dr. Larry Macon, the president of Cleveland's highly-regarded United Pastors in Mission.

And then there was me. To this day, I do not know why the President's secret service agents failed to raise the issue of my background. Perhaps it was out of respect for Reverend Moss and his judgment. Perhaps they had talked to him and been assured that I would not lapse back into my old ways of thinking and acting. Perhaps my positive work in the community since being released from prison in 1989 had outweighed my former delinquency or maybe they figured that as a leader of one of the city's most established churches, I would be beyond reproach and therefore chose not to check my past. Whatever the case, I believe it was an act of God because with all of the weapons and violence charges on my record, it was virtually inconceivable that I would be allowed anywhere near Hillary Clinton. But not only was I cleared to be on the program, I was given special S2 accessibility, meaning that I could go wherever the First Lady went. I still marvel at that, not because I am such a fan of Bill and Hillary Clinton's, but because it amazes me how far the Lord has brought me.

As the program's facilitator, I opened the ceremony with greetings and a responsive reading before introducing the speakers. My excitement increased as the dignitaries I announced grew in stature and significance, so by the time I spoke the words "The First Lady of the United States: Mrs. Hillary Rodham Clinton," I was overwhelmed by a sense of gratification. To my surprise, however, that feeling was surpassed by what I experienced upon handing the First Lady a glass of water while she was on stage. For me, the act was memorable not because I was serving a leading woman - even one as noble as the President's wife - but rather because I was in nearly the same position as the Old Testament prophet Nehemiah, who served as the cup bearer to the foreign king Artaxerxes.

I certainly do not equate myself to that great Biblical prophet, but I do have the same vision that Nehemiah had. As he prayed intently for the restoration of his people, the Hebrews, so do I for African-Americans. While I myself have become greatly privileged, I will not rest until my race as a whole has raised itself from the bottom rung of America's socioeconomic ladder. And like Nehemiah, I see social and political reform for our people beginning with spiritual renewal. Malcolm X believed that if African-Americans embraced Islam, it would change our moral behavior, endear us to the Creator and catapult us toward liberation in every aspect of life. Well, I believe that if we turn toward the Jesus Christ of the Bible - the true Jesus, not the watered-down, misrepresented Jesus of Western culture - that the end that Malcolm envisioned would become a reality. Of course, Nehemiah, invoking the laws of Moses, felt the same way about the plight of the Hebrews. So to find myself following in the footsteps of this prophet of old was both inspiring and prophetic. As soon as I handed the water to Mrs. Clinton, the parallels to Nehemiah began running through my mind and I took it as confirmation of what God can do with anyone, even a former criminal, who is sincerely committed to him.

Obviously, I was not always so committed, at least not to God. During the 1960s and 1970s, I was what today's young folks would call "a gangsta."

9

Stationed in New Haven, Connecticut and the Bronx, and traveling up and down the East Coast, I did everything from gamble away tens of thousands of dollars in a matter of months to rob supermarkets in broad daylight. I toted guns so frequently that they seemed like another clothing accessory and had a reputation for using them at the slightest hint of conflict. Until I was reformed during my final stay in the penitentiary, incarceration did nothing but encourage my reckless behavior. I likened going to jail to a boxer going to his corner during a prizefight. There, I was refreshed, able to analyze what I had done wrong, given better, more pertinent instructions and sent back out to raise havoc. By the time the police finally caught me for good in the fall of 1979, I was done with small-time thuggery and in the process of setting up international drug routes with ports of entry on both the East and West Coasts. Thankfully, those aspirations ended when I was arrested on a North Carolina highway less than an hour after robbing a bank in the town of Goldsboro. I was taken to Wake County Jail in Raleigh to await my trial and a judgment that would become a 30-year prison sentence.

Months later, after listening to an evangelist preach a three-hour sermon through the bars of a 16-man cell area, I committed myself to the Christian faith that my mother had tried to instill in me decades before. That put me on the path toward inner renewal and led to many wonderful opportunities on which I have been fortunate enough to capitalize. Even so, after becoming, to my knowledge, the first and only inmate ever to be ordained as a minister in the Federal Prison System, earning a master's degree from Case Western Reserve University, writing and publishing a book, starting a non-profit organization, and studying toward a Ph.D., I am not without scars from my past.

Chapter *I*

I KNOW WHY THE COUNTRY BOY WALKS SO SLOW

My options seemed to have dwindled down to two: life in prison or death. I had no presuppositions about death but after spending four years in prison, I figured it could not be any worse than being jailed. "Chances are it's even better," I said to myself. There was not much time to deliberate. I had to make a decision fast. A state trooper was on our tail, and I was sure that a police roadblock had been stationed just minutes up the highway. So, in keeping with the reckless way in which I had long been living, I reached into the satchel that held the tens of thousands of dollars I had just stolen and pulled out two pistols. For all intents and purposes, I had chosen death. When I uncovered the gleaming 45-caliber Smith and Wessons, thrusting them against my chest with all the histrionics of a Cowboy, my partner, Jack Best, threw his head back toward the top of the car, rolled his eyes and mumbled to himself, "My world." That let me know that Jack felt I was about to get him killed.

The thought of death had never entered Jack's mind when I asked him to assist me in robbing a bank in Goldsboro, North Carolina. Knowing that I was a veteran of such crimes, Jack thought this would be another easy and successful heist and quickly agreed to pick me up in a second getaway car. The scheme had called for me to take the bank alone, ditch my car near Jack's home and then hop into his car for a cruise to Fayetteville, which is about 60 miles southwest of Goldsboro.

11

Everything was going as planned until I uncharacteristically discarded evidence along U.S. Highway 13. Like an ill-prepared novice, I tossed the wig I had worn during the stickup out of the passenger's side window. As I watched the wind blow the wig into the center of the highway, the thought of how that would look to a state trooper performing a sweep maneuver made me realize that I had just made a monumental mistake. Whenever a robbery took place, troopers immediately conducted what was known as a sweep by driving north, south, east and west on every major thoroughfare in the vicinity. Even if they had little evidence to go on, they would drive at a high rate of speed, hoping to come across something suspicious or to force someone to react to them. And quite naturally, an afro wig blowing along the dividing line of the highway was suspicious.

Sure enough, soon after I dropped the wig, an oncoming state trooper flew by us en route to Goldsboro. As seasoned professionals, Jack and I had expected this and made no exaggerated movements; and Jack, of course, made sure to adhere to the speed limit. But the trooper spotted the wig and, since ours was the only car he had passed, made a screeching U-turn that let us know we were suspects. To double check, I told Jack to speed up. When he did, the trooper followed suit. Then, I told him to slow down at which point the trooper backed off his pedal. That's when we were certain that things were about to get complicated, that we could either turn ourselves in or partake in a showdown against the local sheriff's department, state troopers and FBI agents.

When I pulled out my guns, Jack knew that I had opted for the showdown. But he wasn't so brazen. A career criminal like myself, Jack was one of the coolest men I have ever known. He feared no man, least of all a cop, but he did not like guns. He was into safe crimes - those that were not likely to get you killed - such as selling drugs and pimping women. He always used to say that too many things can go wrong with a gun. But I did not share that opinion. I lived for firepower, often carrying AK-47s, sawed-off shotguns, nine millimeters and pistols, all while wearing a bullet-proof vest. Still, I knew I was not capable of taking out a dozen or so cops.

I knew Highway 13 as well as anyone, having driven it day and night while making my rounds from Goldsboro to Fayetteville to Raleigh to collect money from the drug pushers and prostitutes who worked for me. So though it was still out of view, I knew a sharp turn was approaching and that the cops' roadblock was likely to follow. I told Jack of this and then tried to sell him on the idea of a shootout.

"Look Jack, you're my friend, and I don't want you to die, but I ain't going back to prison. I'd rather die."

"Well, I wouldn't, so put 'em away," he shot back, beads of sweat racing down his forehead. "They'll blow both our heads off. Prison is better than death, man. And plus, if we escaped once, we can do it again."

We went back and forth a few times and then I grudgingly put the guns back into the money bag between my feet. My decision had nothing to do with my own desire to live, but was totally based on Jack's. He was my best friend, and I could not take his life just because I had nothing to live for. "I love you too much to get you killed," I blurted out, not really intending to verbalize my feelings. Relieved, Jack cracked a smile and sighed, "My world."

When we rounded the curve, there it was: a police roadblock that looked straight out of a Hollywood movie. Squad cars were parked on the highway, blocking every inch of the road. Cops stood resolutely behind their vehicles, their pistols and shotguns aimed in our direction. Clearly, there was no getting past them. As Jack hastily stopped the car and jumped out with both hands raised to the sky, I sat there contemplating, calculating my chances of winning this lopsided battle. In another time of year, I would have been able to kick open the car door, roll into a ditch and run off into the fields. But this was the fall, and all of the crops had been harvested, leaving nothing but clear land for acres and acres. As I waited for Jack to leave the danger zone, I sensed that the police were in the same mode as I. They too were waiting for Jack, and more importantly, for the state trooper who had been trailing us, to clear. As the trooper grabbed Jack and began walking him away from the line of fire, I realized that I was going to be fired on whether I made a move or not. I no longer had two choices. Now I had to shoot.

Just then, at the moment I had committed to go for my guns, the passenger door swung open and a hand grasped me firmly by the arm, accompanied by the words "Get into my car. I'm not going to let them hurt you." It was a state trooper who had sneaked around to the rear of our car while I was focusing on the armed policemen in front of me. For a couple of reasons, I did not resist or even attempt to go for my guns. First, I knew I was trapped. But beyond that, I found the trooper's grip to be somewhat comforting and protective. He did not grab me in confrontation or even draw his gun from his holster, so I was not intimidated. Then, when he led me to his car, he actually shielded me from the other cops, most of whom

13

remained steady with their guns pointed at me. I gathered from his badge that his last name was Albritton and I later found out that he was a Christian. I believe God used him that day as my guardian angel.

As I sat in the back of Trooper Albritton's car, peering through the dust covered window, I was engulfed by a state of numbness. I was so out of it that I almost felt like I was high. My condition was the result of the disturbing thoughts that raced through my head. Obviously, I was distraught about returning to jail, particularly since I had been so close to obtaining the type of wealth I had always lusted after. I dreaded going back to that restrictive, controlled environment. Faced with the reality of spending perhaps the rest of my life behind bars, I wondered how it had come to this, how my life had gotten so far out of hand that I was willing to give it up by engaging in a gunfight I knew I could not win. As Trooper Albritton began driving me away, I thought all the way back to my childhood for an answer.

Like many African-Americans, I was raised by a spiritual mother. The Freewill Baptist Church in Maury, North Carolina that we attended met just once a month, but whenever that Sunday rolled around, my mother, Ida Mae Olds, made sure she was there with her children. My father, Willie Gray Olds, almost never went to church. He had seen too much hypocrisy and too much money being passed from the pews to the pulpit to attend faithfully. Ultimately, he passed that attitude on to his seven sons, though not intentionally. I also had two sisters, Christine and Julia, which brought the total number of children in my family to nine. My father also had a son named Earl Freeman with another woman before marrying my mother, but Earl did not live with us. Marvin, my youngest brother, died of pneumonia when he was about 11 months old. Because of the lack of health care, infant mortality among Blacks in the South was high. Every family I knew had at least one child die as a baby. Later I would use those family tragedies to assume multiple identities and thereby enhance my criminal activity.

Marvin was my parents' last child so I grew up as the baby of the family. Of my five older brothers - Rufus, Aaron, Willie, James and Douglas - only three are still alive. Earl, my father's oldest son, was a Korean war veteran. He died from one too many bouts with alcohol. Rufus was killed in a car accident in 1953, and James died of cancer in 1994. My sister, Julia, died from lupus in 1981.

I was born on November 11, 1949 in Farmville, North Carolina, a town of less than 5,000 people. My parents named me Mark Carven Olds, but for the first 22 years of my life, my official name was Baby Boy Olds. In those days, the doctors who assisted in childbirth were responsible for filling out the birth certificates, and when it came to Black people, White doctors would sometimes rush through the process and record the first name simply as "Baby Boy" or "Baby Girl." For that reason, the family Bible, where the family tree was recorded, was regarded as the most legitimate record of identification among Blacks. In 1972, as I was nearing the height of my criminality, I used this travesty to my advantage by changing my legal identity to Carack McVen Olds, a name I came up with by rearranging my first and middle names as given by my parents. It was not until 1992 that I finally had the name on my birth certificate changed to Mark Carven Olds.

My first home was on a farm behind what was called "the ice house." The ice house played a significant role in the commerce of the community because that was where people literally went to buy ice. This, of course, was before electricity became prevalent in the rural South so ice was extremely valuable as a mode of refrigeration. Most families had a small piece of furniture they stored ice in to preserve their perishable goods. While the wealthiest people had electric refrigerators, most common folks made do with these ice boxes. And we certainly qualified as common, since my parents were caught up in the same unjust system that shackled many Black people during those days: sharecropping.

From what I saw, the word "share" had nothing to do with this shady business. "Slavecropping" would have been a more appropriate term. Under this system, Black families would rent a farm from a White owner or more commonly, a White middleman known as a subleaser or overseer. I did not know this then, but the Whites with good sense went off to college and became judges, congressman, doctors and the like. The ones who were not as sharp stayed in town, rented land from wealthy owners and became overseers. Of course, we didn't know these overseers were considered lowly by highbrow White folks so we respectfully referred to them as "Boss man," even though in reality they were a mere step above us on the social ladder. With this racially-biased, three-tiered system in place, it is easy to see why there were rarely any profits for the Blacks who actually worked the land. The system basically allowed Black families to make just enough money to survive. In a good year, a family might make $1,000, but more often than not, it was closer to $400. Sometimes, it was nothing.

Sharecropping was actually just a slightly kinder, gentler form of slavery, as there were many similarities between the two systems. For in-

15

stance, a Black sharecropping family could be thrown out of its home on a White man's whim. Blacks had no legal recourse because there were no written contracts and because the local judicial system was incredibly unjust. The reality was that, in the rural South, Blacks still had few, if any, rights that a White man was bound to respect. There also was the exploitation of children through free labor. That was commonplace, as Black boys and girls worked the fields while the family was paid as if only the father had worked. The solution to this was not as simple as a Black man deciding to keep his children out of the fields because again, if the White overseer was not pleased, he could simply toss the family off the land. I remember coming home from school, changing my clothes and heading straight to the fields, where I put in two or three hours of work before dark nearly every day.

The most popular crop in our area was tobacco. Tobacco season lasted from February, with the planting of the beds, to the end of the harvest in late August. After that, we would break for a week or two before harvesting the peanuts and the corn. Then, in late October and November, it was time to pick cotton. Though the winter months were slow, the overseers continued to profit off the Blacks by running up a tab at the local store. Because the stores would not sell anything directly to Blacks, we had to establish an account through the overseer that would allow us to purchase groceries and other necessary items. The overseer would collect on his tab during the tobacco market in early September. For example, if your crop sold for $10,000, half of the profit would automatically go to the overseer. Out of the $5,000 that remained, the Black family would have to pay for half of the fertilizer, half of the seed, and the sum total of whatever items they had purchased during the winter. This system might not have been so pernicious if the overseers had acted with integrity, but they would falsely inflate the Black family's bill to take 80 to 95 percent of its profit. Asking for an itemized statement did no good because the overseer would simply produce a bogus bill.

Having witnessed these practices for years, I cannot honestly say that any of the overseers were kind. But different ones treated us with varying degrees of civility or wickedness. One of the most nefarious was a man named Ralph Stokes, who was known throughout the county as R.R. Stokes. No one knew what the other R stood for, but we used to call him "Roguish Ralph" because he was always stealing from folks. His one act of benevolence each year was to give us a $4 box of oranges for Christmas. But after he had ripped us off all year long, it was hard to be appreciative. I was about 10 years old when we worked for Ralph and I interacted personally with him only once. The incident left such an impression on me that I can recall it as if it happened yesterday.

At the time, I was a solid student who was exceptionally good with numbers. My mathematical ability came in handy in the system we had for working the tobacco fields. My brothers would bring the tobacco from the fields, and the women would put it on sticks outside of the barn. At the end of the day, we usually had anywhere from 450 to 500 sticks. There were four rooms in the barn, and my job was to keep count of how many sticks we had so at the end of the day the guys would know how many to hang in each room for curing. Because I was so good with numbers, I would always keep the count in my head instead of writing it down on paper. Usually, my mother or someone else in the family would ask me for the count and I would proudly rattle it off with no problem. But on this day, it was Ralph who asked me for the count, and as soon as he got near me, I froze.

I can still hear his booming voice loud and clear, saying "How many sticks do we have boy?" Part of my fright may have been because Ralph was 6-feet-4 inches tall and spoke with forcefulness and authority, at least around us. But most of it was because he was a White man who was standing over me, making a demand. My mother, calling me by the initials of my first and middle name, kept saying, "Go ahead M.C. Tell him how many sticks there are." But I just went blank. I went to pieces. I could hear my mother saying my initials, but all other mental apparatus had shut down. I started to write numbers on the ground to add them, thinking that if I could see them, I could add them and not have to look up at that imposing figure staring down at me. But as his shadow covered the numbers I had scratched on the ground, I got this awful feeling in the pit of my stomach. When I could not produce an answer, Ralph just laughed, as if pleased that he had intimidated me.

Because of our size, my family had it good compared to many share-croppers. Large families were able to rent large farms, so when most of my brothers were at home we stayed in big houses and were able to keep a relatively nice car. We also were one of the first Black families to get a television set. People would come from miles around to watch our T.V. When a popular program such as "The Ed Sullivan Show" or "The Nat 'King' Cole Show" was on, we would have as many as four or five families crammed into the living room of our home. The only two Black shows at the time were Nat 'King' Cole's and "Amos and Andy." Both shows were hits in our house, even though the buffoonery of "Amos and Andy" promoted every destructive stereotype that had been cast upon Black people. I think Blacks watched it despite its negative portrayals because we were just happy to see our people on television, particularly when cast as something other than the servants of Whites. Nat 'King' Cole's show, on the other hand, was what I would call a role model show. He sang and played the piano and interviewed guests - all on *his* show. My introduction to the concept of boycotting came when Budweiser dropped its sponsorship of Nat's show, thereby forcing it off the air. In protest, Black men throughout the country stopped drinking Budweiser products.

The cars and television were about the only signs of advantage we had since there was little variety in the clothing styles of sharecroppers' children. We all shopped at the same few stores, which usually were owned by landowners, so everyone wore the same drab shirts and pants. I look back and laugh because in school it actually looked like we had uniforms. You could identify the sharecroppers of a particular region, whose farm they lived on, and which store they shopped at all by the clothes on their backs. In my area, our outfits consisted of a pair of brown or gray slacks, a pair of "Western" brand blue jeans, a flannel shirt, some brogan shoes and a tobogan hat. Luckily, I was able to break the monotony every once in a while by wearing some of my brothers' old hand-me-downs.

Every two or three years, my family was forced to move because the landowners did not want us to stay in any one place for too long. Even so, I still saw nothing but the same North Carolina farmland because we always moved within the 20- to 25-mile radius of Greene and Pitt counties. And unlike the typical American family, we did not move up; we moved down. Whenever my brothers turned 15 or 16, they would go up North, which of course lessened the amount of help my father had on the farm. So every couple of years, as my father's value to the landowners decreased, we moved onto a smaller farm with a smaller house. By the time I was a teenager, home was a tiny place and new cars were a thing of the past. The days were past when my father purchased a new car every other year, that ended in 1955 when he purchased his last new vehicle: a Pontiac Star Chief. While the Pontiac was nice, my father's dream had been to buy a Cadillac. But my mother told him that the White folks would shoot him if they saw him driving around in his own Cadillac. They laughed about it, but judging by his decision, there obviously was some truth to her statement.

In my adolescent ignorance, I did not have much respect for my father. My disgust for sharecropping led to a dislike for him, as I concluded that he was not able to financially provide for us. But as I have grown older and more knowledgeable, I have developed great respect for him. A third-generation free man, he went to school through the eighth grade. He had a rigid upbringing that he never talked about, but I learned from other family members that his father, Granson Olds, worked his boys like slaves. Granson Olds was a landowner and one of the most respected men in his community. Because he had the ability to negotiate and settle people's disputes, he was renowned for his wisdom. On Sunday afternoons, dozens of people would travel from the surrounding areas to hear him speak. Despite his favorable reputation in the community, my grandfather governed his house so strictly that when he died, his children did not want to claim anything he owned. As for my grandmother, all I know about her is that she died when my father was young.

Because of the way he was raised, my father never laid a hand on us. But we were afraid of him nonetheless. He stood 5 feet 8 inches tall, weighed 155 pounds and looked like someone had carved him out of a piece of granite. I spent 16 years of my life in prison with guys who lifted weights everyday and never saw anyone as awesomely built as him. He was the strongest little man I have ever seen. While my brothers and I would lose our breath just walking unencumbered across the plowed ground of our farm, he would put a 200-pound bag of fertilizer on each shoulder, balance them and move gracefully through the uneven soil, whistling as he went. His strength must have come from his many years of farming. I bet he was a wonder during his younger days because he was a tireless worker in his 30s and 40s.

My father had a unique way of dealing with the overseers: he would never let them into our house. Whenever one came up the driveway, my father rose quickly and met him outside. For years, I thought he was kowtowing to Whites but later I understood the reasoning behind his actions. With his makeup, he was not going to let a White man come into our house and talk down to him in front of his family. My father would have gone off on a White man for doing that and that would have gotten us kicked off the land. So he chose to meet them outside and made sure that their conversations were always out of the earshot of his children. For that reason, I never heard a White man say anything disrespectful to my father. But I do remember one incident that must have been a heated exchange. I could not

19

hear what was being said, but I could tell by the gestures of both men that they were arguing. When the White man left, my father went and got his shotgun. The overseer never came back, but we moved the next year.

While my relationship with my father was strained as a child, my mother and I had a special bond. A deeply religious woman, she always seemed to be praying and fasting, and even though everyone else in the house thought it ridiculous, she paid tithes to the church regularly. Her spirituality did not stop her from whipping us, though, as she adhered to the paraphrased Biblical quotation "spare the rod, spoil the child." Since my father refused to hit us, he would simply report us to Mama. At 5-foot-5, 150 pounds, she was able to put the fear of God in us.

My mother's father was named Mark Tillman Wilkes. A first-generation free man and a landowner, he also was held in high regard throughout his community. He was among the three founding fathers of the Maury Chapel Freewill Baptist Church, to which many of my family members still belong. Like Granson Olds, Mark Tillman Wilkes was rigid in the running of his household, to the point that his wife, Mary Wilkes, referred to him as Mr. Wilkes.

It was not uncommon in those days for Black men to rule their homes in a somewhat despotic fashion or for Black women to refer to their husbands as Mister. I believe this was due partly to their adherence to the Bible, where Abraham was called Lord by his wife, Sarah, and partly to the injustices that Black men experienced within the majority society. After being mistreated all day by the White man and his racist system, Black men could only receive affirmation of their value and manhood at home from their wives and children and within their particular community. So, many times the wife would give the man the respect he could not find elsewhere by calling him Mister. It is unfortunate that many men behaved so brutally toward their families, but I believe that is where they drew their strength from, where they were allowed to display their leadership. Having just come out of slavery, few of them comprehended how to build and maintain loving familial relationships or understood that they could have more effectively obtained the respect they craved by displaying affection rather than cruelty.

In my extended family, all of the women went to church while most of the men stopped going during their teenage years. This is still the case among many African-Americans as Black women outnumber Black men by more than a 4 to 1 ratio in the church. On any given Sunday, you can drive through a Black neighborhood and see churches filled with Black women and their children. I often look at the young boys who are there without their fathers and lament because I know that as soon as they can make their own decision about attending church, most of them will choose to stop going. Some of these boys will grow up to become great professional athletes and entertainers, but they likely will not keep the values they were taught in church because there was no man in the house to provide a godly example. In the worst-case scenario, some will get involved in crime and end up dead or in jail.

Where I came from, it was customary to attend church once a month because one preacher usually had four separate congregations. So he would have his First Sunday church, his Second Sunday church, his Third Sunday church and his Fourth Sunday church. Of course, televisions and telephones were not popular so going to church was a social event. In addition to being the spiritual headquarters of the community, the church building was the social hub, where folks from separate counties gathered to share information.

The prevailing theology of that era stated that a child's sins were upon his parents until the age of 12. So anyone who died before turning 12 would automatically go to heaven. Thus, whenever children began approaching their 12th birthday, they were rushed to the baptismal pool so they would be safe if they died after 12. I was baptized early, at age 10, and at the time, I did not have the slightest notion of the true meaning of salvation. I simply did it because it was time for me to join the church on my own, not because I had seen the light. I still was too young to tell my mother that I wasn't going to church so I really didn't have any say in the matter; I would be baptized and that was that. The only spiritual instruction I received after baptism was from a deacon who told me that, since I was now a full-fledged member of the church I could no longer play marbles because that was gambling.

As I grew older and began developing my own opinions about church, I concluded that it was a scam set up by the preachers to control people. One reason I felt this way was because all of the preachers I knew, married or not, were dating my cousins, and from the looks of things, everyone else's too. I watched how the sisters catered to the preachers, and at times it made me envious and other times upset. It was easy for me to see that their Sunday declarations of prayer and purity were nothing more than holy-sounding lip service. Upon realizing that, I tuned them out completely.

21

One day, my insolence toward preachers angered one of my aunts when I refused to clean the pastor's spittoon. I thought the way he hacked into that thing during his emotionally arousing sermons was disgusting and I told her as much, saying "I ain't putting my hands nowhere near that spit." From that day forward, I was labeled as a rebellious child because I did not want to wait on the preacher. My disregard for church manifested itself in other, more destructive ways a few years later. After I turned 14, my friends and I would go to church whenever there was an evening service - during this period, many churches held midweek prayer meetings - and steal gasoline from the preacher's car. We targeted the preacher's car because we figured he could afford the most gas. Stealing the gas was incredibly easy. All we did was suck on a rubber hose, stick it in the gas tank and watch as the gas came pouring out. My companions were old enough to drive, so the gas allowed us to roam the county free of charge.

Despite its many deficiencies, at least the church was a Black-owned, Black-run institution. It was the only organization of consequence in the rural South that was funded entirely by Black dollars and therefore was free to speak with its own voice. The schools were segregated so they certainly were Black, but the ramshackle books were outdated ones that the White schools no longer wanted. In essence, the White folks determined our curriculum. Even after the Supreme Court's ruling against "separate but equal" schools and the subsequent Civil Rights Movement, our schools remained either all Black or all White. The government may have been going into the urban areas of the South and desegregating schools but no one was riding into Farmville, Snow Hill and Bethel, North Carolina forcing Blacks and Whites to sit down in class together.

It would have been nice to have gone to the schools that were closest in proximity to us, regardless of their racial makeup, if only to eliminate those two-hour bus rides. I used to get up at 6:00 in the morning, catch the bus at 6:30, pass a few White schools on the way, and arrive at my school at 8:30. Avoiding those long and boring bus rides, however, was my only motivation for integrating with White folks. They didn't want to be with us so I didn't want to be with them. That was my take on the situation. When the local leaders tried to follow the law and place some of us in a White school, I wasn't even considered. My name was never mentioned in the same breath with integration. They did take a few of my female cousins of the same age, though. They put them on the bus with about 50 White kids, and the White kids tormented them fiercely. On the ride to school, in the classroom, on the

22

playground, and on the ride home, they relentlessly threatened them, calling them every racial epithet in the book. It was so bad that my cousins returned to the Black school after only three days.

It would have surprised no one if my cousins had been maimed or killed while attempting to integrate the schools. Occasional White-on-Black violence was an accepted part of life. The Ku Klux Klan was still powerful in our area and once a month its hooded members would march or form a motorcade through the Black parts of the county, just to show us that the country's inclinations toward racial tolerance had done nothing to change their views or diminish their strength. I can recall a number of lynchings by the Klan, the most gruesome of which was performed on Delbert Lee, a teenager who was the same age as me. Delbert was always interacting with White folks and probably considered many of them to be his friends. He used to coax Black girls into messing around with the White boys. That's where his value was to his so-called friends. But evidently, some Klansman didn't like the fact that Delbert had made a practice of crossing the color line. So one night, they kidnapped him, beat him to the point of death, and then ran a pipe up his rectum. While a wave of horror swept over the Black community, the local police department neglected to conduct even a scant investigation. The predominant feeling was that Delbert had brought misfortune upon himself by hanging out with White folks. The incident only served to heighten the already prevalent sentiment among Blacks that if you get involved with Whites, something tragic will eventually happen to you.

Though cavorting with White folks was the furthest thing from my mind, my parents worried that something similar might befall me because, my earlier episode with Roguish Ralph notwithstanding, I rarely displayed the typical deference that most Blacks did for White people. I was always saying that I wouldn't let them do this or that to me and oftentimes grew visibly angry when discussing them. My attitude had been shaped by my frequent trips to see my brothers, Willie in New York City and Aaron in Washington, D.C. When I turned 11, I began spending every summer with Willie in New York. I believe my parents sent me up there so I would be exposed to something other than a sharecropper's existence.

Willie was 13 years older than me, so he had left North Carolina for the Bronx in the late-1950s. Like most of the guys who migrated from the South, he was grateful for the opportunities he found up North and showed it by working hard at anything and everything. That was typical of Southerners in New York so employers often preferred to hire them over the locals. Though there was still plenty of racism up North, the society had a different feel because the discrimination was less blatant. Compared to the South, you witnessed little overtly racist treatment by Whites and hence, little overtly submissive responses from Blacks. A more sophisticated mind would have seen the tension beneath the facade, but being a youngster from the South, I did not pick it up.

When I visited Willie in 1962, he was working in a factory. One day he promised to take me to see the San Francisco Giants play the New York Mets at the old Polo Grounds. Up to that point, the only ballpark I had ever seen was a barren pasture in Maury, North Carolina. That's where they used to play games on what could be referred to as baseball's version of the Chitlin' Circuit.

With the integration of professional baseball in 1947, the Negro Leagues had disbanded, but scores of informal minor leagues continued to thrive in the Black communities of rural North Carolina. Every little town had its own team made up of players in their teens and early 20s. Games would be played on Sundays. There was no official way of paying these minor leaguers, but the teams would always bet on the game, with the victors splitting the winnings among themselves. Few teams had uniforms and there were no stadiums, just barren fields with bases. Some fields had wire that served as a backstop behind home plate and homemade bleachers, but for the most part, the hundreds of fans in attendance stood along the foul lines, enjoying the barbecued pork and corn liquor that was sold by vendors. And while all the players, managers, vendors and organizers were Black, there was always a healthy number of White people in the crowd. They could not get enough of watching Blacks play baseball in the dynamic, carefree way that made the Negro Leagues so lively.

Though they may sound bush, these minor leagues were actually a testament to the entrepreneurial spirit of Black people. In fact, before Jackie Robinson broke Major League Baseball's color barrier, leagues like this served as the minors of the Negro Leagues. There was plenty of talent on display in those pastures. Jim Ray Hart, who went on to play third base for the San Francisco Giants, played for a team from Snow Hill. And he had two older brothers who, though they never played professionally, were reputed to be better than him. I never played in the league but as soon as I was old enough to stop going to church, I was there to watch as often as possible.

Willie was aware of the enthusiasm I had for baseball, particularly for my favorite player, the Giants' Willie Mays, and he knew how much of a thrill I would get out of attending a game at a Major League stadium, so he purchased two tickets for a Mets-Giants game one afternoon. To his surprise, though, his supervisor would not give him the day off. He even threatened to fire Willie if he left work that afternoon. With a wife and child at home, Willie could not afford to lose his job, but he felt such a binding sense of obligation to keep his promise to me that he left the factory and never returned. I didn't know any of that at the time but when I found out years later, I viewed it as a prime example of the loyalty that has always existed among myself and my brothers. No matter what the endeavor, no matter how strange or off the wall it was, we could always count on one another for support. We never expressed our love for each other verbally; we just acted it out. When I found out that Willie had sacrificed his job just to keep a promise to me, I was greatly moved. He knew how much it would mean to me to return to the South having seen Willie Mays play. He knew the type of lasting effect that would have on a poor country boy from North Carolina, so he spared no expense to see that I enjoyed that experience. And I honestly believe that my other brothers would have done the same thing.

Fortunately, everything worked out for both Willie and me. He quickly found another job, and I got to realize the dream of every American boy - seeing his hero play in a Major League game. Mays was not the star of that day's game - his teammate, Chuck Hiller, hit the game-winning home run in the 10th inning of a 2-1 Giants victory - but he still was the coolest guy in the world to me. My fondness for Mays went beyond his playing ability. In my eyes, he was a Black man who had the world by the throat, even the racist world in which we lived. He was the first Black male fashion model that I can recall, and I used to dream of the day when I'd be able to wear the types of Petrocelli and GGG suits that he sported routinely. Though we waited for him after the game, I was unable to get his autograph but I did get to see him in person, which up to that point was the highlight of my life.

The summer before, I had seen the world middleweight champion, Sugar Ray Robinson, getting his hair conked at a barbershop in Harlem. When he left the shop and drove off in a pink Mercury automobile, I almost flipped, especially because there was a six-foot blond sitting in the front seat beside him. That was the first time I had ever seen an interracial couple, in real life or in the movies. Where I was from, a Black man could be lynched for even looking at a White woman, so to see Sugar Ray with his arm around a gorgeous blond in broad daylight blew my mind. It was really baffling because he wasn't looking around for White men and didn't appear to be nervous at all. After seeing that, I knew why he was the middleweight champion of the world. He had to be terrible.

The sightings of these two world famous Black men, combined with what I perceived to be a lack of blatantly racist attitudes, led me to believe that New York was some sort of Black promised land. This was especially true after reading in the newspapers about Cuban president Fidel Castro's stay at the Black-operated Theresa Hotel in Harlem. I read that on a trip to the United Nations, Castro chose the Theresa over a plush downtown hotel because he said he wanted to be with his people. That impressed me and I brought it up a few years later in an eighth-grade history class in North Carolina.

We were discussing communism and democracy when I asked the teacher, Ms. Viola Vines, if she would rather be the leader of a communist country or a second-class citizen in a democratic country. You would have thought that I had committed a criminal act the way Mrs. Vines tore into me, raising her voice while telling me how awful those communists were, how poor everyone in Cuba was and how they didn't have any freedom. As she shouted, I thought to myself, "That sounds a lot like what Black folks are experiencing here in America." I responded to her tirade by saying that Castro, as the leader of a communist country, was getting respect all over the world so I would rather be in his shoes than to be living here. Then she started again, railing at me about how great things were in America and how fortunate we were to be Americans. While she eloquently defended the rights that I didn't think she had, I sat there thinking, "Doesn't this lady see the poverty, the discrimination, the lynchings, the Whites with the best of everything and the Blacks with the worst of everything?" It truly struck me as odd how a Black person could feel so patriotic toward a country that displayed outright hatred for her and her people.

Though I never did, I would have loved to have posed that same question to Willie Morris, my sixth-grade home room and world history teacher. Based on what he had to work with, Mr. Morris taught his subject well. Of course, the books he used said nothing about Africa's glorious past and instead misrepresented it as the "dark continent." I have often wondered whether he was ignorant of the former civilizations of Africa or knew the truth and simply chose not to tell us because he thought it would cost him his job. I would bet on the latter because I cannot see how a man as intelligent and as thorough as he was could have had no knowledge of Africa's rich history.

During my younger years, I liked school because it was a place where I could excel. I attribute that to my father, who always encouraged us to read the newspaper. I did not realize it then, but he made a huge financial sacrifice to make sure that our family had a daily subscription to the Raleigh News and Observer. He always wanted us to know what was going on outside of our small community, so every day after he read the paper, we read it. When my older brothers began moving away and the money situation got tighter, we had to cancel our subscription; but I would still buy the paper as often as possible. In fact, the first crime I ever committed was stealing the News and Observer. It cost a dime to get the newspaper out of the boxes, but pennies worked just as well. So I regularly bought the papers at a ninety percent discount. I also was able to read a lot of books, thanks to the bookmobile. When I was in the seventh grade, this library-on-wheels began moving throughout the county. The librarians-in-transit would bring books to one person's home and, for three or four hours, everyone in the community would be able to check out books.

One great thing about those segregated schools, particularly on the elementary level, was that, while they lacked courses in Black history, they gave us a solid foundation in reading, writing and arithmetic. They also provided us a corps of teachers who sincerely cared about us and had our best interests at heart, even Ms. Vines. Because we were all Black and all fighting against a clear and common enemy, the teachers had a vested interest in seeing us succeed, which created a true sense of camaraderie at the school. In most instances, the teachers were from the area, so they either went to school with our parents or taught our parents. In this close-knit community atmosphere, it was nothing for a teacher to give us a whipping at school and then send us home to our parents for another one.

That is not to say that our school system was totally inclusive because it wasn't. One of the saddest legacies of American slavery is the rampant division within the Black community. That much of White America views the Black race as a monolith proves how ignorant many Whites are of African-American culture. In reality, that notion could not be further from the truth. Among other things, the infamous Willie Lynch speech of 1712 and the subsequent application of its thesis by Southern slave owners did much to dissolve any semblance of Black unity, during and after slavery.

Lynch's speech, a portion of which has been circulating throughout Black America for the past few years, was directed to slave owners in Virginia who were having trouble with unruly slaves. Lynch was a renowned plantation owner in the West Indies who treated his slaves so brutally that the term "lynching" was taken from his name. He addressed the issue of slavery in a seven-page speech that promised to "have a fool-proof method for controlling" slaves. He added that if his plan was "installed correctly it will control the slaves for at least 300 years." In a nutshell, Lynch's diabolical scheme instructed slave owners to magnify the differences between their slaves. "These methods have worked on my modest plantation in the West Indies and they will work throughout the South," Lynch said before giving a list of differences: "age, color (or shade), intelligence, size, sex, size of plantation, attitude of owner, whether the slaves…have fine hair or coarse hair…" Before concluding Lynch stated, "Don't forget, you must pitch the old Black against the young Black male and the young Black male against the old Black male. You must use the dark-skinned slaves against the light-skinned slaves…" Obviously, it has not yet been 300 years since Lynch's speech, and clearly many African-Americans, after having this destructive attitude passed down from generation to generation, are still divided over their differences, one of the most emphasized of which is skin color.

Perhaps predictably, light-skinned Blacks have been viewed as superior to dark-skinned Blacks since slavery; the obvious reason being their closer physical resemblance to Whites. This warped way of thinking has infected every sphere of Black life, from conceptions of beauty to educational opportunities to socioeconomic status. For instance, drive through the government-owned housing projects of any major city and 95 percent of the Blacks you'll see will have brown or dark skin. Where I was from, light-skinned Blacks did not have a lot to do with dark-skinned Blacks. One girl I grew up with committed suicide because her mother would not let her date a dark-skinned boy. The same dynamics were at work up North, where Black women chased after Puerto Rican men because they had straight or curly hair. A lot of those sisters wanted nothing more than to get pregnant by a Puerto Rican so their babies would have "good hair." This type of discrimination was prevalent even within my own family, where relatives treated my brothers who are light-skinned differently than those of us who are dark.

Back then, the significance of skin color and other distinctions became more of an issue with age. As Blacks went from being children to teenagers to adults, they became increasingly aware of their menial position in society and more troubled about their prospects of attaining a respectable standard of living. This state of precariousness came into play during my high school years when I was victimized by what I call the "Black aristocrats," which included the educators, because I was the son of a sharecropper.

When it was time for me to go to college, I had no idea that student loans were available because the teachers had kept such information hidden. If you were not a part of the Black aristocracy, they didn't tell you about those loans. When I discovered this years after I had left high school, I was terribly disappointed because I couldn't believe our teachers would do that to us. I think they felt like they had no other choice because they were vying for limited resources. Though they may have been near the top of the Black socioeconomic ladder, the aristocrats still were struggling financially; especially the teachers, who could not afford to send their children to college on their small salaries. So without the loans, their children would not be able to go to school either, and since there was only so much money available, they felt like they had to eliminate a certain number of us from contention.

If I had known what was going on at the time, I might have thrown in the academic towel much earlier; but being ignorant of their deception, I waited until high school to stop applying myself. Though I continued to get above-average grades, I honestly cannot remember learning anything of substance after the seventh or eighth grade. At that time, I became more concerned with emulating my older brothers, only one of whom had graduated from high school, than with studying.

All of my brothers had reputations for getting the girls and beating up the guys, so when I came along, everyone assumed that I was as tough as the rest of the family. The problem was, I was much smaller than my brothers. They all reached full size - about 5-feet-10, 170 pounds - by their 14th birthdays. I, on the other hand, was 5-foot-5 and extension-cord thin when I entered high school. So, to overcompensate for my lack of size, I fought more than anyone. It didn't take much at all to get me riled; a dirty look, a smart remark, a rumor was all the provocation I needed to go off. Though most of my fights were against Blacks, a group of four or five of us would cut class every now and then to go and fight the boys from the nearby White school. While it was never stated publicly, I think we all got a feeling of retribution from whipping them.

My most hostile act as a schoolboy occurred in the ninth grade, when I threw a brick at a female teacher for disciplining me in front of my classmates. Fortunately, my aim was as bad as my intentions, and no one was hurt. It's hard to believe I did something so ferocious at such a young age, but it shows how wild I had become. For my actions, I was rightfully expelled and forced to attend school in another county.

Because of my smallish stature, I never competed in any of the school's athletic programs. It wasn't until my home became the penitentiary that I began playing organized sports on a consistent basis. But I got involved in school sports in other ways. Still somewhat a mathematical wizard, I became what I believe was the first statistician in the history of the H.B. Sugg High School football team.

Though I never played organized football, I knew the sport well. It was one of my favorite subjects to read about when the bookmobile came around. I remember shocking the coaches and players by presenting them with statistics such as average yards per carry and punt. I even recorded each individual play and how successful it was and gave the coaches a detailed synopsis at halftime. Pitt County football had never seen anything like it, and that was one of the first mental achievements I ever took pride in. Those natural organizational skills, which I later honed behind bars, are what gave me a small degree of marketability upon my final release from prison.

I was the only child still at home during my high school years so my family no longer had value as sharecroppers. My father began doing construction work and odd jobs and my mother's first job off the sharecropper's role was as a maid for a Dr. Smith and his family in Snow Hill. My mother was very intelligent and her career as a maid was short-lived. She quickly moved from being a maid to a baker at the local high school to a social worker for the county. With her smarts, boldness and dedication to justice, she played a huge role in improving the way migrant workers were treated in eastern North Carolina. Her accomplishments taught me a great deal about the transitory stages one encounters in life and how it is important not to let others hinder the potential that lies within you. My mother also provided a great example of Christian faithfulness, consistently doing volunteer work at Maury Chapel as the secretary in charge of both records and finances. That experience proved valuable when she entered the workplace because it had developed her administrative and communicative skills.

During her time as Dr. Smith's maid, my mother would often bring home hand-me-down clothes from his children. But the last things I wanted to wear were a White boy's retreads. Having spent a few summers in New York, I had developed an appetite for stylish clothing and a foul idea for obtaining them. The old clothing catalogs that Spiegel's, Alden's, Montgomery Ward and other national department stores used to send to people's homes always came with credit applications. I knew this because I had watched my brother, Douglas, complete the credit applications while ordering clothes for his wife. So to improve my wardrobe, I began filling out applications in every catalog I could get my hands on. In the spaces designated for information about one's occupation, I wrote that I worked at Collins and Aikman's in Farmville, which was where Douglas worked.

When the clothes began coming in, I went from wearing flannel and denim to being the best dressed guy in the school. All of a sudden, I was wearing clothes that were actually color coordinated. For my prom, I ordered a white sports coat and black slacks, which made me the envy of all the brothers. If my parents ever wondered about my sudden upgrade in clothing, it was news to me because they never said a word about it. Perhaps that was because the bills always came to me. But since I was an unemployed child, I never paid a cent. It was what I would have referred to later as a clean getaway. I have no idea what those stores concluded about me or their lost clothes, but the situation never caused me any trouble.

That was my first premeditated and organized criminal act, besides stealing the 10 cent newspapers. The ease with which I carried it out led me to engage in more illegal behavior. Soon I was regularly siphoning gas from the preacher's cars, stealing corn from other farmer's storage barns, and selling it and shoplifting other items. I often found the courage to go through with such acts in a bottle of beer or wine, as I was now drinking alcohol regularly. But I had never seen as much as a leaf of marijuana or any other type of drug.

Oddly enough, my two closest friends at the time never joined me in my felonious activities. It was like I had two sets of companions: one group that I got wild and rowdy with, and then Jasper Ormond and Edwin Gay, confidants with whom I could talk seriously. My hooligan friends were older guys who let me hang out with them because they knew my brothers and because I always kept them laughing with my seemingly endless supply of jokes. But Jasper and Edwin were true friends.

I was so young when I met Jasper that I cannot remember a time when I did not know him. He lived in Maury, near the church my family attended, so I would visit with him after service. Our relationship was somewhat unique because his family was a part of that Black aristocracy referred to earlier. But unlike others in their class, the Ormonds never treated me as anything but an equal. Jasper's father was a school teacher so Jasper had an entirely different approach to education than I did. While I believed in going to school merely to get a job and survive, he understood that getting an education positioned one to make choices about how he would lead his life, that it enabled a person to have a say in his future. College was always a part of Jasper's plan - once he even spoke to me about graduate school, though I had no idea at the time of what he was talking about - and he ended up going to North Carolina A&T. While there, he was not only a scholar but a terrific second baseman on the baseball team. He now has a Ph.D. and works for the government in Washington, DC.

Edwin was just as bright as Jasper and even more strait-laced. Tall, handsome and blessed with a beautiful singing voice, he had his choice of the finest girls in the school. Edwin defied all the stereotypes of the times when light-skinned, curly-headed guys got all the pretty girls. On the contrary, his complexion was deep chocolate and his graceful way of walking and talking made him a hit with the girls. That's why we nicknamed him "Smooth." Edwin seemed to have everything going for him, which I guess I noticed because in a strange sort of way, I saw myself as his protector. Consequently, I never let him get involved in any of my wrongdoing, or anyone else's for that matter. After graduating from high school, Edwin earned a Bachelors degree from North Carolina A&T State University and then entered the Air Force. It was on his way home from the military one weekend that tragedy struck and took his life. The victim of a deadly automobile accident, he is someone I often think about. I wonder why he died despite following all of the rules, and why I lived despite breaking them.

My relationships with Jasper and Edwin combined with my fondness for reading were probably the reasons I maintained strong grades in the midst of my budding corruption. By the time I completed the 11th grade I had fulfilled the state requirements for graduation. A North Carolina accepted practice stipulated that if you completed 16 units in the core courses, including at least four units in English, you were to be considered a high school graduate, diploma or not. Once I found that out, I set my mind on finishing in three years. So the summer after my sophomore year, I took an

English class to earn the necessary credits for graduation. Then, after my junior year, I never set foot in high school again. I never received a diploma, but I was a legitimate high school graduate, and that was good enough for me.

Chapter *II*

THE BRONX STAR

I was now 16 years old and faced with the question of what I was going to do with the rest of my life. I had applied for acceptance to a few historically Black colleges in North Carolina, but while my grades were decent, my failure to complete a fourth year of high school led them all to turn me down. That being the case, I weighed my two choices: stay in North Carolina, work in the tobacco fields and end up like my father; or go up North, away from the blatant racism of White Southerners, and find a job with at least a hint of a future. It was a simple decision.

At the time, moving up North was the thing to do. Every year, scores of Black high school graduates and drop-outs from the rural South would migrate to New York City, New Haven, Connecticut and Philadelphia. Compared to the limited opportunities we were used to, life up North seemed lucrative. It was commonplace for guys to leave our area with minimal academic qualifications and come back to visit months later with a new car and the finest fashions of the day.

Months earlier, one of my cousins, Roy Barrett, had done just that, surprising everyone with his apparent wealth by returning from New Haven in a brand new Ford Thunderbird. In keeping with the custom of the time, Roy had visited Farmville for the Memorial Day weekend. In those days, Black folks always returned to their hometowns on holidays and during their vacations. This was before time shares, cruises and trips to the islands. Blacks returned to their Southern roots like other immigrants made trips to the old country or whatever their native land.

Roy was only about four years older than me, so when he returned in such style I took extra notice. He said he worked at a munitions plant in New Haven and he told engaging stories about the bundles of money he made. All the evidence he needed was in that big brown Thunderbird. Though he had not been very accomplished in high school, Roy was a smash hit in Farmville in May of 1966. After being gone for only two years, he came back wearing hip clothing and driving a stunning new car. When it was time for Roy to go back to New Haven, half of the brothers in town wanted to go with him. Indeed, when he finally took off, there were so many guys in that car that people were literally hanging out of the windows.

It was with such delusions of grandeur that I left for New York City in August, several months after Roy had returned in a blaze of glory. But my cheery optimism vanished quickly when I stepped off the bus at the Port Authority in midtown Manhattan. Though I had been to New York on numerous occasions, I suddenly found myself frightened and perplexed. It was as if I was overwhelmed by my independence. When I had visited New York in the past, I was a child on vacation, with no responsibilities or cares. While I went on daily searches for fun, my brother Willie and his wife took care of me, providing my meals and money. Even though I would be staying with Willie, who by this time was separated from his wife, I no longer was a little boy whose mistakes would be covered by his guardians; nor did I know if this stay would be temporary or permanent. All I knew for sure was that I had to find a job, and fast.

The legal age for securing a meaningful job was 18, so with me being 16 years old and baby-faced, finding work was not easy. I told employers that I was a high school graduate but of course, I could not validate my claims. As my fruitless job search went on for weeks, I began wondering what to do. Still, at this point the thought of a career in crime had never entered my mind.

My first job turned out to be working as a scout for Willie during a weekend gambling excursion in Stamford, Connecticut. All of my brothers - Willie, James, Aaron and Douglas - were accomplished gamblers and on this occasion, Willie was providing me with "on-the-job training." Obviously, I had no money to throw into the pot, so Willie gave me the responsibility of surveying the area. My first duty was to watch his money and how all bets went down. If there was a heated dispute, Willie had to be able to rely on my telling him the truth and on my ability to accurately repeat everything that had occurred. Next, I had to scrutinize the curious creatures who never placed a bet, yet always hung around, standing in the oval of the dice game. These guys were either potential robbers or leeches, and being ignorant of them could cost you your money or even your life. Willie told me to keep track of their whereabouts, particularly when they made their exit. This was serious business and my charge was to remain sober, patient and disciplined. Gambling sessions could last all weekend.

As part of my training, Willie later questioned me about what I had seen. While that may sound elementary, it was anything but. He taught me that playing cards and rolling the dice were only small parts of gambling. Becoming adept at studying the behavioral patterns of people was essential to a gambler's success.

Willie explained that different gamblers have different motives, and that it was imperative to understand what made a man bet his hard-earned money on a game of chance. In many cases, a brother gambled simply to supplement the income of his low-paying job. In this way, playing poker, dice or the numbers was an investment. During this era, before Blacks began obtaining mutual funds, pension funds and stock portfolios, the safest investment for many was to have one number that they played daily. Therefore, having a good relationship with the numbers runner or the stationary banker was critical. Sometimes, if a day approached and a regular gambler was without money, credit would be extended to him if he had a history of consistently playing the numbers. Similarly, when the gamblers who were working men stopped by to play before going home for the evening, they had to be given assurances that if they lost all they had, they would be able to borrow enough money to feed their families. This was an important lesson to learn because most working guys lost much more than they won, and it was a good public relations move to keep their business by lending them money after their losses.

I learned that perhaps the key factor in becoming a proficient gambler was recognizing when someone else had reached his rhythm and subsequently shaking him from that state. All good gamblers have a rhythm. They aren't in it all of the time but when they are, watch out. A gambler being in a rhythm is similar to a basketball player being in "the zone," when every shot he throws up seems to fall through the hoop. The rhythm gambler is not counting the dollars on the table or thinking "I can't afford to lose this bet." He is almost oblivious to his surroundings. Totally focused on the game, he is confident that his card is coming (poker) or that he is going to hit the next number (dice) every time. Breaking a gambler's rhythm while keeping him in the game is an art form because the one thing you do not want to do is force a gambler in a rhythm to leave the game while he is winning. This is where knowing the personality and psyche of a competitor comes in handy.

Later, when I became a crackerjack gambler, I would always try to shake the confidence of a competitor who was in a good rhythm by saying things like, "Man, you worked hard all week and you're gonna bet that much money on one roll of the dice." Or if he was a working man with a family, I would say something like, "Man, if you lose this one, your wife's gonna lock you out the house." All I wanted to do was get him thinking about the consequences so that doubt would enter his mind and affect the pace at which he played.

Some guys rhythm was based on their betting at a certain level. For instance, some brothers felt comfortable betting $20 all night, but if you could get them to up their ante to $50 they became frazzled and started pressing. Usually, an attack on someone's manhood - "When you're ready to start betting like a man instead of playing all that chump change, let me know" - would get a brother to start playing beyond his means. Then there were the guys who built toward their rhythm by betting in a hurry. Once their adrenaline started pumping, they liked to play fast. To break that, I learned to grab the die, hold it for a few moments and start talking to them: I'd bring up a current news event or something happening in the world of sports, anything to keep them from dictating the tempo of the game. Whenever I gambled, I never allowed another guy to play at his own design. That's a lesson I kept later, when I started playing chess in prison. If I was going to play somebody who was better than me, I would never play him on his bunk. I would always play him out in the yard or on my bunk to strip him of any kind of advantage that might make him feel comfortable.

On our way to Connecticut that night, we passed numerous gambling spots and I wondered why we had to leave the city for my indoctrination into the underworld. I later realized that gambling was only our second reason for being in Stamford. Willie's first priority was to meet up with a young lady whose house was adjacent to the corner on which we were playing. As he gambled, Willie waited for the woman to signal from a particular window that her man had gone to work. When the time came, Willie ambled over to the house, officially ending my first lesson in gambling. If there was one thing Willie loved more than gambling, it was women. With his bronze complexion, striking good looks and six-foot, 170-pound frame, he attracted females like a magnet.

Despite his frequently hazardous behavior, Willie never got heavily involved in major types of crime. The only illegal operations he performed were running his own gambling spots. Willie's places were always hot because his generosity and charming personality made people want to be around him. When he was winning big, it was nothing for him to buy food for others and even pay someone's rent or car note. Though many of Willie's debtors were people he beat continuously in craps and poker, they never stopped hanging around him. It was as if they actually enjoyed losing to him. His most prolific scam took place at 854 Freeman Street in the Bronx, where he opened a storefront shoe shine stand that fronted for a gambling spot. It was there, in a poorly ventilated 12x12 foot room behind the stand, that I developed the gambling skills that eventually led people to call me "The Bronx Star."

But on that night in Stamford, I felt like anything but a star, especially as I dawdled on the corner waiting for Willie to finish his business. As I stood by lethargically, feigning interest in the dice game, I heard a voice hollering my name. When I looked up, I saw six of my former running buddies from down South riding by in a convertible. Their familiar faces halted the loneliness I was beginning to feel and put me at ease. One of the brothers in the car was Joe Charles Hopkins, Jr., a favorite cousin of mine. He and the rest of the guys had left the South a few years earlier and were now living in New Haven. We talked and caught up for awhile, and then they invited me to ride to New Haven with them. Since I had no job prospects in New York, they didn't need to ask me twice. Sprinting across the street, I yelled up to the window of the room that Willie was in and told him I was going to New Haven with some homeboys. I never received an answer but I knew I would have his blessing. This impromptu trip marked the beginning of what would become a nomadic existence for me.

With a population of about 130,000 and a downtown area that consisted of only a few department stores, New Haven was much less intimidating than New York. It had a substantial population of Blacks, most of whom

39

lived in one of three areas: Dixwell Avenue; Newhallville; and Congress Avenue, also known as The Congo. I took up residence with Joe Charles at 69 Arch Street in The Congo. The more congenial surroundings and the presence of my friends from the South made me hopeful that I would fare better than I had in New York. And I did.

I quickly found a job making $2.25 an hour as an X-ray file clerk at the Veterans Administration building. I was living rent-free with Joe so besides the small cost of food, I had no expenses. I still had the desire to attend college in the near future so if I had been smart I would have saved my money. But at 16, I wasn't smart.

Bringing home $70 a week and living free-of-charge made me something of a high roller, especially for someone who should have been a senior in high school. Joe's wife, Blanche, and his three children, had gone down South for a few months, so there were actually seven guys, all native Southerners, living in his small third floor apartment. There was myself; Kent Streeter, whose bodybuilder's physique made him a lady killer; Bernard Bullock, whom we called Slack because his pants never quite fit in the butt; Otis Barnes, who was tall and quiet; "Rabbit" Davis, Otis' nephew and clone in every way; and Joseph "Blue" Taylor, a married man with an excellent job at the Pratt and Whitney aircraft plant. Blue's wife and kids were in North Carolina and he was saving money to bring them up North. Then, of course, there was Joe Charles.

I was a fan of Joe's from way back. He was a few years older than me and grew up in the same North Carolina farmland as I had. What made Joe such a hero to me was his incredible fighting ability. He was a small guy, about 5-foot-6, 140 pounds, but I saw him beat down six-footers on a regular basis. At the time, it was popular to say that, pound for pound, Sugar Ray Robinson was the world's greatest fighter, but I believed that title should have gone to Joe Charles. I have no doubt that with the proper training, he could have become a world champion. Physically, he was gifted with great strength and phenomenal hand speed, but it was his knowledge of how to fight that made him so devastating. He was like a boxer in that he treated fighting like a science. He knew that most guys in the streets were out of shape and tired quickly, so a lesser fighter with stamina could often outlast a real tough guy. He also had rudimentary boxing skills in that he could jab and follow with hooks, crosses and uppercuts. He never wasted punches and, unlike many guys who closed their eyes and flailed about wildly when angered, Joe always kept his eyes open and stayed alert during a fight. He also knew how to probe his opponent for weaknesses and then exploit them. Once, I saw him overwhelm a burly 6-foot-3-inch guy by getting him on the ground and nullifying his height advantage. Joe and this guy were in each others' faces, talking smack and braced to fight, when Joe kicked the guy in the ankle with his right foot and made him trip over himself. By the time the guy knew he was falling, Joe was on top of him, hammering him with rapid lefts and rights.

Despite many impressive victories like that one, Joe knew he wasn't invincible. After teaching me all of his tricks about fighting, he made sure to tell me that nobody can win every fight, especially small guys like us. "No matter how skilled you are, you just can't beat some big guys," he would say. So Joe would fist fight only when he knew he could win. For the towering guys that he could not punch out, he carried a knife.

Outside of fighting, Joe's achievements were not so notable. He could not get a high-paying job because of his criminal record. Though he had never committed a major crime, he had just enough small-time arrests and convictions to keep him from landing the type of government job that he coveted. None of that lessened my admiration for Joe, though, and in an effort to be like him, I started carrying a knife for the first time in my life.

In most cases, seven young men with an apartment all to themselves are going to party. And we did just that, turning 69 Arch Street into a frat house. One night, we decided to throw a party for the neighborhood women. No guys besides us were invited, just dozens and dozens of women. We chipped in about $30 apiece and planned the Congo's biggest party of the summer. But shortly after the music started pumping and the liquor began to flow, our plans began going awry. First, there were just as many men as women pouring into our place. We initially tried to keep the guys away, but it really was no use. It was futile to try and keep brothers away from wine, women and song. Once we accepted the fact that there would be competition for the ladies, we settled in and began to groove. But then a couple of brothers jumped bad with Slack, provoking Kent, the muscle man, to get involved. Heated words led to a push, then to a shove, then to an all-out riot. It was the seven of us versus The Congo. It was wild. It seemed like brothers were coming at me from all angles. I had just started carrying my knife weeks before and now I was clutching it like it was my best friend. Blade in hand, I began swinging like a mad man. I probably stabbed five or six brothers, including Blue Taylor by accident. When things calmed down, blood was all over the place, the house was wrecked and brothers were staggering away while gripping knife wounds. The emergency room at Yale New Haven Hospital was full that night, and it was all because of us. Fortunately, no one died and none of our brothers were seriously injured.

Things changed drastically after that. None of the girls would enter our pad for fear of their lives. Kent, deciding the fast life up North was too dangerous, went back to North Carolina and married his high school sweetheart. Slack and Rabbit split from The Congo and relocated to New York. Blue moved in with his sister a few blocks away. Otis joined the Marines. And Joe's wife, Blanche, came home. Peace had returned to the Hopkins house, and not a moment too soon. Though I had enjoyed our wild lifestyle, I soon began to realize that I was better off without it. Having settled down, I now had time to think things out with a clear mind. Much of my maturation was the result of Blanche's return.

Blanche was a beautiful woman who gave birth to her first child before she graduated from high school. She was probably 16 or 17 when she first got pregnant by Joe and two or three years later, they married and immediately began making more babies. Though I believe they had a lot of love for one another, the pressure of raising three children on Joe's slim wages often got the best of them and led to intense arguments. I think Blanche realized that most of their problems were the result of mistakes they made when they were younger. And as I was still a teenager, she wanted to help me avoid the same pitfalls. She never actually told me that, but I could tell by the way she interacted with me. She treated me more like a son than a cousin who was only a few years younger than she was. Like everyone else, she could see that my admiration for Joe was going to lead me into the same pent-up situation that he was in and she wanted me to have something better. She really tried to enlarge my perspective on life before I got trapped in a frustrated marriage or some other circumstance that would zap me of my potential. Her presence went a long way in helping me become a young boy again because around her I didn't have to be hard. Before, I was always trying to impress the older guys, trying to show them that I wasn't a little kid anymore. But having a strong and caring female in the house returned a sense of order to my life. I was appreciative at the time but also torn between wanting to do something constructive with my life and wanting to have fun.

For a short time at least, Blanche's influence won out. I began reading again, taking special interests in politics and philosophy, and decided to return to the South to study psychology at North Carolina A&T in the fall of 1967. Of course, there was one small problem: a year ago, the school had rejected my application. But being a gambling man, I thought it was a sure bet that A&T would accept my family's money and chalk my registration papers up as being lost. So in August, one year after I had enthusiastically bolted from the South, I left New Haven and headed home with every intention of doing right.

At the start of the school year, my parents and I drove to A&T and got in line to register, never letting on that the school had already denied me entry. Things went smoothly, and the registrar, unable to locate any previous paperwork regarding me, accepted me without hassle. We enrolled in the school's budget payment plan, which called for us to pay tuition at the beginning of each semester and then $100 in each successive month for room and board. If we fell behind in our payments, we would have to pay off our debt before enrolling for the next semester.

Though I had been such a hoodlum the past few years, I entered A&T with tunnel vision: I was there to study, get good grades and become a psychologist. I don't know if I had gotten my fill of partying in New Haven or what, but I was a changed man. If my friends from up North had visited A&T, they would not have recognized me. I was not partying at all. Drinking and smoking were the last things on my mind. I wasn't even chasing girls. I was all about the books. Even the discovery that A&T did not offer undergraduate degrees in psychology did not deter me.

Some of the credit for my new outlook on school had to do with my renewed relationships with Jasper Ormond and Edwin Gay, both of whom attended A&T. Jasper was a sophomore who excelled in the classroom and on the baseball field, and Edwin's prominence in a campus singing group made him one of the school's most popular freshman. Though I wasn't an athlete or a singer, the bond we built as youngsters remained strong and we spent most of our time hanging together. The peer pressure I received from them was positive, and I remember striving to succeed in the classroom in order to contribute something constructive to our threesome.

But just because I was now applying myself didn't mean that things came easily. It wasn't long before I realized that my years of academic indifference, not to mention my year away from school entirely, had taken its toll. I did well in the general courses such as history, but my prowess in math was long gone. Since the entry-level math class was full, I was forced to enroll in a remedial course, but even that was above my head. I was still good with numbers but I was completely lost when it came to trigonometry, algebra and geometric proofs and formulas. Part of the reason I was dumbfounded had to do with my Chinese instructor, the first non-Black teacher I had ever had. I understood less than half of the things he said. If I had had a solid grasp of the material, I might have been all right. But since I didn't, his heavy accent made it all but impossible for me to get out of the dark. Nevertheless, I plugged away and for two months operated as a solid college student. I did well on all of my midterm exams except for math and I somehow managed to pass even that.

Having successfully completed my first quarter of classes, I was filled with a sense of pride as I went home for Thanksgiving. It was great to see my parents, especially since I felt like I was making them proud. Though my sister Christine was their first child to go to college, I was the first son to attend. Of course, becoming the first to graduate was the goal, and that challenge inspired me greatly.

However, my excitement about school soon turned to indignation after I intercepted a letter intended for my parents in the mail. Since the return address on the envelope said North Carolina A&T, I figured the letter had something to do with money. My family's poverty and how it could potentially jeopardize my chances of completing college was never far from my mind, but still I was startled when the letter stated how much money we would have to pay before I could start my second semester. Tuition alone was $447, plus room and board. On top of that, we would have to pay an additional $300 for room and board for the three months I had already spent at school. Knowing my parents would not be able to pay even half of that, I contemplated the hard truth: I was done as a student in academia.

Though I had known beforehand that this was possible, even likely, I was not prepared to accept it now that it had become a reality. I did not know what to do, where to go, who to talk to, or scream at, or hit. So many feelings welled up inside of me that I felt I would explode. Sometimes I wanted to go outside and run as fast as I could, as far as I could, for as long as I could. Other times, I wanted to hit a wall or go hide and cry. I was frustrated because I thought I had finally gotten my life and my priorities in order and very angry at my family's never-ending financial problems. And I was upset with myself for having wasted all the money I made in New Haven on beer, wine, clothes and craps. I regretted not having saved that money for my college education.

After sorting out my feelings as best as I could, I decided not to say anything to anybody. In fact, my parents never found out that I even knew about the letter. They may have noticed that I was a bit withdrawn during the holiday but they never found out why. In hindsight, I see that keeping my feelings bottled up inside was not a good thing because sooner or later they were bound to come out.

Knowing this would be my last semester no matter how well I did in class, I returned to school as a different person. I guess you could say I went back to being the old Mark. I regressed back into my former ways, skipping classes and partying because after all, what was the point? I started carrying my knife again and reacquainted myself with alcohol. I even cut down on my time spent with Jasper and Edwin.

One night, a group of guys in my dormitory threw a party, and one brother was extremely generous with the whiskey. There were no girls around, but in my naiveté, I didn't even realize that the brother pouring the booze was gay. That possibility never crossed my mind because I had never come across a young homosexual. The only ones I had ever seen were old men, and I actually thought it was something that happened to you later in life, if ever. Anyway, that brother succeeded in getting us drunk but before he could attempt anything perverted, a fight broke out with me as one of the main participants.

There was one guy in the room who thought he was the baddest thing in North Carolina because he knew karate. Why he began picking on me, I don't know. I guess he looked around and, seeing that I was tall, thin and heretofore known as a bookworm, figured I would be the easiest one to whip. Eager to demonstrate his skills, he provoked me by saying something about my mother. In the Black community talking about somebody's mother is a declaration of war, so I told him that if he knew what was good for him he would shut his mouth. Surprised but not frightened by my boldness, he got more fired up and started cursing and calling me names. By that time, I knew we were going to fight, so as he was running his mouth, I was deter-mining my mode of attack. Every lesson Joe Charles ever taught me was running through my mind. I knew about this dude's karate so I figured my best chance was to end it quickly, before he had a chance to start kicking

45

and chopping. So without word or warning, I jumped up, cold-cocked him in the face and then stabbed him in the head with a knife I had brought from New Haven. It was over in a matter of seconds, as I pounced on him before he got a chance to throw a blow.

He wasn't hurt seriously and his wound required only a dozen or so stitches, but naturally, that did little to quell the anger of the Dean. Appalled at our conduct, he expelled both of us, thereby ending my college career before the close of my first semester. I returned home in shame around Christmas, faced with the same dilemma I had confronted a year earlier: stay down South or go up North? Once again, I chose the latter.

It was January of 1968 when I headed back to New Haven. I saw no reason to go to New York since my last experience there had been so humbling. Having landed a good job in New Haven as a 16-year-old, I figured I would really clean up now that I was older and looked more mature. This time, I would not be that shivering, insecure little boy who got off the bus in New York City. With everything I had experienced, the year-and-a-half since I first gave it a go up North seemed like two decades. My mentality had shifted 360 degrees. While I felt like the prey on my first trip, I felt more like the hunter this time around.

In less than a month, I secured a job making bullets at a factory for $125 a week. I was staying with my cousin Joe again, but this time I did not let Blanche dictate my lifestyle decisions. The way I saw it, I had tried to make it her way and had failed because of my family's poverty. I took great consolation in the fact that I had attempted to do the right thing. It dulled my sense of remorse when hustling and committing crimes because I reasoned that I had no other alternative. I still treated Blanche with respect and appreciated her concern, but if I was ever going to make it, I knew it would be as a hustler.

While Blanche hoped against hope that I would stay out of trouble, Joe helped lead me the other way. He talked about me returning to college and having a career some day, yet continually drew me into poker games and other night-life activities. We hung out constantly, as Joe tried to get away from the daily grind of marriage and I started to feel my oats. Though I was just 18, I had no interest in high school girls. I was making good money, using fake identification that recorded my age as 22, and running with cats in their early and mid-20s. I was now beginning to operate like an adult and as such, looking to attract women, not girls.

Most of the money I made went toward gambling and buying clothes. I was way out of my league in terms of gambling, and the older brothers used to gladly take advantage of my inexperience. As I handed them my 10 and 20 dollar bills, they smiled and offered words of consolation, assuring me that all young gamblers take their lumps and that eventually I would improve. Even Joe didn't mind taking my money at cards.

Although I wasn't as naive when it came to buying clothing, I was close. This was before credit cards but not before credit, so after Joe co-signed with me on an account at Backers Clothing Store, I began buying new threads every week. Each time I received my paycheck, I would treat myself to an outfit. Still a little bit country, I dressed in tacky, trendy stuff at first, wearing lots of loud colors and fly-by-night fashions. But hanging out with adults refined my tastes. The older women let me know in a hurry that faddism would not cut it, so I picked up the quality and toned down the colors. Of course, a couple of years later in the 1970s, loud colors and wild styles would be in.

In the midst of all this carousing, I still took time to read. It was an outrageous contradiction that was not lost on my partners. They would laugh at me for buying newspapers the morning after I had gotten drunk or spending hours at the library before a party on Saturday night. Reading was not something I forced myself to do in an attempt to stimulate my mind. It was a desire that had become natural. Because my father had made it a part of my daily routine while growing up, it was now a habit. I didn't feel right if I didn't know at least something about what was going on in the world.

My reading made me appear intelligent in the eyes of those in my crowd, particularly Joe. He always encouraged me to save my money to re-enroll in college. They really wanted me to better myself. That might sound strange considering how much we drank and gambled, but it's the truth. A lot of them felt like they had missed their own opportunities to become legitimate successes, but that I was still young enough to do something special. Regardless of what my peers were saying, though, college was the furthest thing from my mind, in part because I felt like the stabbing incident made me an untouchable in the eyes of most schools.

Black people were making plenty of headlines in 1968 so I read more fervently than ever. Two of the biggest stories of the year were the assassination of Dr. Martin Luther King Jr. and the emergence of the Black

Panthers into a sociopolitical force within America. Though I appreciated Dr. King's bravery and brilliance, at the time I disagreed with his nonviolent philosophy. I just couldn't understand how a man could ask Blacks to "turn the other cheek" in the face of White people's merciless brutality. I certainly was no Bible thumper, but one verse of scripture I knew well was "an eye for an eye, a tooth for a tooth." I felt that if White folks beat on us, we should beat right back on them. I might have gone along with Dr. King's urgings of nonviolence if he had a White counterpart who was preaching nonviolence to Whites, but since that was not the case, I leaned more toward the Panthers. I thought their social programs like "Feed the Children" were excellent and I loved the fact that they seemed to put fear in the hearts of White people. Though I questioned whether they could back up their big talk, I thought it was high time that Whites experienced what it felt like to live every day under the threat of random, racially-charged violence; or in other words, what it felt like to be Black in America.

Because I enjoyed sports so much, athletes who spoke out against racism had a substantial impact on me, especially Muhammad Ali. Ali was to me at 18 what Willie Mays was to me at 12. He was the man. I remember making a sign that read, "Ali Is Still My Champ!" after he lost his first fight to Joe Frazier in 1971. I loved Ali because he was the strong Black man that many of us could not, or more accurately, would not be. When he refused to join the United States Army and fight in Vietnam because "them Viet Cong ain't never called me no nigga," he showed the system that he was just as bad outside of the ring as he was inside of it. No one could make him do anything he didn't want to do. The fact that he sacrificed his career, his world title and hundreds of thousands of dollars in an act that brought him nationwide criticism and scorn showed that he was not the White man's slave or tool. Even to this day, that serves as a great inspiration to me because if Ali could give all he had for his belief in Allah, then I can give all I've got for Jesus Christ.

Two other athletes who displayed a tremendous amount of courage in drawing global attention to America's racial injustice were the Olympic sprinters Tommy Smith and John Carlos. After taking the gold and silver medals in the 440-yard dash, Smith and Carlos stood on the victory podium in red, white and blue. But to show that they would not perform for America without exposing its despicable history of race relations, they shot their black-gloved fists into the sky during the playing of the national anthem.

When those brothers did that, it was the greatest feeling of unity and pride that I had ever experienced as a young Black man.

Even though Smith and Carlos were not members of the Black Panthers, their actions made me respect the brothers in the Panthers and listen more intently to the things they said. But while I admired the Panthers, I never thought twice about joining them because I thought many of them were hypocrites. Most of the ones I knew dated White women, and it was common knowledge on the streets that they were involved in crime. Lots of their members in New York robbed Black night clubs and dealt drugs. Some of their corruption might have been the result of the prevalence of FBI agents in the group since, by the time the Panthers were finally dismantled, there were more agents in the movement than actual Panthers. Before the Panthers came along, there were hardly any Black federal agents, but after their rise the bureau started going onto college campuses and recruiting Blacks. There was no shortage of Blacks who were willing to cooperate, and in an effort to diminish the Panthers' effectiveness and reputation within the community, those new agents may have committed crimes in the Panthers' name.

To a lot of Blacks, the Panthers' corruption was not disheartening because everybody in New York seemed to be involved in some form of illicit behavior. Some who drove trucks pilfered their products and sold them on the side. Brothers who worked in the garment district ripped off suits and dresses. Even the always polite, conservatively dressed, non-cursing brothers in the Nation of Islam were dirty, selling dope down on 116th street in Harlem. Black folks felt like, "Hey, the White man has gotten over with all sorts of crimes, so why can't we?"

The one time I questioned the Panthers' call to arms was when Dr. King was shot and killed. That was a terrible time for Blacks, and I think White folks were trying to appease us, hoping and praying that we didn't go berserk. The day King was killed, the foreman at my job asked me if I wanted to go home. I had not yet heard the news of King's death, but when I looked around and saw all the Blacks leaving the plant with their heads down, I joined the procession. I was crushed when I heard what happened and not just because we had lost a great leader. In some strange way, I felt like I had contributed to Dr. King's death by making a living from making bullets. It was one thing for a criminal to be killed with a bullet but for a preacher of nonviolence, a man who had not lifted a finger in anger to anyone? I had a hard time justifying my job after that, and for a while, I didn't have to. For the next week or so, every time we went to work, hundreds of Blacks would be demonstrating down the block from our factory. Presented with the perfect excuse to take the night off, all of the Blacks would leave as if they were going to the demonstrations. In actuality, most of us went straight to the bars.

Though I was beginning to develop a sense of Black consciousness, I was far from acquiring a revolutionary or moral voice. In fact, my moments of deep reflection about the struggle were heavily outweighed by my periods of foolishness. Part of my problem was that there was no one in my circle with whom I could discuss these issues. I often wished that Jasper and Edwin had been around at this time because I could have seen us staying up late, spending hours dialoguing about such topics. My friends up North were not so inclined. Sure, they recognized and disliked racism and supported anyone who spoke out against it, but they could not intelligently analyze the times or the movement because they did not read. All they knew was what they happened to catch on television or heard in the streets. The only thing brothers did less than read was vote.

At that time, I did not know one Black person up North who was registered to vote. In fact, I knew very few Blacks at all who voted. My mother and father registered to vote for John F. Kennedy, but that was the first time I recalled seeing Black people vote. I knew a few other Black Southerners who, out of principle, always made sure to vote. After being denied the privilege for so long, they were determined to stand up and exercise their right. But the Blacks I knew in the North were not so sentimental. Politics was of very little concern to them. The popular opinion was that politics was something White folks did to keep Black folks broke. The chief concerns of Northern Blacks were more elementary: things like daily survival, getting a job, getting a car, getting some clothes or having a drink. The whole concept of voting was foreign to them. I think that stemmed from the fact that they had little, if any, civic orientation. Most of them did not understand how the government functioned, especially on the local level, so it was hard for them to believe their one vote could make a difference. Racism, both past and present, also discouraged many people from voting because they believed that the White man's system was rigged to keep us down regardless of who was in office.

Another key factor in the political indifference of many Black Northerners was that, upon migrating from the South, they often lost their affiliation with a large, organized church. At least that was the case in the circles I ran in. All of the people I knew down South who voted went to church, and it was the church's emphasis on social and political issues that motivated them to do so. To this day, the church is the political hub of the Black community, and back then it was even more so. So if you were not involved in a church, you were not likely to receive any direction concerning politics. For many of the Blacks who left the South, gatherings such as rent parties replaced the church as the center of the socialization process. In addition to gambling and helping the host pay their rent, people went there to exchange information. That's how folks found out who had just come up from down South, who had died down South and things like that.

It really was a sad state of affairs because Blacks who moved up North and left the church became disenfranchised both spiritually and politically. When that happens, you are, for all intents and purposes, a lost people, a people separated from God and from the world's system. Without a strong faith in God and without the understanding or protection of the system, you become prey. That's what happened to me and my running buddies. We were being raped of our intellectual faculties and our potential because we were living in a senseless hustler's world.

Despite my interest in legitimate social issues, I delved deeper into that world with each passing day. After working a couple of jobs, buying some nice clothes and making a few friends, I soon felt comfortable enough to return to New York. Every weekend, a couple of my boys and I would drive to the city on trips that served both social and business purposes. The social part included gambling, drinking and meeting women. My business affairs consisted of buying suits, dresses and shoes on the so-called "black" market and selling them for a profit in New Haven. After only a few weekends, I realized that I was making more money hustling clothes than I was on my job, so naturally the next step was to quit my job. Now, for the first time in my life, I was a full-time hustler.

Consequently, I took on a hustler's attitude toward women. No longer was I looking for love or someone to talk to in my interactions with females. I now was after sex and access to money and shelter. I was aided in my mischief by the fact that the depletion of desirable Black men that today is such a problem in the African-American community was just beginning to take root. Much of this was related to the Vietnam war. First, an inordinate number of brothers were being drafted into the military, which meant at least two years away from home. And secondly, the economic boom that resulted from the war led to a proliferation of illegal drug activity in the Black community, which in turn led to unprecedented numbers of Black men being carted away to prison.

With the economy in the inner city thriving, organized crime saw great potential in putting heroin in the Black community. This criminal element had always had a presence among Blacks but with so much money available they expanded their activity. More significantly, new international heroin routes were opened up because of the war. In the 1950s and 1960s, most of the drugs in the inner city could be traced to the French connection. But during Vietnam, heroin started coming in from Thailand, China and other Asian countries. Some of the biggest traffickers were members of the U.S. Military, particularly those who had spent time in Bangkok. As a result of all this, more brothers on the streets had an opportunity to get a piece of the action, more and more poison began flowing into the Black community, and the number of Black men in prison began to swell. Up to that point, the prison population had been mostly White, particularly up North.

With fewer Black men to choose from, many respectable Black women who owned cars and solid well-playing jobs were left without a man. That made it was easy for charlatans like myself to step in and fill the void; as long as that void was physical rather than spiritual or emotional. As far as emotions were concerned, I was as cold as the bottom of the sea to women. I felt that to become emotionally attached to a woman was to sound one's death knell on the streets. Decked in fine clothes, laced with money and armed with numerous surefire lines, I was able to make a number of women "my girl." That gave me access to three or four apartments in New Haven and New York, meaning I didn't have to worry at all about rent.

This mentality was not something I created but rather something I picked up from watching the older, more polished hustlers. They always had women around, but it was clear who was in charge and who needed who. This attitude among brothers is still prevalent today, as evidenced by much of the rap music. The male rappers, particularly the "gangstas" or modern-day hustlers, talk about Black women as objects of pleasure to be used and not loved. It's sometimes even seen as a weakness to be in love. I believe this mentality, at least in part, results from slavery, when it was beneficial or necessary to sever all emotional ties. The brother who attached himself emotionally to a woman was often crushed when the slave master would rape her or ship her off to another plantation. So to maintain his strength, or at least the guise of it, a man would use a woman for sex, food, or a warm bed to sleep in, rather than experience intimate love with her.

Though I was making money hustling, there was still a part of me that wanted to earn a legitimate living. At night sometimes, when I was alone with my thoughts, I would muse about how much I enjoyed my one semester at A&T and how stimulating it would be to discuss social issues in an intellectual setting. Most of the time, I would cut short such thoughts by telling myself that it was an impossible dream, but one night I refused to stop imagining myself in a college setting. I thought about being in a class of 20 students, holding discussions about racial injustice in America and poverty in the Black South. I thought about being like my childhood friend, Jasper Ormand, and earning a degree. I thought long and hard that night and when I woke up the next morning, I decided to give school one more try. The big question, however, was would they give me one more try.

Since North Carolina was the only state that would recognize me as a high school graduate, my college choices were limited. So I went home for Mother's Day 1968 and told my mother I wanted to go back to A&T. The timing seemed perfect because she recently had heard about a student loan she thought we would qualify for. To have more leverage, we decided not to contact the school until we were sure about the loan. While waiting for word on the loan, my mother sent me back up North, but this time to Philadelphia, where I would live with my Aunt Mittie and Uncle Elbert Williams.

My parents continued to send me North because they were oblivious to what type of life I led up there. For the most part, relatives in the South were ignorant of how corrupt their sons, nephews or cousins had become in the North. Since we always came back with money, nice clothes and no jail time, they figured we had legitimate jobs. It never occurred to my mother to keep me in North Carolina for the summer. As far as she knew, the last bit of trouble I had gotten into was in North Carolina, so she thought she was keeping me out of trouble by sending me away from home.

While my mother and I agreed before parting that I would find a job, stay with Aunt Mittie throughout the summer and return to school in the fall, I had other plans. Just because I wanted to go back to school did not mean that I had become a saint. Staying with my relatives and returning to school was fine. But finding a job? I had learned how to survive up North without employment so I didn't think that looking for a job was necessary.

I felt the same way about church. Though my mother didn't mention it, I knew my aunt and uncle were very religious and would expect me to accompany them to church every Sunday and perhaps on a weeknight. But I hated church even more than I hated work. One of the great things about being on my own up North was that I never had to attend church. Sleeping late on Sundays felt extra good because all of my life I had been forced to rise early to go to an hour's worth of Sunday school and a church service that seemed to last all day. In New Haven and New York, I didn't even know where a church was. If I passed one by accident, I didn't look for the name, try to find out who the pastor was, peak through the windows, or attempt to listen to the music. I wanted no part of church. I didn't even want to hear the word "church." But since my mother and relatives felt differently, I was forced to perpetrate a fraud.

In those days, there was such a thing as church attire. When I was down South, we didn't dare wear our flannels and jeans on Sunday. We wore the best outfits we owned, part of which was always a white shirt. I figured it was the same way up North, at least in the Black churches, so my plan was to leave all of my white shirts in North Carolina. This would of course keep me outside of the church walls, and thwart my job search since in those days, no self-respecting person would show up for an interview without wearing a white shirt. So with my bags packed, my white shirts hidden in my closet, my plan in place and my smile stretching from ear to ear, I kissed my mother, shook my father's hand and hopped on the bus to Philadelphia.

Almost as soon as I arrived, Aunt Mittie and Uncle Elbert began pressing me to find a job. But their persistence did not bother me since I had what I believed to be a fool-proof plan to avoid work. Easing into my scheme, I left the house each weekday as if I were looking for a job; of course, I always had on something other than a white shirt. Instead of going on an interview, though, I would spend the day familiarizing myself with the city, its clothing stores and its women. Then I'd go back home at the end of the day and tell my aunt and uncle that I had no luck finding a job. This lasted for a week because after hearing my excuse for not being able to go to church - no white shirts - we all laughed and came to the conclusion that my inappropriate attire was the reason I could not land a job. So we called my mother and told her that I forgot my white shirts. She said she'd put them in the mail as soon as possible. That gave me a few more days, but I extended

54

it by hiding the package of shirts when it arrived. Since both my aunt and uncle worked, I was the only one at home during the day, so when the package came in the mail, I was there to receive it and stash it in the basement. Every day, my aunt would ask if the package had come, and every day, I would say no.

Finally, my aunt and uncle, insisting that I do something other than lay around the house, began having me run errands for folks in the neighborhood. Uncle Elbert even loaned me his car to do so. To my surprise, this assignment played right into my hands. As I mentioned earlier, I was now strictly into older women. I didn't even know how to relate to high school girls anymore. In Philadelphia, my devilment sank to a new low as I began sleeping with married women. Most of my escapades took place while I was supposedly running errands. For instance, one guy wanted me to teach his wife how to drive a car, but we ended up having a sexual relationship. Men would trust me with their wives because at 18, I still looked young and innocent and also because I was "Brother and Sister Williams' nephew." And since I played the respectful, naïve country boy role to the hilt around the husbands - complete with "Yes sirs," "No sirs," and a bowed head - they never suspected me of a thing.

Since I was not looking to fall in love or become emotionally attached to anyone, I found married women to be the perfect partners for me. We both were looking for a solely physical relationship with no strings attached. Adultery soon became the norm for me as I began dating married women and prostitutes almost exclusively. I can count on one hand the number of single women who weren't hookers that I dated over the next 10 years.

I never did get a job that summer, and I think my aunt and uncle were glad when I went home around Labor Day. My trip to North Carolina would be a short one, though, as I learned that my family's request for the loan had been denied.

Now, it was official: I would never attend college again. If I was going to be successful in life, I was going to have to take another avenue. I had just the one in mind too. Within days, I was back in Philadelphia, staying with my aunt and uncle. But they weren't about to fall for the same mess this time, so before they made their inevitable demand that I get a job, I bolted. Their niece, Betty Pearl, who was a few years older than me, was dating a guy who was a truck driver. While he was visiting her one night, I asked him where his next stop was. When he told me he was going to New

York City that night, I sprinted into the house, packed my bags in less than two minutes and left Philadelphia for good. I moved back in with my brother Willie in the Bronx and once again immersed myself in the stagnant, party culture that seemed to have everyone I knew locked in its grip. I gambled on the weeknights and attended rent parties, where I gambled some more, on the weekends.

About a month or two later, I returned to New Haven and found a good job at an accounting firm. I was doing both the right thing and the wrong thing at this time: working a legitimate job by day and gambling profusely by night. My style was cramped briefly around the first of the year, January of 1969, when I received notification in the mail that I had been drafted by the U.S. Military. For a week or so, I worried myself sick, going back and forth in my thoughts about staying or going. But after hearing my peers talk about how simple it was to dodge the draft, I figured I would challenge the Army to find me first.

Though I was working a solid job, my night life demanded that I carry a knife and it wasn't long before that blade pointed me straight to the military. A few weeks after being drafted, I was pulled over for a minor traffic violation that turned major when the police officer discovered that my driver's license was invalid. When the officer searched me and found a six-inch blade with a double handle in my back pocket, I was charged with possession of a deadly weapon and arrested for the first time in my life.

In those days, before non-violent offenders were about to be sentenced to jail, the judge would often give them the option of going into the service instead. That's one explanation for the strong criminal element in the military. While I had absolutely no desire to fight for America, the thought of an existence behind bars was even less appealing. So when the prosecuting attorney stated that my charges would be dropped if I entered the military, I jumped at the chance to join Uncle Sam's Army.

Chapter *III*

DRESSED TO KILL

If ever there was a person the Army regretted forwarding a draft notice to, it was me. That's an exaggeration of course, since I did not commit murder or any other heinous crimes during my enlistment. But short of performing such an act, I was as much of a royal pain in the Army's collective behind as is possible. Indolent and unruly, I was a horrible soldier. I paid attention to the survival skills, but with everything else, I was totally derelict. When the sergeant said move, I stood still. When he said run, I walked. When I stood at attention, my posture was incorrect. When I did push-ups, my head was too low and my butt too high. On the shooting range, I stole ammunition. Seemingly every other week, I went AWOL. In total, I was absent without leave five times during my less-than-two-year stint in the military. And, as if my decision to hinder my own progress was not enough, my tumultuous behavior had an adverse effect on the morale of the entire group.

The root cause of my poor conduct was my inability to follow orders, which was nothing new. As far back as I can remember, I had a deep-rooted aversion to obeying the commands of any adults besides my parents; and obviously, I went behind even their backs on a regular basis. While my ungovernable attitude knew no racial boundaries, it was especially sensitive to White men, who not surprisingly, accounted for all of the commissioned officers.

Spending so much time in the North had made me forget what it was like to be around White people, particularly Southern ones. In New York, I hardly ever interacted with White folks. In my section of the South Bronx, Black people could go weeks without seeing a White person. Those who did cross our path were usually downtrodden, from the neighborhood and conditioned to relate to us equally rather than derisively. Occasionally, a political caravan, full of smiling White faces, would come through the neighborhood of Franklin Avenue and 170th Street, but there was no interaction. New Haven was similar, but because it was smaller we did at least see Whites on a consistent basis. But even there, I did not develop any relationships with them. Other than the police and other authority figures, my partners and I rarely had White folks to contend with.

With my attitude toward authority, the military and White people in general, no one would have ever suspected me of being a volunteer. But I was, and not because of my day in court. Whether I answered the draft call or volunteered, my criminal charges of possessing a deadly weapon would be dropped, so that was not a factor in my decision. What led me to walk into the recruiting station in New Haven was my reluctance toward serving in the military down South. As a volunteer from the North, I would be based in nearby Fort Dix, New Jersey. But as a draftee, my basic training would take place at the installation closest to my home town, which for me was in Fort Jackson, South Carolina, where both rednecks and racism were celebrated with vigor. I had no doubt that I would either kill or be killed before completing basic training if I was based in the heart of the South, with bigoted officers hollering and screaming orders in my face. That feeling was so strong that I chose to volunteer for three years rather than accept two years through the draft.

One of my friends from New Haven, James Jefferson Joyner, a.k.a. J.J. or "Kitten," was having the same dilemma. J.J. was an old friend from Farmville, North Carolina who had moved up North about the same time as I had. His birthday was just 10 days after mine, and he shared my fears about undergoing basic training in the South. Like many young Black Southerners, he possessed my distaste for following the orders of White people. For us, surviving Vietnam was secondary to coming through a racist basic training unscathed. Besides, Vietnam might as well have been on another planet as far as we were concerned. We were at war every day on the streets of America so the last thing on our minds was fighting some Vietcong. We could not have cared less about who America had a beef with because we had a beef with America.

58

So to settle our predicament, J.J. and I volunteered under the Buddy-Buddy Plan, meaning we would always be based together during our first three years. This was favorable for a couple of reasons: one, because J.J. was a good friend; and two, because he could fight like a pit bull. He actually resembled a pit bull in that he was short and stocky. Black as the night sky, he was powerfully built and tenacious when he fought. He literally refused to lose, sometimes engaging in street fights for up to an hour. I knew a partner like him would come in handy in the Army, where I expected to have more than my share of scraps.

There was also a humorous side to J.J., which is what drew me to him down in Farmville. We both loved to tell jokes, though our styles were totally different. I told stories, while J.J. was a one-line specialists. Playing the dozens was and still remains an art form in the Black community, and J.J. would have cats crying with his quick wit. Everybody knew not to get J.J. going because he would make you look like a fool in a hurry.

Having entered as volunteers and avoiding the South together, J.J. and I were calm and confident upon our arrival at Fort Dix. But that feeling quickly abated when, to our surprise, we found that there was little difference between being based in the North or the South. There were yelling, screaming, domineering White Southern officers in both places. Just the sound of their Southern accents drove me crazy, bringing back memories on which I did not care to reflect. It was not unusual to find myself reliving memories of when I was a 10-year-old boy who had been rendered inoperative by the imposing presence of "Roguish Ralph." Instead of being shackled by fear, though, I was chained by the protocol of the military. Either way, I saw it as an unfair system that was stacked against Blacks and forcing me to take orders from a White man.

I wasn't the only African-American who was uncomfortable with the racial dynamics of the military. After all, it was 1969 and most Black men had been affected in some way by the various movements and personalities that had been fighting for the freedom of our race. Whether it was Malcolm X calling the White man "a blond-haired, blue-eyed devil," Martin Luther King proclaiming the day we would be "free at last," Stokely Carmichael demanding "Black Power," Huey P. Newton and Bobby Seale brandishing firearms in black leather jackets, or the race riots that had razed parts of several American cities, someone or something had touched a nerve in most members of the Black male population. As a result, we were determined to touch the members of the White male population. With our fists.

Every chance we got, J.J. and I attacked some White boys. We never ganged up on just one, as they were prone to do to us. Instead, without any fear whatsoever, we challenged them to fair fights. The general feeling among Blacks was that, all things being equal, we could whip the White boys every time. Evidently, they felt the same way since they would never utter a racial slur or joke unless they had an unfair advantage. Whenever the number of Blacks and Whites in a room was close to equal, they were quiet and polite. But if they got one or two of us alone, all of a sudden they waxed tough. As with everything, though, there were exceptions. I discovered this one day when coming across an ornery and robust White soldier from Alabama. Somehow, he and J.J. had gotten into an argument and he took it to another level by shoving J.J. Even though the guy was almost twice the size of J.J., I figured that he would get socked around in a matter of minutes. But when I saw him taking J.J. apart, I jumped in, thinking I was coming to the rescue. Instead, I turned out to be just another body for him to pound on. He handled both of us reputed street toughs with his bare hands. He was the strongest White boy I had run into in all my life.

That fight marked one of the last times I saw J.J. in the military. Because of our unruly behavior, we were separated after basic training. He was shipped to Fort Lewis, Washington while I remained in Fort Dix. So much for the Buddy-Buddy Plan. I discovered later that we never even had a contract. The recruiting officer had duped us from the beginning, which just added to my distrust and resentment for White authority figures. In actuality, J.J. and I were fortunate to have spent basic training together.

The amount of racial polarization in the military was incredible. Though Blacks and Whites were in the same units and shared the same sleeping quarters, practically everything else was segregated. The only thing that was able to bridge the gap was drugs. On the few occasions that Blacks and Whites were seen together on their own time, drugs were involved. When it came to smoking reefer and shooting heroin, it didn't matter if you were Black, White, blue or green. If you were capable of getting someone high, you were all right with them, if only for as long as the buzz lasted. It was strange to see a mixed group of Blacks and Whites partying together, arms around one another, laughing at the same jokes, singing the same songs. Up to that point of my life, the only thing I had ever seen bring significant numbers of Blacks and Whites together as friends and equals was drugs.

The first White guy I ever interacted with on anything close to a friendship level was John Alligood, a heroin addict from Connecticut. Extremely intelligent and politically astute, Alligood was a conscientious objector who had somehow ended up in the military. He was probably a former college student who got strung out on heroin and watched things go downhill from there. But at that time his brain power was far from diminished. Unwavering in his convictions, Alligood would back up his arguments with real, hard facts. He wasn't just some hippie screaming "I hate the war in Vietnam." He skillfully articulated his reasons for opposing the war from economic, historical and political standpoints. He talked about the exploitation of the Southeast Asians, the puppet governments that had been set up, how the French had occupied the area before the Americans. He was actually the first person to tell me that Vietnam was formerly named Indochina. I would be high as one of the Army's fighter planes while listening to Alligood and often would dismiss his rhetoric as the rants of a junkie, but some of it sunk in and I later realized how smart he really was. One of the things I appreciated about him at the time was his respect for Dr. Martin Luther King and the Civil Rights Movement. He always talked about justice and praised those who fought for racial equality. About halfway through basic training, Alligood split, telephoning his girlfriend and leaving with some friends in a car. That was the last time I ever saw him.

Though I had done more than my fair share of partying since age 16, I had almost no exposure to drugs before entering the military. I was 19 years old before I saw anyone smoke reefer or engaged in the practice myself. It was in New Haven, just a month or so before I was drafted, that a friend named Lamar turned me on to weed. While in the army, I was thankful for that brief encounter with marijuana because it made me look like I knew what I was doing when we got high in the barracks. Most of the guys, White and Black, partied in some way, shape or form, whether it was with alcohol, marijuana, heroin or something else. It's amazing how creative some of those guys would get when it came to seeking a buzz. They made me look reserved for resorting only to beer, wine and reefer.

One guy I became close with named Bo Petty used to drink ungodly amounts of cough syrup for a high. As I watched him down bottles of Robutussin A.C., I remember thinking that something was terribly wrong with him. But despite my reservations concerning Bo's mental state, I could not stay away from him. He was a down home, country player from New Orleans who would keep me entertained with his unusual take on life. Mostly, he talked about relationships between Black men and Black women. He was adamant in his belief that Black women too often castrate Black men mentally and he was hilarious when telling outlandish tales about the lives that pimps lead in New Orleans. He was like one of those street corner philosophers who had weird ideas about everything. He even philosophized about how the value of a real player would increase on the streets because of the great numbers of Black men dying in Vietnam.

With regularity, Bo's speech would become very soft in the midst of a conversation, and you would have to lean in closely to hear what he was saying. At first, I thought Bo was making our conversation personal and I felt fortunate to be drawn into his confidence. Then, I figured he didn't want the White soldiers learning about the ways of the Black world. Later, I even began thinking that he didn't want the square Blacks obtaining his nuggets of street wisdom and applying them back home. Finally, I realized that none of those theories had anything to do with Bo's manner of speaking. Instead, the gallons of cough syrup he had consumed had damaged his voice.

The guys from urban areas usually were the ringleaders of the military's underground drug culture, probably because they had been exposed to more drugs while coming of age in the city. The country boys didn't know what they were doing at first but they caught on quickly and often became some of the most outlandish druggies on the base. While the cats from the city got cool and mellow from a high, the country boys got rowdy and rambunctious. It seemed like they couldn't handle their high because quite a few of them ended up with serious addictions.

The military is where I first began to interact on a steady basis with guys who were born in the city. Almost all of the people I hung out with up North were originally from the South. That's often how it worked during the '60s. If you migrated north from Mississippi, you got hooked up with a crowd that was almost entirely from Mississippi. Even the bars were sometimes segregated by state, as folks from North Carolina would frequent one spot and folks from Alabama another. From my observations, that was because most Southerners lacked the confidence and social skills to mingle with new people.

It was through discussions with my "city-bred barrack-mates" that I first considered the idea of selling drugs. Hearing them use terms like "consignment" and listening to them share stories of the surplus of money they made on the streets sparked my curiosity. But the city boys were not the only ones talking about dealing dope. The brothers on the front lines, those who had been fighting in Vietnam, returned with tall tales about the power and privilege that drugs had afforded them overseas. While many American soldiers were victimized by Vietnamese drug peddlers, who sought to use dope to dull their enemies' senses and gain an advantage in the war, others used the heroin that was so easily attainable to fatten their own pockets. With my sparse knowledge of drugs prior to joining the military, I had been under the impression that heroin was no more potent than alcohol. But after listening to those brothers, I found that I had been mistaken. I soon understood that drugs basically gave you control over people and that selling them enabled you to get whatever you wanted.

I had the opportunity to learn about more legitimate ways of making a living as well. For months, I attended radio operator school at Fort Dix. When they initially signed me up for the program, I thought I was going to be trained to send messages from headquarters, which of course would keep me safely behind the lines of fire. That sounded like a cool profession so I entered the training period with a favorable attitude. Though it was nothing like I expected, I gave it a chance anyway and soon found myself enjoying it. The small bit of schooling and success I had previously had, for the most part, dealt with reading and writing. I hadn't had any technological experience and the capabilities of those man-made machines intrigued me. I had one reservation, though. In every John Wayne movie I had seen, the enemy always shot the radio operator first. My anxiety only increased when my buddies confirmed that communications was indeed the top target on any military's list. When I began seeing brothers come back from Vietnam in body bags, my paranoia grew to unparalleled heights. Though I liked radio operator school, I was not about to lose my life over it. So I decided to go AWOL.

Most of the times I went AWOL were for recreation. Bored and frustrated with military life, I would catch a bus to Philadelphia or New Haven or New York City and hang out with some of my old friends. I knew I would have to return to Fort Dix and I usually did after a few days. One time I stayed away for 17 days, but even then I had no intention of trying to permanently escape from the Army. My excursions never got me in major trouble; a fact that often bewildered me. I honestly believe that, since I was such a nuisance, the military didn't mind letting me go away for a few days as long as I eventually returned. Were it not for the necessity of keeping up appearances, they probably would not have minded if I had disappeared altogether.

63

This time, however, I was serious. I had lived my life recklessly indeed, but death had never crossed my mind. Seeing those body bags changed that. I realized now that the military was no joke, that it was more than fighting, getting high and listening to overblown tales of sexual conquests in enemy territory. I knew I was in a war that potentially could end my life. After sharing my feelings with Bo, I was even more inspired to leave the Army for good. With his low tone of voice and the smell of cough syrup emanating from his breath, he told me, "If you go AWOL again, don't come back. Be prepared to stay. You can make it. You are tall and slim and a good-looking fellow. Use what you got naturally and you will have no problems making it."

The advice sounded good, especially coming from an established player like Bo. I had never really thought of myself as handsome before. I was too busy thinking about survival to be worried about my looks. But with Bo constantly telling me I looked like this cat named Silky, I began to get full of myself. According to Bo, Silky had been some sort of prototype pimp who became a legend from New Orleans to St. Louis. By the time I finished listening to Bo, my head was so puffed up that I thought it was my destiny to become the Silky of New Haven and the Bronx. So when I crept off the base in September of 1969, I did so without plans to return.

I went to New York and as always, stayed with my brother Willie in the Bronx. Rather than admit that I had fled, I began telling everyone I was on my 30-day leave before going "across the pond." After that first month passed, I said I had been given a 15-day extension. When those two lies were no longer usable, I jokingly started saying I had joined President Lyndon Johnson's War on Poverty as opposed to Uncle Sam's War on Vietnam.

I worked the rent party circuit all winter, sharpening my poker skills, and more importantly, my skills of asking women for money. Having gone AWOL, I had not even attempted to find a job and I needed money to feed my gambling habit. Since I was always available when most married men were at work, I had plenty of time to spend with lonely wives, and though their families may have been struggling financially, these women proved to be my greatest source of revenue. I never thought of this at the time, but it was almost as if I was working as a gigolo. Not a high-priced one, mind you. While these married women supplied me with enough money to play small-time poker and craps, I needed to broaden my horizons if I ever wanted to be financially comfortable. When spring arrived, I began to expand my production.

My first move was to start operating crap games on the corner. Though I would play with anyone, I looked specifically for guys who had recently come up from the South. That way, I could instantly relate to them as a "homeboy" and gain their trust. Plus, if they were as country as I had been, they would be too green to know how to play but too intent on appearing cool to walk away. Always able to find a fair number of young bloods, I made decent money with this scam.

According to the protocol of the gambling culture, every block was owned by a street entrepreneur who would collect a dollar for every pass of the dice. He was known as the "House Man" and was responsible for settling disputes and making sure that all bets were straight. Becoming a House Man wasn't merely a matter of the biggest, baddest guy on the block taking possession of a corner, although just about every owner knew how to handle himself in a fist fight. There actually was a procedure involved, the most important aspect of which was to pay off New York's Finest, the local police, so you could deal as you pleased with trespassers and sore losers.

I ran my games on the corner of Franklin Avenue and 170th Street, which belonged to a strapping, 6-foot-5-inch, basketball-playing drug dealer named Robert Moore. I didn't know Robert personally at the time but I was well aware of his reputation. One thing hustlers did besides hustle was play basketball, and Robert was known as one of the best players in the South Bronx. With the moves and skills of a guard and the size and strength of a forward, he should have been on some team's roster in the National Basketball Association. Known as "The Commissioner" for the way he handled his business on the corner, Robert fought just as well as he played ball. He was a merciless brawler who had beaten brothers within a breath of their lives with nothing more than the hands and feet of his muscular, 220-pound frame.

Robert knew I was holding games on his block and didn't seem to mind until I unknowingly hooked up with one of his rivals, a guy named David Mullins. They had been feuding for years, and I got caught in the middle of it one Sunday afternoon. As I was holding a game, Robert walked toward me and said gruffly, "Give me my money." I knew he was just trying to maintain control of his block and the sensible thing to do would have been to pull him over to the side, hand him half of the money and act as if we had a prearranged agreement. That would have gotten Robert off my case and given the onlookers the impression that he and I were working together. But because I didn't like the way he approached me, calling me out in front of everybody, I instead yelled, "What money?"

I knew before the words came out of my mouth that I was essentially challenging Robert to a fight. This was one of those instances where I ignored my cousin Joe Charles' philosophy of knowing what fights you could and could not win. Any fool could see that Robert was too big to try and beat one-on-one with bare hands. But I thought I was invincible. My boldness quickly turned to horror when Robert grabbed me around the neck with the force of a bulldozer. At that moment, two policemen drove by, and I was praying that they weren't on the take. Seemingly ignoring the rest of us, they spoke directly to Robert, asking him if there were any problems. When he looked them in the eye, tightened his grip and calmly responded, "No. I got this," I knew I was in trouble, especially when the cops drove off, and Robert hoisted me into the air by my collar.

Like the cavalry, my brother Willie suddenly appeared on the corner. I would have been relieved if Robert's knuckles hadn't been embedded so deeply into my throat. Willie didn't seem ruffled when he saw me in Robert's grasp, and I began to wonder what was going on. Then, he slowly walked toward Robert and asked if he could talk with him for a minute. Finally, after what seemed like hours, Robert released me and began walking with my brother in the opposite direction. I sprinted away with every intention of settling my dispute with Robert, only this time with a gun. A friend of mine named Earl lived nearby and he had a 25 automatic. But when I reached his place, he refused to give me the gun. There was no way I was going to return to the corner without a pistol, so I just wrote it off as a lost day and went back to Willie's place.

When I saw Willie later and asked him what happened, he told me that he and Robert were hustling partners. They sold whiskey together on weekends at after-hours gambling spots and also had a shoe scam going. My brother drove a truck for a shoe company, and Robert would take shoes off the truck and sell them. Willie told me that Robert knew I was his younger brother and that he had not planned to hurt me. He said he probably would have given me the money back later, but after I jumped bad, he had to save face. Fortunately, Willie showed up and saved my face.

Robert and I eventually became friends and collaborated on a few scams of our own. That incident on the corner was one we often looked back at and got a good laugh from. Years later, after I had built a sizable reputation as a street hustler, Robert said to me one day, "If Earl had given you that pistol, you probably would have shot me, right?" I responded matter-of-factly: "Dead in the chest."

It had been more than six months since I had gone AWOL, and the Army, finally realizing that I was not coming back, sent out FBI agents to find me. They approached my family members one by one, trying to gain information on my whereabouts, but found nothing. My mother was in complete opposition to the Vietnam War, which she termed "immoral." She even encouraged me to flee to Canada, but Canada had no appeal to me. I was too busy reacquainting myself with the streets of New York City to leave the country.

As I became more comfortable and made more connections, I began thinking I had what it took to establish myself in New York's underworld. I began to see what Bo Petty had seen in me. With visions of big-time hustling swirling in my head, I figured I had better get this Army thing out of the way and get the FBI off my back. I didn't need the distraction of them chasing me down before I had even become a major player in the game, so I decided to return to Fort Dix. In July of 1970, a friend of Willie's named Teddy took me back to the Army base. Teddy had volunteered to do this because he was hoping to convince me to use the military as a positive opportunity on the drive up. But I wasn't hearing it. I simply wanted to do my required time and get out, so I could unleash the bona fide hustler that I knew was inside of me.

I reported back to the Army and was immediately thrown into a holding compound for three or four days. While there, I witnessed a junkie kicking a heroin habit cold turkey. Despite my grandiose plans of becoming a renowned hustler, I was still naive in many ways and this was a case in point. When I saw this brother sitting on the floor, crouched in the corner and throwing up, I thought he was just sick. I didn't know he was going through withdrawal. Nearly everyone else in the barrack knew what was happening but no one said a thing. Some of the guys threw blankets over him because he had the chills, but the MPs, the military police, didn't even approach him. Thinking he was sick, I showed compassion and tried to get the MPs to take him to the hospital, but they just looked at me like I was crazy. Years later, I would know of people who died trying to kick heroin in the same manner.

My next stop was the stockade. Giving me one day for each month I was away, they put me in for 10 arduous days. The stockade was a collection of old wooden barracks inside a tight surrounding of wire. It was secured by armed soldiers who stood atop towers watching for a reason to draw their rifles. Since they had not shot at a human being since returning from Vietnam, I figured they were probably hoping someone would run. For that reason, the thought of escape never entered my mind. There were about 30 guys in each barrack, and the lights never went off. The perpetual brightness made you lose all sense of time and left you disoriented. The only way to keep track of days was by the grueling and regimented work schedule. After doing calisthenics in the morning, we were trudged out into the hot sun and forced to work on the rock pile. On one side of the compound, you would use a sledgehammer to crush cement blocks and then pour the dust into a cart. Once the cart was full, you would pull it to the other side of the compound, where another group of guys would turn it back into concrete. Then, in this Sisyphus-like exercise, you reloaded the cart with cement and pulled it back to the other side to start the process again.

The brother I had seen kick the heroin habit was in the same barrack as me. By the time he got himself together, I knew what his problem was and I was curious. All I knew about heroin was what I had heard during basic training. I had never seen its effects firsthand and I wanted to learn more about a substance that could make a man curl up into the fetal position and cough up his insides. In my quest for knowledge, I befriended this brother and we ended up sharing cigarettes and conversation during our evenings in the barrack. At first, all he talked about was the pleasure he received from heroin. He was an entry-level dealer who became addicted to the stuff and now his only concern was getting high as soon as he was released. Knowing I didn't want to end up like him, I pushed him to go beyond the effects of the drug and into the business of dealing it. He then told me everything I needed to know to become a pusher.

I listened with all the attentiveness of a schoolboy as he broke down step by step how to work on consignment. I had learned a few things, including the meaning of the word "consignment," during basic training but I had not received the kind of personal, in-depth instructions that this guy gave me. He told me that working on consignment meant the supplier received two-thirds of the profit and the dealer one-third. So if you sold 15 bags of heroin, you would give 10 bags worth of money to your supplier and keep five bags worth for yourself. It was funny how the dealers in the army

68

used the word consignment. They said the word so often that I actually thought "consignment" was a specifically drug-related term. I didn't know you could have any type of item - shoes, clothes, food, whatever - shipped to you on consignment.

I did not recognize it at the time, but the illegal drug industry was much like the sharecropping system that for decades had shackled thousands of Black families in the South. The dealer was the equivalent of the White middleman and the junkie was in the place of the Black family. So when I decided to make drugs my trade, I unwittingly joined a new sharecropping venture, only this time at a higher rung on the ladder.

Armed with this valuable information, I set my sights on becoming a supplier as soon as possible. Any fleeting thoughts I had of completing my military training were now thrown completely out of the window. Like a college student who had gained the inside track on a prestigious summer internship, I was excited about my new career opportunity.

After I finished my sentence in the stockade, my superior officers presented me with the option of starting basic training over again or receiving an undesirable discharge under honorable conditions. I'm sure they thought I would opt for basic training since being undesirably discharged had such disgraceful connotations that most employers would refuse to hire me. But I was planning to have a thriving career in drug dealing so finding a job was the least of my concerns. Without any sense of shame, I chose the undesirable discharge and left the United States Army in August of 1970, having never progressed beyond the rank of private.

When looking back on my military experience, I certainly do not blame it for my deviant behavior that followed. I clearly was headed toward a life of crime well before I enlisted. But it is undeniable that being in the Army changed me for the worse. Not only did I receive an education in drug trafficking, but, through the process of basic training, I was taught to kill. Obviously, thousands of individuals have completed basic training without developing murderous inclinations, but for someone like me, who was already violent and malicious, it seared whatever principles I had and infused in me a more destructive mindset.

People think fighting in Vietnam is what turned men into animals, and in some cases, that's true. But in other cases, basic training is what desensitized them to the possible elimination of someone's life. That's where I first thought about killing someone. Before, when I was angry, I thought about

69

knocking a guy out or stabbing him with a pocket knife, but during training, I began fighting to kill. I equate it to college, where you are trained in a field and then sent out to perform a job. If you have paid attention and done your homework, you are prepared to do the work whether you get a job or not. It was the same thing with basic training. All of us were trained to kill but only some of us were sent to Vietnam. Those who went to Vietnam acted out what they had been taught over there. Those who didn't, had the capacity to act it out elsewhere. After being discharged, I acted it out in the South Bronx, which I imagine was at times as hostile as Vietnam.

Chapter *IV*

CRIMINAL MINDED

Y ou would have thought I was leaving the Army as a decorated war hero, the way I strutted proudly out of Fort Dix, smiling widely, with head held high, chest out and arms swinging. I marched better that day than I ever did during basic training. Having fully surrendered myself to the idea of a life of crime, I left without reservation or regret. No one - not my parents, not my cousin Joe, not my brother Willie - could have convinced me that I had made the wrong decision. I now had plans and a future that seemed more secure than ever before. This was not school, I thought, where financial lack was always a concern, and my destiny was not in my own hands. Nor was it some dead-end job that would lull me into a boring, mundane lifestyle while fighting to stay above the poverty line. This was a sure thing.

Fueled by the stories of my drug-dealing friends in the military, my imagination ran wild. Money, power, women, the finest cars and fashions - all of it would be mine once I settled into my new career. I was willing to work hard to become successful, to stay up late and awake early, to cover any dangerous, downtrodden part of town necessary, to overcome what- ever obstacles I would meet on the streets. I did not want to become just a hustler. I wanted to become *the* hustler.

By this time, I had developed a perspective of life that matched me against two opponents: the system and poverty. Therefore, being undesir- ably discharged did not bother me in the least bit. The way most of my peers and I saw it, I had beaten the system. I had refused to be the White man's soldier, his puppet. I was too Black for him. He could not handle me. I had scored points against the system by taking his discharge. And as a hustler, I would do the same against poverty.

Obsessed with my crooked ambitions, I wasted no time before attempting to get into the mix. Experience had taught me that New York was not the place to begin. I expected to make some mistakes, and the Big Apple, especially the rotten part in which I roamed, was too unforgiving. So I set my sights on New Haven and hooked up with Joe, who was now driving cabs and pushing dope for a living. What I did not know was that Joe was also pushing dope into his veins. A full-fledged heroin addict, Joe was putting his profit right back onto the streets by getting high. Even though his addiction was obvious, I never thought of him as a junkie. I thought of him more as a guy who liked to party hard. This was because the Joe I knew had always been in control - he ran his household; he decided when his wife and kids went down South; he determined the direction of his crew in New Haven. Plus, he had been the baddest and wisest street fighter around, knocking out dudes nearly twice his size and smoothly avoiding the battles he knew he could not win.

But one day while driving his cab, Joe failed to use the discernment that had left him undefeated in the streets. The details I received were sketchy, but I know that a passenger tried to play Joe for a chump by refusing to pay his fare. When Joe told the man he would pay either in dollars and cents or flesh and blood, the passenger, underestimating Joe because of his size, laughed in his face. Within seconds, Joe turned the guy into a victim, beating him so badly that he was given a 90-day jail sentence for assault with a deadly weapon. Joe did his time in the local jailhouse at 245 Whalley Avenue, where he befriended a career junkie named Rolo. They were released on the same day, and instead of going home to see his family, Joe went with Rolo to check out this heroin high that he had heard so much about. Joe found the heroin to be as powerful as Rolo had promised and, like his new friend, ended up hopelessly addicted to the sensation it produced.

Though heroin had changed Joe quite a bit, it never changed the way he treated me. To him, I was still his little cousin, still the kid whose eyes beamed with admiration every time Joe looked into them. Joe knew I idolized him, and with his life falling apart bit by bit, I don't think he wanted to lose his one big fan. So at my request, he introduced me to two of the most prolific pushers in New Haven, the guys who could teach me the drug trade: Matthew Bethea, known on the streets as M.B., and Sylvester, who was simply called "Vest."

M.B. and I became extremely close over the years. We shared an honesty that was foreign to most gamblers and dope dealers. He taught me the trade and didn't get jealous when, by following his instructions, I became larger than him. While M.B. had significant status in New Haven, what kept him from truly going big time was his addiction to heroin. Again, my country boy naiveté blinded me to what M.B. was. I hung around him for years, including some time we spent together in prison, before realizing that he was a junkie.

M.B. and Vest turned me on to the richest crap tables in New Haven's Black community, and it was at such places that I began to establish my identity as a hustler. When it came to gambling, I had a unique quality that escaped most brothers. It was called nerve. Nerve was the ability to remain undaunted when making big bets, and win or lose, I never seemed frazzled. When I won big, I remained calm, acting as if the winnings meant little to me. When I lost big, I fronted like my cash flow was endless, like a couple thousand dollars was mere chump change. I enhanced my persona by always arriving alone, which made me mysterious and led everyone to assume that I was some real bad character. Since I was betting big and living in New York, most people figured I had made some big score in the city and was hiding out in New Haven while things cooled down. Remembering the lessons I learned from Willie, I always gave liberally after winning. In addition to supporting the myth that I was some big hustler, my generosity made me a favorite among the guys and served as my personal system of checks and balances. Lending money assured me of leaving a game ahead, since I wasn't foolish enough to bet someone I had just given money to.

My stature and charisma gained me the respect of Melvin Long and Irvin Brown, the kings of the New Haven dope game. They figured I was well connected in New York, and though that was far from the truth, I said nothing to diminish their opinion. Soon, we were holding discussions at bars or after crap games about merging our businesses and becoming major players in the East Coast drug trade. They thought I was their big break. Realizing that I would soon be revealed as a fraud if I did not produce tangible evidence of my wealth, I decided to lay low until I came up with a plan.

73

A few weeks later, I lucked up and came into some money by, of all things, being in a car accident. I was riding in a car with Joe and another cousin, Gene Suggs, when Joe, who no one ever accused of being safe behind the wheel, slammed on the breaks after seeing someone who owed him $20. His abrupt stop caused the car behind us, a late-model Cadillac driven by a White man, to slam into our rear. No one was injured but when I moved to get out of the car, Gene grabbed me and said sternly, "If you get out of this car, I'll slap the taste out of your mouth." Knowing this was a potential gold mine, Gene told us to wait in the car until an ambulance came. All three of us visited the emergency room and then went off to meet with Gene's lawyer, who advised us to sue. I was so excited that I took the first settlement they offered; it was $3,500. Of course, in 1970, $3,500 was a great deal of money, enough to legitimately reconstruct my life with by going back to college. But I never even entertained the thought. My mind was focused on instant gratification, and four years of college seemed like a lifetime, especially when I knew of a much faster way to make money.

I received my check in December and at once began investing in the ghetto version of the stock market: gambling. Within days, I was in the Bronx, cramped into that musty, smoke-filled room behind my brother's shoeshine stand on Freeman Street. That room, which consisted of nothing more than a crap table and the seemingly built-in smell of reefer, became everything but home to me for the next six months. I can honestly say without fear of exaggeration that I won and lost more than $125,000 over that half-year.

With so much money coming in, I put my thoughts of entering the drug game on hold and adopted gambling as my full-time occupation. This was unusual because most gamblers had another source of income, whether legal or illegal. One day, a seasoned hustler from Farmville, North Carolina called "Bro Gay" said to me, "Mark, you got to figure out a way to get money. One day, the (gambling) draw is going to be empty, so you got to have another way to get money, be it women, drugs or stickups." Since Bro Gay was an older player, I respected his advice, but I was on such an incredible roll that I ignored it and poured all of my energy into the games.

I approached my profession with all the diligence of a high-ranking executive in a Fortune 500 company. Along with shopping and sleeping, it was one of the three staples of my life in 1970. I was so addicted to the dice that I didn't even make time to chase women. My work week usually began on Thursday and ran through Sunday. Most of the guys with legitimate jobs were paid on Thursday, so from then on it was non-stop betting around the clock. I gambled so much on those days that I did nothing but sleep on Mondays and Tuesdays. Wednesdays were usually reserved for shopping. Spending a couple grand a week on clothes, I was always decked out in new suits, wide-brimmed hats and suede and lizard-skinned shoes.

I rarely dined out because I viewed it as too time-consuming and basically lived off of whatever I could find at Willie's store in front of the gambling room. Mainly, I ate salted pumpkin seeds, roasted peanuts in the shell, Almond Joy candy bars and 7-Up. Willie eventually bought a pressure cooker, and sometimes a bunch of us would chip in a few dollars and buy some ox tails for him to cook. That was the closest I came to having a decent meal when the betting was heavy.

Christmas of 1970 was indicative of our fanaticism. With the forecasts calling for a treacherous snowstorm, about a dozen of us headed for the back room on the afternoon of Christmas Eve. Before long, everyone was locked into the action, and by the time someone looked at his watch, it was early Christmas morning. Guys started panicking then, knowing that they had to get home to play Santa Claus for their children. When a couple of them began heading out, though, they were met by fierce winds and snow gusts that could nearly knock you off your feet. It was a complete whiteout, and you couldn't see further than two feet in front of you. Thankful for an excuse to stay put, the brothers ran back into the room and resumed play. I ended up spending Christmas Day with Willie, Bro Gay and a group of characters named School Boy, Pretty Willie, Cadillac the Super, Bean Head, Ronnie Fort Knox and Bobby "Double O" Hargrove. We had no tree, no turkey, and no gifts or family, but every last one of us had a ball. The stakes were especially high over those two days since guys came loaded with holiday money that was meant to buy gifts for their wives and children. Instead, it was thrown rashly into the draw and, in most cases, lost. When the games finally ended the day after Christmas, I left the room with about $9,000 in my pocket.

It was a strange mix of guys who gathered over on Freeman Street. Some portrayed themselves as hustlers who were trying to win enough money to go and play in Harlem, where the real money was, while others held down regular jobs in factories, restaurants, barbershops and the like. As was the case that Christmas, it was not uncommon to see guys jeopardize the livelihood of their families at the crap table.

A brother we used to call Jackie Boy did just that the week after the two-day binge over Christmas. It was New Year's Eve, and he and his wife had planned to treat a couple from out of town to dinner and dancing. Not coincidentally, Jackie Boy picked a joint located directly across the street from our gambling room. Just before they entered the spot, Jackie Boy slipped across the street to add to the $300 wad he was carrying for his wife and dinner guests. Unfortunately for him, his typically horrible luck on the table didn't change with the New Year, and he lost every dollar he had. Terrified and desperate, he began begging for money, telling us that his wife was going to kill him and that he would pay us back with interest. Guys laughed so hard that tears rolled out of their eyes. But while the mood was festive and light, nobody gave Jackie Boy a dime.

Another guy who was as awful and addicted as Jackie Boy was Mitch, the subway operator. Mitch appeared to be a hard-working, sensible family man, but when it came to gambling, he lost all discernment. Paid every Thursday, he would go straight from work to the gambling spot, where brothers would chew him up like a stick of bubble gum. Without fail, he would gamble into the wee hours of Friday morning and leave empty-handed, his week's pay having been divvied up among four or five hustlers. Consequently, he ended up borrowing thousands of dollars from loan sharks. Unable to win and therefore, pay back his loans, a stressed-out Mitch eventually had a heart attack and died.

Mitch was one of four guys in our circle to suffer a heart attack as a result of gambling; five, if I count myself. It happened to me when a small-time hustler named "Fly Guy" beat me out of $3,000. I couldn't believe Fly Guy had come up with that type of money and more significantly, duped me. As soon as the realization of losing hit me, I felt my heart jump, and for seconds that seemed more like hours, it didn't come down. When it finally did, I just sat there in shock. I don't think anyone else realized what was happening to me because they were all busy shouting and "giving five" to one another. I never went to see a doctor about it but I'm convinced that it was indeed a heart attack.

It's hard to explain why I was so drawn to gambling. I guess it was the excitement of winning. Then again, my appetite was just as strong during losing streaks. Something about throwing the dice with all that money on the line, with all those people around, with brothers bragging and playing the dozens, was exhilarating. It was like being on a roller coaster. The thrill of winning five or ten thousand dollars in one night was indescribable. Up to that point, I had not yet become deeply involved in drug abuse, but later when I did, nothing, not cocaine or heroin, gave me more of a high than gambling.

Some brothers were strung out simply on watching the action. There was a group of about five or six guys who would stand up against the wall as long as a game was going on. They smoked, drank, ate pickled pig's feet, pickled boiled eggs and candy, all while watching the competition. It was like they were watching a football game on television. I don't think they could have had more fun at the Super Bowl. Each guy had his favorite players, and they talked more trash than the guys playing the game. They even gave everyone a nickname. I had two: M.C. for Mark Carven and "The Bronx Star."

For the most part, the atmosphere in the room was friendly. We all were from the South and everyone knew each other, so we knew that all of the loud talk was in jest. Every once in a while a newcomer would come in and start acting like a knucklehead and get beat down, but fights were basically a rarity. Besides friendship, another reason for the relative calm was the fact that everyone carried a gun. It was hard to meet a brother who didn't have at least one pistol on him. The dynamics of power on the street had changed. It was no longer about being big and burly and able to knock somebody out with your fists. Former chumps and sissies became tough guys because they carried guns. Since I had been making lots of money, I toted more heat than most, owning sawed-off shotguns, nine millimeters, 38 revolvers and 25 automatics. I didn't pack at all times but at night, I rarely left home without at least a shotgun and a 38. When out on the town, I would wear a black leather maxi coat with my guns tucked underneath it.

Early in 1971, I got on a hot gambling streak and started cleaning up. I was winning every day and making more money than anybody on Freeman Street. That's when the leeches started urging me to go to Harlem to play with the big boys. The leeches were those who hung around the crap games smoking reefer but never bet. Most of them were junkies who didn't have enough money to support their habits, so they would try to latch onto the winners and use their money to get high. They did this by feeding your ego, saying, "You da man!" and things like that. They always seemed to know of a better game with more money where you could easily double or triple your winnings. Willie had told me never to listen to the leeches, that they can break your bank faster than the worst losing streak. But in my cockiness, I disregarded his advice. What they were telling me sounded good, so I began hanging with them.

It was the leeches who took me beyond smoking reefer and into heavy drugs, namely cocaine. When the betting got slow on Freeman Street, they would take me to another spot, saying "You can win big over here M.C. You da Bronx Star." They would pass the reefer around in the car and tell me, "Look, when we get there, you're going to meet this guy from Colombia. I know you don't do drugs, but just take one little hit because you don't want to offend him or have him thinking that you're the police." That's how I first got tricked into snorting cocaine. And once I started getting high on the white powder, I started becoming much more generous with the leeches.

The first time we ventured down to Harlem was the first time I had ever seen a circuit for a gambling game. All of the big-time drug dealers were there, betting thousands of dollars a pop. One of the first things I noticed was the way people were dressed. Everybody was sharp. On Freeman Street, I had always been the smoothest dressed dude in the joint, but in Harlem I just blended in with everyone else. The big thing at the time was fur. If you really wanted to appear wealthy, you had to have a fur coat, a fur hat, or a fur something.

The crap games in Harlem were different from those on Freeman Street, which is why I never won big down there. First of all, Harlem was the first place I had ever seen a stick man. A stick man was someone who would shake up the dice and throw them into your hand before you shot. Once you caught the dice, you had to toss them over one line and make them roll across a second line and hit a wall in order for your shot to be valid. On Freeman Street, we had played that only one piece of dice had to hit the wall. That's why I was so good, because I could make one die stay on five, while the other die hit the wall. That way, I never crapped out. But in Harlem, my signature shot was gone, so I had no chance. Eventually, they changed the rules on Freeman Street too and put an end to my days of winning thousands down there.

Once, when I was down in Harlem with Bro Gay, whose real name was Bob, I began reflecting on the craziness of the life I was leading. It was early spring 1971 and Marvin Gaye's hit single "What's Going On" was playing on the jukebox. We were getting high on reefer and I started tripping on how easy it was to win or lose thousands of dollars in the under-

78

world. One day you could be broke, languishing in poverty, and the next day you could buy anything you wanted, and vice versa. What gripped me was that Marvin seemed to be speaking directly to me because I didn't have a clue as to what was going on. I was lost. I had tens of thousands of dollars, but no idea of what to do with it. Sure, I bought clothes, but beyond that, I didn't know what to spend my money on. I hadn't even gotten hip to buying jewelry and cars yet. Nobody I knew owned a house. None of my partners knew anything about investments. Most of the guys I hung with had the same backwards background as I did. Many of the brothers in Harlem, who had gone to prison and learned what to do with their money, were more sophisticated. They owned brownstones or lived out on Long Island. But us brothers on Freeman Street were not as progressive. I had enough money to go anywhere I wanted, but besides gambling spots, I had nowhere to go. I knew it wasn't natural to spend 96 hours a week, cramped up in a tiny room eating food from a vending machine, but that was what my life had become. Whatever promise I had once displayed had deteriorated into nothing, leaving me stuck in a world where scheming and conniving were the ultimate virtues. I truly was wondering "What's Going On?"

I continued to wonder the same thing upon my return to Freeman Street. Though I knew the change in rules would make it more difficult for me, I did not expect to become a total loser. My luck having run desert dry, I began losing on a regular basis, dropping hundreds, sometimes thousands, of dollars a day. By May, believe it or not, I was broke. Not short on cash, not low on funds, but broke. Penniless. Completely out of money. The man who months earlier had been sent off to Harlem feeling like a king now felt as foolish as Jackie Boy. In need of money, I decided to pay Robert Moore a visit.

I approached Robert and asked him to give me a package of heroin on consignment. Having become a friend of mine since our first encounter at my corner crap game, he obliged and sent me out to make some money. But I knew that dealing on the streets would leave me broke or in jail, so I promised myself that I would never push dope on the corners; and in all my years of dealing, I never did. Instead, I enlisted others to do the dirty work for me. My underlings went to New Haven to sell my product, but poor timing foiled our plans.

Several locals had recently died from heroin overdoses, so the junkies were being picky. They were looking for that "killer dope" and nothing less.

Whenever someone overdosed on heroin, rather than staying away from the pusher who sold the stuff, the other junkies pursued him feverishly because he had that "good poison." The feeling was that his dope would really make you high, and that the only reason someone died from using it was because it was so good that they took too much. The product I had was decent, but the brother with the killer stuff was getting all the business. The only customers my guys got were the junkies who were sick and on the verge of going into withdrawal.

One thing I learned quickly about heroin was that it crossed all racial and socioeconomic lines. You had street junkies, who didn't have a place to stay. You had those who were addicted, but were able to keep up their appearance. They always had a scheme, such as shoplifting and selling the stolen goods, to get money to finance their habit. Then you had the hustlers, prostitutes and working people who were addicted. The addicts who held down jobs would take a shot in the morning and a shot at night, and that would keep them from going into withdrawal. You also had a lot of middle-class White folks coming into the community to buy dope. Beyond that, you had the dealers themselves. I was unaware of this for most of my tenure on the streets, but most pushers had incredible heroin habits, even though they would never allow junkies to sell their product. I learned about this in the late 1970s when a panic broke out, meaning there were no drugs on the streets. Anyway, out there on the corners hunting for dope with the rest of the junkies were the dealers, many of whom looked as hopeless and as disheveled as the street junkies.

While in New Haven, I bumped into my old friend J.J., whom I had entered the Army with on the Buddy-Buddy Plan. J.J. had been wounded in Vietnam and given an early discharge. He wasn't dealing dope himself but he informed me that the South was a dope pusher's paradise. Drugs that sold for $2 a bag up North was selling for $10 and $15 a bag in North Carolina. Plus, because of the dearth of drug treatment centers in the rural South, the rule was once a druggie, always a druggie. Whereas junkies in the North could receive help for their addiction, junkies in the South basically had to stay hooked. As twisted as it now seems to me, back then I considered that to be good news.

But before I could begin dealing in North Carolina, I had to get my hands on enough cash to buy some dope. It was one thing to ask for a package on consignment when your destination is 75 miles away in Connecticut, but quite another when you're going 450 miles into the South, particularly when you're relying solely on the word of a friend who doesn't sell drugs.

In search of easy money, I got dressed to the nines and went to a crap game on the upper Eastside of the Bronx. For the first time in awhile, luck was on my side, and I was able to clean up just like in the old days. Ecstatic about being back on the winning side, I began talking exceptional trash. Though I was 21 years old, I could have passed for 16, and my big mouth and youthful appearance did not sit well with one of the older hustlers in attendance. Thinking I was a loud-mouthed kid who could easily be punked, he picked up the draw after I had won a bet. Without hesitation or a word, I clocked him with a straight right hand, tackled him around the legs, and began pounding him. I was incensed, not only because he had tried to take my winnings, but because he had broken my rhythm on what I knew was going to be a hugely lucrative night. Though I had clearly shown that I was not to be trifled with by the time I was pulled off him, I was not satisfied. The viciousness that I became known for years later had started to take root, and I wanted to let everyone know that M.C. was for real. For some reason, I was not packing a gun that night, so I left and went to Freeman Street to get one. When I arrived, I ran down what happened to be an old friend, and he let me borrow his .38 caliber pistol, saying "You gotta do what you gotta do." I had carried guns for a long time but up to this point, I had never used one. Still, there was not the slightest bit of fear or apprehension in my mind. My intentions clear, I returned to the game in the Bronx and, as soon as the door opened, was rushed by the guy I had beaten up. I pulled out the gun and started firing haphazardly. The 30 or 40 people in the room went ballistic. Folks were screaming, yelling and diving on the floor. I still don't know how many people I shot, but the legend of the ferocious M.C. was birthed that night.

To avoid any trouble that might result from the incident - be it from the police or a vengeful group of hustlers - I left the Bronx in a hurry and headed for North Carolina. I didn't get a chance to pay Robert his money, but I would deal with that later. I figured I would make a killing selling drugs down South and would have his money plus interest within a few weeks. My first move upon arriving in North Carolina was to contact my cousin, Elvin "Slim Poppa" Bryant. He had started hustling in Greensboro during the mid-'60s, and I reckoned he could teach me the ins and outs of the Southern dope game, not to mention hook me up with some product.

Slim Poppa was more than happy to teach a family member the trade, and my first lesson was on how to cut heroin. My second was less definitive and consisted of him overcharging me for bad stuff. Slim Poppa smiled in my face and played me for a fool. But in a strange way, I appreciated his chicanery. It taught me that a hustler is, first and foremost, a hustler, and that in most cases, friendship and even blood does not change that. Months later, after I had learned the game, I asked Elvin why he had played me. Flashing the same devilish smile he had used to con me, he replied, "I was wondering when you were going to catch on," and left it at that. My recognition of his deception gave me respect in Elvin's eyes, and he soon began treating me as an equal rather than a subordinate.

The Southern drug trade was not as profitable as I had been led to believe, and I was unable to make large sums of money. But my clothing told a different story, so my reputation was more sizable than my action. In those days, certain clothing was available only in hot spots like New York City, Los Angeles or Detroit, so with my wardrobe full of big-city fashions, I looked like a movie star compared to the best-dressed hustlers in Greene and Pitt Counties. My animated dress code begged for confrontation and provoked jealousy and other forms of hostility in the minds of some hustlers. For one, it screamed that I had money and at the very least, it made me a tempting target. It also enticed anyone who thought he was bad in his own right to prove it at my expense, perhaps to show that better clothes don't make a better hustler. That type of thinking is probably what led to my first shooting in the South.

One of my cousins, James Saunders, dropped me off in front of a Farmville nightclub one night, and when I got out of the car and headed toward the entrance a stranger started challenging me. I didn't know if he had mistaken me for somebody else or what, but when I turned around to see what he was talking about, his partner began loud talking me too. Before I could respond, he pulled out a knife and began gesturing like he was about to cut me. Having started my night with the intention of partying and having a good time, I was not in the mood for conflict. So in an effort to end things before they got messy, I pulled out my pistol and shot into the sky. It was clear that this dude's deadliest weapon was a knife, so I thought my shot would scare him into rethinking the situation and going about his business. Instead, the brother with the knife responded to my shot by saying, "Don't do that," while his friend worked his way behind me. The brother with the knife continued to bait me and in an obvious sign of ignorance, said I didn't have the guts to shoot him. So without so much as a thought or a blink, I shot him in the abdomen with my .25 automatic, sending the roughly 250 witnesses, including the jive-talking brother who started the confrontation, scurrying for cover. In addition to establishing me in Eastern North Carolina as a no-nonsense type of hustler, the shooting added fuel to the already burning belief in Pitt and Greene Counties that the young men in my family wouldn't think twice about drawing a pistol and putting a bullet into someone's body.

Though there were plenty of eyewitnesses, my demeanor was cool for a number of reasons. First, I didn't think the guy was dead, so I didn't think it was a big deal. It was only a .25 caliber gun, and I had purposely aimed away from his head and his heart. I thought I might have to pay a fine, pay his hospital bills, or do some community service. I certainly wasn't expecting major trouble. Unfortunately, the bullet hit a vital organ inside of his body, and he died from internal bleeding (I learned later that with small caliber weapons, the wound closes quickly, disallowing the blood to flow out of the body and causing people to bleed to death internally). My second reason for thinking I would be safe was that I didn't think anyone would testify against me. I was thinking like I was still in New York, where Blacks were steadfast in their refusal to cooperate with the police. I forgot that in the South, Blacks readily complied with the law, if for no other reason than fear.

So, secure in my safety, I returned that night to my parents' home as if nothing had happened. It wasn't until I awoke the next morning that I realized the severity of my actions. I opened my eyes and policemen were everywhere. It was like a scene from a movie. There must have been close to 12 cops surrounding me. Playing dumb, I asked what I had been charged with. When they replied, "Murder One," shock waves ran throughout my body. They began reading me my rights and asked if I wanted to tell them what happened. I responded defiantly, telling them to talk to my lawyer. They responded by escorting me to a squad car and shipping me off to jail. Unaware that the Supreme Court had overturned the death penalty, I thought my life was at risk.

One of my cousins (remember, my family was known for shooting folks) had recently been acquitted of killing someone. He recommended that I get his lawyer, Roland C. Braswell, to defend me. Braswell was viewed as the

Perry Mason of Eastern North Carolina, so I knew I was in good hands. He was unable to make it to my initial hearing, but his assistant, Tom Strickland, who later became a state senator, represented me in his place.

Naturally, I described that evening's events as favorably as possible. Even without my embellishment, the facts, for the most part, were on my side. The guy, who turned out to be a well-known troublemaker, had a knife and I fired a warning shot. With the evidence pointing toward self-defense, it would have been hard for them to convict me of murder. After I spoke to my lawyer, they let me out on bond, and later, I had a one-day trial. I was found guilty of involuntary manslaughter and given five years probation, a couple of fines, and the responsibility of paying for my victim's funeral. Instead of being thankful, though, I began thinking I was invincible. "They simply can't put me in jail," I said to myself. "I'm the baddest man in North Carolina." So as I walked out of the courtroom in a cocky strut, I shouted, "I ain't gonna kill him and bury him too!"

Though I had gone to North Carolina with big-crime on my mind, my time at home with my parents and friends made me realize that you should never jeopardize your home base. In other words, you always need to be able to return home. So even though I dealt drugs in North Carolina, I never sold much heroin in the vicinity of my upbringing. It wasn't that I was concerned with what people thought of me, but rather that I knew it wasn't wise to be wanted by the law every place. You had to have a safe haven somewhere. So over the years, whenever I got in trouble up North, I always went to North Carolina to lay low for awhile.

I returned to New York after my trial, figuring that Robert Moore had cooled down by now; if not, I thought I would be able to round up enough cash to pay him off. But to my surprise, Robert didn't even want his money back. My shooting spree on the upper Eastside of the Bronx had gained me newfound respect on the streets. Fearing that I might start shooting over the smallest dispute, Robert and others didn't want any trouble out of me, just like I didn't want any trouble out of them. Robert now saw me as his equal, so much so that he even put a few hundred dollars in my pocket.

Despite my freshly-acquired status as a ruthless killer, I found the money-making opportunities in New York to be limited. Eventually, I realized this was because Richard Nixon had been elected president of the United States, and an economic backlash had ensued. Back on Freeman Street, most of the working guys who used to come by and gamble on Thursday nights had been laid off by their employers, so their money was not there for the taking. We also found out that some of the guys who had pawned themselves off as hustlers were not really hustlers at all. They had acted like the money they carried had been won on the streets when in actuality, they had earned it honestly at work. With the recession in full swing, they lost those jobs and became real hustlers in the sense that they were unemployed.

Times were even hard for the true hustlers. The passing of Nixon's "No Knock" law gave police the right to break into the homes of anyone who was suspected of selling drugs. Of course, the inner-city Black neighborhoods were the main targets, so police were knocking down doors at random, whether they had legitimate suspicions or not. Also, under the leadership of Governor Nelson Rockefeller, New York passed the mandatory life-sentence law, which stated that if you were caught with as little as one ounce of heroin, you automatically received a life sentence in prison. Those two laws changed the entire face of the drug game. Times were so tough that some hustlers started driving Pontiacs and Buicks instead of the standard ride for the ghetto's rich and famous, the Cadillac.

In a truly disturbing development, the powerful dealers began recruiting teenagers as runners because they came cheaper, asked fewer questions and possessed, loyalty that was absolute. They also were exempt from the Adult Life Sentence Law that existed in New York state. With slim chances of becoming successful in a legitimate arena, kids were easily drawn to the high-rolling lifestyles that the top pushers flaunted. Because the competition to land a gig running for a major dealer was stiff, many teenagers were merciless in killing for the man they worked for. They felt like they had to be extra treacherous to set themselves apart from the other wannabes their age. That's how some of the most barbarous men I've ever met were initiated into the killing game. I knew a guy named Chris who started that way. Later, when he was about 26 years old, he killed 10 people in one shooting binge in Brooklyn. One of his girlfriend's family members had crossed him, so he stormed into their apartment and started blasting. As far as I know, he's still in jail to this day.

In August of 1972, while I was in New York trying to get drugs, my first child, Tawanda Lashon Ormond, was born. Though most of my relationships with women had been pointless, Lashon was not the product of a meaningless fling. Her mother, Cleaster, was the first woman I ever fell in love with. I met Cleaster in North Carolina after fleeing the Bronx and the repercussions of my first shooting. She was a beautiful, intelligent woman from a solid family. She was a first cousin to my childhood friend, Jasper, and actually grew up in the same church as I had. But because she was a few years younger than me, I had never noticed her. She knew who I was, though. Guys used to refer to her as the barbecue girl because her grandfather sold delicious barbecue in Maury. Whenever J.J. and I hung out, we always made a point of stopping by the barbecue shack to see Cleaster. Both of us had eyes for her and like everything else at the time, I viewed her as a trophy, as something to be won. When it became clear that I was Cleaster's choice, I teased J.J., saying my "mack" was stronger than his.

But before long, Cleaster became more than a prize. Her warm personality disarmed me in a way that was comforting. Around her, I didn't have to be the big, bad hustler. I could just be Mark. In a way, being with Cleaster reminded me of being with Edwin Gay and Jasper. None of them were caught up in the wild, mischievous lifestyle that I had fallen into, and a part of me liked being around positive people. My feelings for Cleaster tore me in half because, as a hustler, it wasn't cool to be in love. With my street mentality convincing me that I had become weak, I thought I had slipped and made a mistake by falling for her. We even talked about marriage, but in the end, my lust for the underworld won out over my love for Cleaster. She wanted me to be responsible and get a job, but I couldn't see the point in getting some low-paying, dead-end job when I could make real money on the streets. To her credit, she refused to put up with my ignorance, eventually ending the relationship while I was in jail, months after Lashon was born.

Obviously, my relationship with Lashon has never been what it should have, since I was locked up for the majority of her first 17 years of life. When not behind bars, I would do my best to cram all the things I had missed into a few precious moments. While on escape from a prison in North Carolina, I took her shopping for school clothes when she was seven. Most of my partners thought I was being foolish, that seeing her was too dangerous. They would say, "Send the money, man. It's too risky to go yourself." But they didn't understand what those few hours with Lashon meant to me. Almost every time I went to see her, I showered her with gifts of money, clothing and toys. I thought that might make up for my absence, but we were never able to establish the emotional bond that comes natural to most children and their parents. One of the most rewarding aspects of my born-again experience has been the revitalization of my relationship with Lashon. Over the past decade, we have made progress in building a true father-daughter relationship, a development for which I continually thank God.

As I mentioned, I ended up in jail shortly after Lashon's birth. My incarceration was the result of my having become a stick-up man. As drug trafficking slowed to a crawl, I turned to robbery as a way to make a living. I didn't really want to pull stick-ups but I had to produce some income; one reason being that my use of cocaine and heroin was on the rise. I hooked up with a guy named Larry Sears, who could only be described as a stick-up fanatic. Totally out of control, Larry would rob any place and any person. Even when we were just hanging out, not planning to commit a crime, he would pull a hold-up. There would be times when we would be in a clothing store. As I was trying to buy an outfit or two, Larry would pull out his gun and rob the clerks. I had made it a rule not to rob clothing stores because I liked shopping at them, but Larry was unconscious. I couldn't even send him into a store to buy a pack of cigarettes because he would stick the people up. His motto was "I ain't paying for nothing." Being a stick-up man, especially one with a partner like Larry, meant being ready at all times. Carrying a gun was no longer a choice, but mandatory. Whether early morning, mid-afternoon or late at night, I always had to be packing a gun.

That was my downfall, as I was arrested on December 10, 1972 for possession of a deadly weapon. I had gotten into an argument with some folks – I don't recall what it was about – and was heading toward their place to settle our dispute. I was carrying a sawed-off shotgun, but I didn't intend to use it unless it was absolutely necessary. As soon as I stepped onto the street, the cops, having been alerted by my adversaries, pounced on me.

I was taken to the Brooklyn House of Detention at 275 Atlantic Avenue and placed in a cell for 23 hours a day. Though it wasn't my first time being in a cell, it was the first time I had been in a major lockup situation. The reason for the 23-hour lockup was that, in those days, anyone arrested for gun possession or a violent crime was put under observation and suicide watch. Under this strange system, the guards would release you from your cell for one hour each day to take a shower or walk up and down the range. There were usually two guys to a cell, and they would allow four guys out of their cells at once. Eventually, I developed the opinion that the 23-hour lockup might as well have been 24 hours. After a week or two, I began thinking, "What's the point of going out for one hour? Why shower if I'm not going anywhere." So sometimes, they would open my door, and I would just yell out my cell number so they would close it right back.

It was in the 23-hour lockup that I adopted the policy of sleeping away my first 72 hours of jail time whenever possible. I did this for two reasons: first, I was tired; and second, I was hoping when I woke up, my nightmare would be over and I would be free. At this point, jail was not a reflective experience for me. Later, when I started going to prison on what seemed like a regular basis, I would ponder and contemplate my past and future. But at this stage, jail was just an obstacle, another hurdle I had to clear en route to becoming a major hustler. The thought of going to jail never scared me. I definitely hated it, but because I believed I was tough enough to take care of myself, I never feared being incarcerated. Being isolated didn't bother me either. Some people always have to be surrounded by others, but I've never been like that. I've always felt like, "If people are around, fine. If not, that's fine too."

Once the authorities began processing me for trial, the experience turned 360 degrees from one of isolation to one of smothering confinement, as I was shipped back and forth between Atlantic Avenue and Riker's Island every other week for the next few months. The two places could not have been more different. Whereas Atlantic was like being stranded on a crude and deserted island, Riker's was like being stuck on an overcrowded subway train.

They woke me up every morning at 5:30, handcuffed me and drove me to Riker's, where I was thrown into a holding cell with dozens of other convicts. Smoke was everywhere, as just about every guy in the cell, including myself, lit cigarettes to pass the time. Under the circumstances, hygiene wasn't a major concern for most of us, so the combination of heat, sweat and body odor created a horrendous stench. The putrid atmosphere, plus the unsavory paper-bag lunches they tossed out, all but destroyed my appetite as I anxiously waited for them to call my name and, quite literally, set me free.

The holding cell also served as a soapbox for members of the Nation of Islam. A series of zealous Muslims would preach almost every day, vehemently rebuking White America for its mistreatment of Blacks and spouting their infamous White devil rhetoric. While they may not have landed many converts, they were always able to captivate the majority of us. They spoke with such eloquence, fearlessness and passion that it was impossible not to be impressed. Of course, the police were always around, but their presence only served to embolden the Muslims, whose proclamations grew louder and bolder as the number of police increased. Above all, the Muslims were entertaining and their preaching was often the highlight of the day.

The nearly unbearable experience of the congested holding cell plays a large role in the plea bargaining process. Most guys don't want to go to trial anyway, so after months of this long and repetitive process, they're usually ready to plead guilty just to get to prison, where the atmosphere is not as confining.

Since I had violated my probation in North Carolina and was caught in possession of a deadly weapon, I recognized that my chances of walking away without doing any time were slim. So while in the holding cell, I came up with the asinine idea of claiming to be a drug addict. After I stated my case, the administrators at Riker's questioned me and concluded that I was indeed hooked on illegal substances. I didn't know whether to feel happy or insulted. Regardless, I thought I had pulled a fast one when they sent me to the Arthur Kills Drug Rehabilitation Center on Staten Island, but I didn't realize that being a certified drug addict would further tarnish my already soiled record. I remained at the center, receiving treatment for a problem I did not have, until June of 1973. That's when my probation officer from North Carolina came to get me and put me before a judge. Amazed that I had abused the rather lenient sentence I had received for involuntary man-slaughter, the judge violated me within a matter of minutes. As brazen as I wanted to be, I told the judge I would appeal the decision. I was given an appeal bond and days later, after my mother's nephew paid for my release, I was back on the streets.

I knew I had no grounds to win the appeal and viewed the bond simply as a way to buy myself some time and perhaps come up with a plan to avoid real imprisonment. I decided to look for an underhanded lawyer who, for a fee, would fix my predicament. That type of counsel is not hard to find, and I soon came across one who told me that for $10,000 he would make sure I got off scot-free. I told him he'd have his money within six months.

By this time, my stick-up partner, Larry, was in jail himself, having been shot and arrested in the middle of a robbery. With my right-hand man out of commission, I hooked up with a super tough thief named Jamaican Cecil. Our main focus was on gambling spots like the one on Freeman Street.

Shuttling between New Haven and New York, we would hit small poker games, strip everyone of their weapons and leave with all of the money. This proved to be rewarding, and I soon had the $10,000 and then some. But in running a few background checks on my lawyer, I was informed that he probably would not get me off, that his plan all along was just to trick me out of my money. So I decided to take my chances as a fugitive. When my crooked lawyer finally called to tell me about my upcoming court hearing, he said I should expect to receive a six-to-eight-year prison sentence. I told him I was on my way, but he should have known better. After all, I was a convicted felon who had attempted to bribe him: I wasn't playing by the rules. So instead of heading to court, I slipped away to New Haven and continued to run with Cecil.

One night, we busted in on a gambling spot after the game had ended and all of the hustlers had gone. The only person left was the guy who had run the game and ended up with most of the money, probably by cheating. I had seen him before but I couldn't put my finger on where, so I figured that we had gambled together at some time. At first, I didn't think he recognized me, but when he began looking at me strangely, I knew he had placed me. In the process of robbing him, we beat him severely and since he had seen our faces, we contemplated killing him. Jamaican Cecil wanted to pop him, but for some reason – perhaps because he was crying - I wouldn't let him pull the trigger, even though I knew he could identify me to the police. So we left him there, sobbing in his own blood.

I never thought the guy would rat on me because hustlers usually don't report being robbed. They are either afraid to go to the police for fear of being arrested themselves, or embarrassed about being victimized and intent on administering their own form of justice. This time, however, was different. This guy, who knew my brother James and had seen me hanging with him on the New Haven poker set, went to the police the next day. So, unbeknownst to me, a warrant was issued for my arrest. Weeks later, I was apprehended by police in front of M.B.'s home in New Haven.

The cops took me to jail and charged me with robbery and kidnapping. Moving someone from one room to another is considered kidnapping. Hoping that my case in North Carolina would somehow vanish, I didn't tell anyone that I was already wanted for arrest. I thought I'd be able to get this case dismissed if I could get someone in contact with the guy we robbed. So I put the word out on the street that I would give him his money back plus interest if he would drop the charges. I had brothers approach him like this: "Hey, you're both hustlers. You can settle this on the street like men. There's no need to bring the White man into it." But he refused to play along because of the way we had disrespected him, so I was forced to come up with another strategy. Knowing there were no witnesses to the crime, I decided to play my word against his.

My plan worked better than I expected because the victim failed to show up for any of the three hearings. By the time the trial rolled around, I was confident because he was nowhere to be found and I had witnesses ready to claim that I was somewhere else at the time of the robbery. But while I'm in court thinking I've got it made, my victim walks in by accident, looking for another case. They were about to throw out my case when the police recognized him and put him on the stand. Of course, he identified me as his assailant, but since the case was so shady, they offered me the opportunity to cop a plea for one-to-two years. Inspired by how well bluffing had served me in the past, I told them, "No! And I'm suing ya'll for false arrest." I know my victim must have thought I was the boldest, craziest brother he had ever seen.

Before we went to trial, the court discovered that I was wanted down South. My case crushed, they added a three-to-eight-year sentence to the one I already had in North Carolina. I was furious, madder than I had been in years. I couldn't believe I was about to do real time. I had been moments away from freedom, at least up North. If it weren't for the freak accident of that guy wandering into the courtroom, I would have been back on the streets. With my distorted way of thinking, I actually felt like I had been wronged. I was in such a foul mood that it was only a matter of time before I did something stupid; a matter of days to be exact.

Back in jail, waiting to be transferred to prison, and still fuming, I sat in the back of the recreation room playing cards. There was a specified time period in which the convicts could go to the commissary to buy food, deodorant, toothpaste and other items. To go, you had to sign your name to a list, but I had been too busy playing spades to sign up. As the end of the time period drew near, I decided to go and buy a candy bar. I arrived at the gate just in time to go, but the guard wouldn't let me pass because I hadn't signed the sheet. So I pushed past him and attempted to slide through the small opening in the gate. Naturally, he grabbed me and when I felt his hands on my arm, the fuse that had been burning in me since being sentenced to prison blew. I swung at the guard with my right fist, and before he could respond, a full-blown riot broke out. Motivated by my gall, convicts

91

began attacking guards and heading for the commissary. I couldn't even throw another punch before being engulfed in the mayhem. The ruckus lasted for about five minutes, with no one getting seriously injured. Following the fight, they shipped me to the Connecticut State Prison at Somers as fast as possible. Even so, the news that I had incited a riot reached the inmates at Somers before I did.

Chapter V

DOING TIME

Prison and jail are as different as high school and college. Jail, where people are sent to await trial, is worse in the sense that it is more congested and confining. County or municipal jails are almost always overcrowded, and the conditions border on the deplorable. The atmosphere is teeming with tension because men who are used to releasing their aggression through fighting, roaming the streets, having sex or playing ball, are given little room or opportunity for all but the most rudimentary physical exercise. And the food, which is doled out in tiny portions, is horrible.

Added to these taxing external factors is the mental strain of watching individuals constantly come and go, some making bond and others being released by the courts. This procession of characters cuts deeply into the mental and emotional state of the person waiting for his future to be determined by the charade of a trial or a plea bargain. On top of that, jails are so constructed that one may go months without seeing the sun. This dreadful experience works toward cracking one's psyche and, in many cases, forever changing his way of thinking, for better or for worse.

The dynamics that lead those in prison to commit suicide, have emotional breakdowns, turn state's witness, or become philosophers, militants, professional criminals, religious converts or law-abiding citizens all have their roots in jail. Prison only nurtures and cultivates the seeds planted in jail, the amount of time spent in prison determining how polished, eccentric or erratic the harvest from the original seed. After months in jail, any type of release, whether it be into society or a prison, is a relief.

Somers Prison was unique in that it was not extremely violent. In my two years there, I never saw one stabbing incident. When guys fought, it was a fist fight. Even raping a guy was looked down upon. That, of course, is not to say that there was no homosexuality, but it was nothing compared to what I would see later in other prisons.

At Somers, perverted convicts would not violate inmates as much as they would subtly court them, like a guy wooing a girl on the outside. If someone started doing favors for a guy or became protective of him, that was his way of making a pass at him. Most of the guys into that sort of thing went after the known homosexuals or the 19 and 20 year olds, who by convict standards were seen as innocent. The young boys would not always know the rules of the game, so if a guy got friendly with them, stood up for them in a dispute, or gave them some cigarettes, they would not realize his intentions. As a result, they would let it continue. Then later on, when the older inmate started looking for something in return, the young guy would be shocked. But by then, it was too late. He had let the older guy look out for him as a man does for a woman so now he had to continue playing the part. The thing about Somers, though, was that if you were not a homosexual, or weak-minded enough to be coaxed into that lifestyle, you didn't have to worry about any nonsense. It wasn't in your face all day, every day.

I never had any problems at Somers because I had two of the most important things a convict can have: a reputation and a posse. With numerous hustlers whom I had gambled with already there, my reputation as an accomplished fist fighter preceded me. And the news that I had jacked a prison guard and started a riot at Whalley Avenue, which spread like a virus across the East Coast penitentiaries, only enhanced my notoriety among the inmates. Soon after arriving at Somers, I fell in with some of my old homeboys - Face Clemmons, Melvin Long, Irvin Brown and M.B. - and we watched each other's backs.

When I first entered Somers, the Muslims were probably the strongest group in the place. This was 1974, a year before Elijah Muhammad died and the Nation of Islam splintered into sects, so every Black Muslim in the joint was a member of the Nation. But I was never attracted to the Nation, which strikes me as odd because I had always been one to keep up with politics as they pertained to Black folks. At Somers, I became even more in tune to my Blackness by reading books such as *The Autobiography of Malcolm X* by Alex Haley and *Manchild in the Promised Land* by Claude Brown. Through my reading it became clear that, even though I had been living in urban areas, I was still very much countrified. I had maintained a farmboy mentality because nearly everybody I hung around with up North had been born and raised in the rural South, just like me.

Existing alongside my country mentality was a slave mentality. I had never thought of myself as being afraid of White people because I had always been eager to fight against White boys while growing up and in the military. But fighting is pretty childish, and when it came to interacting with Whites as a man, I couldn't do it. If I wasn't high, as I often was in the military, or enraged and ready for a confrontation, I was extremely uncomfortable around White folks, particularly those in authority. This condition was so embedded into my psyche that I was not even aware of its existence. I would just subconsciously drop my head and mumble in the presence of the White security guards or prison administrators. I could never approach them as an equal.

I did not realize that I had a slave mentality until an observant inmate brought it to my attention during a dispute. We had gotten into a heated argument over some trivial matter and I was about two seconds from attacking him, when all of a sudden he blurted out, "Look at you. You ready to kill me. But you can't even look a White man in the eye!" Stunned, I forgot all about hitting him, even though my rage grew stronger. Noticing that I was taken aback, he went on, "I been watching you and every time you talk to a White man, you look straight down to the floor."

He could not have thrown a punch that would have stung me as much as his words had. I felt like I had been stabbed, like he had really whipped me. I was supposed to be one of the baddest dudes in the joint, but this brother had stripped me of all my toughness and made me look cowardly in front of the throng of inmates that had gathered.

I felt like killing him but I couldn't move a limb. His words had paralyzed me because I knew they were true. From that day forward, I vowed that things would be different. Not only was I determined to look White guards and officials in the eyes, but I was determined to beat them down if necessary. If one so much as looked at me funny, I made sure to show the brothers that I wasn't afraid of him by getting in his face. I became obsessed with proving that I did not have a slave mentality, though at the time I did not know to call it that. If I had dealt with this new revelation in a positive manner, my transformation might have begun many years earlier. But I dealt with it negatively.

My first related incident took place about a month later in the cafeteria. Having already eaten one dinner and desert, I reentered the line and reached for another ice cream cup. Second helpings, however, were not allowed, so a young officer who looked to be about 21 or 22 years old, hollered out harshly, "Put it back!" Of course, everyone heard him and grew silent.

I had been waiting for a moment like this ever since that inmate had called out my slave mentality. That White boy was the only officer in the room so, I knew that if I disrespected his authority it would be his word against mine. Eager to display my fearlessness, I walked over to him and said, "Let me speak to you for a minute over here," before taking him to a secluded area near the kitchen. He had only been on staff for a few weeks and didn't know better than to go somewhere alone with a convict. But once we were by ourselves, he realized that he had made a mistake. I could see that he was frightened so, knowing I had the upper hand, I looked him squarely in the eyeballs and said firmly, "Don't you ever speak to me like that again." I didn't hit him, didn't push him, didn't even raise my voice. But he knew, I knew and the inmates knew, that I had stood up to a White officer.

Even though I won that small battle, a respected group of older, wiser prisoners told me later that I had made a mistake. They understood why I didn't want to take any mess from a guard, especially a White one, but they also understood that showing up a White boy wasn't worth receiving more time. They told me I would have to adjust my attitude in order to get out of prison, that the silent route was the way to go, and that I should never say a word to an officer. That way, the guards won't have any reason to say anything to me. "Don't joke with them or think you're doing yourself a favor by getting chummy with them," they told me, "because they'll turn on you in a minute." These seasoned prisoners understood that the guards were looking for reasons to add time to our sentences because keeping convicts in prison was how they fed their families. Their words led me to stop interacting with guards altogether.

I had started hanging with these "professional" criminals about a year or so into my incarceration. My entry into this elite group was due in equal parts to my reputation for roughness and my perceived intelligence. In addition to reading a lot, I worked at the prison school, where the little education I had put me head and shoulders above most of the inmates. Since these professional criminals were thinking convicts, they decided to invest in me in order to tap into whatever knowledge I might have. But while I had more of a standard education than they did, they were far more schooled in the ways of sophisticated criminality.

Most of the professionals were in their 30s and past the point of doing crime for the thrill of it. To them, crime was a means to an end, so they worked toward solidifying plans and schemes to legitimize their efforts. Not into foolishness and random crimes, they spent countless hours preparing themselves to make enough money off one big sale or heist to buy a bar, dry cleaners or laundry mat and go legit. They even spoke of sending their children to private schools to give them the resources and opportunities that they never had. That might sound like a strange objective for hardened, streetwise criminals to have, but the professionals understood the importance of being able to maneuver within the American mainstream. That's why, unlike the majority of the prison population, they had developed skills that, though elementary to most American adults, escape scores of Black men behind bars and on the streets. I'm talking about simple tasks such as balancing a checkbook, buying a house on credit, and obtaining a title for an automobile.

When I was running the streets of New York and New Haven, most of the people I came into contact with lacked these basic system skills. They were very adept at sustaining themselves outside of the system, having had years of practice on the streets, but they had no idea of how to function within the American mainstream. They were so concerned with merely surviving that they never developed the abilities necessary to operate within the nation's economic system. For example, brothers often survived by scrounging up enough money to buy a car from a friend. But they never learned the proper procedure for purchasing a car within the existing system because they didn't purchase insurance or go to the motor vehicle department to have the title changed. That was one of the many tragedies plaguing the African-American community during that period – that so many brothers and sisters did not know how to function within the system. Because of that, they struck some as being feeble-minded, but their intelligence was evident in their ability to subsist for years without the benefits inherited by those within the system. Sadly, this is still the case with many African-Americans.

Those are the types of discussions the professionals engaged in. Though they intended to gain wealth through crimes outside of the system, they also studied tax codes and other things they would need to know when producing a visible means of support. They were very intelligent brothers. Through our sometimes surprisingly in-depth conversations, I learned that being behind bars does not have to put an end to one's criminal activity on the outside. By maintaining his network while in prison, a brother could set himself up to have a new car and thousands of dollars in his pocket within 30 days of his release. Through frequent phone calls to their partners, wives and girlfriends - using coded language, of course - these professionals continued to handle their business on the streets while in prison. In fact, being incarcerated actually helped them increase their number of contacts.

These brothers also had a systematic approach for dealing with women. As hustlers, they would put many of their possessions, such as cars and apartments, in the names of women they were dating. For that reason, the professionals avoided sisters with "street mentalities" and instead went after educated and respectable women, who were less likely to draw suspicions from neighbors and the police. Listening to these crime kingpins made me recognize the importance of setting goals and having a plan. Before, I had plans to become a drug dealer or a stick-up man but never made precise, step-by-step outlines for my activity. I soon realized that instead of squandering $125,000 in a year, as I did in 1971, a man with a plan would have used it to set himself up for the next decade.

An integral part of the professionals' plans for life after prison was the recruitment of runners or street dealers. The professionals were looking to supply the product to dealers, not traffic it on the corners themselves: and what better place than the penitentiary to find ambitious young dealers? With a resume of felonies and defeated foes, the professionals had most of the young boys in awe of them, so the youngsters considered it a privilege to have the opportunity to run for them. That allowed the professionals to pick and choose from among some of the finest dope dealers in the Northeast. The recruitment process was not trivial, either. Guys didn't just pick young cats they knew from the neighborhood. Observing how the youngsters handled themselves in the yard, they studied their personalities, searching for mental toughness, fortitude, persistence and loyalty. They evaluated guys in earnest, as if recruiting prospective management trainees for a major corporation.

The opportunities to scrutinize an inmate's abilities were plentiful because of the booming drug business that operated inside of the prison walls. Because of their numerous contacts outside, the professionals nearly monopolized the trade and beneath them were the contraband hustlers who worked to impress the professionals and gain influence within the prison population. It was amazing how much these contraband hustlers wanted to be bigwigs in the prison. While the professionals sat atop the inmate hierarchy, they were essentially unconcerned with what went on in the prison. They were more interested in establishing themselves on the outside.

Though I was young and not yet a professional, I never thought of hustling contraband in the joint. It didn't make sense to me. So what if you made a lot of money while incarcerated? You certainly couldn't buy a car or clothes or take it with you upon release. Maybe I would have considered it if I had had to work to impress the professionals, but I doubt it. Don't get me wrong. There was much money to be made in prison hustling, but I was doing my best to serve good time and get out as soon as possible. I definitely did not want to risk catching another case while incarcerated, as I had done at Whalley Avenue.

I also refused to use drugs in prison. Getting high behind bars seemed like a no-win situation to me. Since I knew I had to constantly look over my shoulder to protect myself, I wanted to be as alert as possible. The prevalence of the drug trade was one of the things that surprised me the most about prison. I had heard from people that drug use in the penitentiary was rampant, but it was hard for me to believe until I saw it for myself.

With the help of guards and visitors, inmates were able to have their drug of choice as often as they liked, presuming they had some means of payment. Most of the drugs came in through the guards. After feeling out a guard, studying his personality and casing him for criminal tendencies, a convict would approach him with an offer of say $1,000 to bring in a package of heroin. Precious few guards had the convictions to refuse such a proposition. In fact, many would look for opportunities like that in order to make extra cash. That's the painful irony about prison; that plenty of the guards are as corrupt as the inmates.

Though I was smart enough to avoid selling or using drugs, I had in no way learned my lesson, unless of course, my lesson was how to become a better criminal. Besides the true religious converts, usually the only inmates who realize that crime doesn't pay are the ones who are left out of the in-crowd, the ones who don't know how to communicate and therefore don't learn anything from the wiser convicts. Without false hope, their isolation forces them to straighten up. On the other hand, I, the popular prisoner, was up to my forehead in false hope. I thought I was seeing clearly when my vision actually was more blurred than ever. Consequently, like a high school honor student, I listened, kept my mouth shut and took notes. I knew I would be transferred to North Carolina soon, so I was intent on learning how to recruit. I savored every moment with the professionals because as soon as I was shipped down South I planned to become one myself.

After two-and-a-half years, my experience at Somers ended. It was terrible, to be sure. All time behind bars is. But compared to what I was about to go through in North Carolina, and what I would see later in Lewisburg, Pennsylvania, it was tame. Somers actually gave me the wrong impression about prison. There, you could talk to guards any way you wanted to. That episode in which I took the young guard behind a door and reprimanded him would have gotten me thrashed in North Carolina. All of this led me to believe that prison really wasn't that bad; losing your freedom and being away from family and friends was difficult, but the actual experience behind the walls wasn't that tough. Soon I would realize the error of my thinking.

I was moved to Central Prison in Raleigh, North Carolina to serve my six-to-eight-year sentence for probation violation. After a night in a county jail, I arrived early the next morning and quickly rescinded my previously nonchalant attitude toward prison life. My new place of residence was so overcrowded that they didn't even have a cell for me. Instead, there were dozens of bunks spaced a-foot-and-a-half apart in the middle of this huge cellblock. There must have been about 600 men in my wing alone, which in itself had to be some sort of building violation. But the administrators didn't care. Prisoners meant nothing to them. That was evident by the way they threw me into the cellblock.

There was no orientation, no escort to a bunk, just a burly guard pointing the way into this vast expanse, telling me to find a space and slamming the gate shut. With my belongings in my arms, I looked forward and saw hundreds of Black men staring at me like I wasn't worth the dust on the bottom of their shoes. Black men. All Black men. I would find out later that the administration purposely segregated the prison: Blacks on the east side; Whites on the west. Knowing that the minorities on each side would be abused mercilessly, they would always throw a couple of White boys they despised in with the brothers, and vice versa.

When I began walking toward the collection of bunks, the initiation began. CP was a multi-tiered facility, and the guys on the higher levels were hooting, howling, whistling, cursing, propositioning and flinging things at me. I was called every derogatory name imaginable. Homosexuals were yelling out, "Fresh meat! A new boy!" It was so loud that I couldn't hear myself think. The inmates on my level were silent but by no means oblivious to my entrance. They were staring coldly at me, looking for my reaction to the heckling. How I responded would tell them all they needed to know about how strong or weak I was. Knowing as much, I showed no emotion whatsoever. I just kept looking ahead and walking forward. But inside, I was tripping. I had never heard or seen anything like this. Somers now seemed like day camp. I said to myself, "Man, this is real prison."

At about 11 o'clock, we were sent to lunch in the mess hall and I encountered more shock. I was standing in line when a guy walked up and cut in front of a bunch of inmates. I heard this brother in front of me say to his friend, "Man, I told him about disrespecting me." The next day, the same guy cut in the front of another line, provoking the brother he had upset the day before to walk up to him and stab him. He didn't say a word, or make a scene, just calmly sliced him up. I don't know if the guy died, but blood was everywhere. I was amazed. I had thought that I was ruthless. I noticed that no one else was as astonished as I was. Apparently used to such haphazard acts of violence, the other prisoners knew exactly what to do. As the orderly wiped up the blood, everyone hastily ate their meal, aware that we would be temporarily locked in our cellblocks until the inmate who was stabbed was identified.

Later on, I found out that CP got even more disgusting at night, especially for those of us who had to sleep on the bunks in the middle of the cellblock. Guys on the upper level would roll up toilet paper, light it on fire and throw it down on you. Even worse, they would sometimes masturbate into paper and toss it down over the balcony.

Life at CP was sickening. It was the filthiest place I ever had to live. Because we were allowed to shower only once a week, there was a repulsive stench everywhere. And unlike Somers, you couldn't scare the guards into making things more humane because they were all about 6-foot-6-inches tall. Of all the prisons and jails I stayed in, CP was the only one that led me to write my mother a letter asking her to pray that I was sent to another facility.

I thank God that He always looked out for me in the penitentiary. Knowing I would one day serve Him, He protected me from the more horrifying aspects of incarceration. He did this by making sure I had connections everywhere I went. In every institution, without fail, I found a group of brothers I had run with on the streets. They were always prominent prisoners, so hanging with them gave me a measure of respect inside the joint. In CP, I met up with some of my partners on the third day. A guard was calling out the names of the inmates who had received mail, and one of my old partners known as "Hook" heard my name. From the upper tier of the prison, he ran down, screaming, "Where's Mark Olds? Where's Mark Olds?" I recognized the voice instantly and hollered out, "Hook, is that you?" I was overjoyed to find that one of my old hustling buddies from North Carolina was in there. Through Hook, I discovered that a lot of my homeboys were in CP. Among others, there was Trick Dupree, Buggie Blount and Bank Robber from Wilson, North Carolina. Seeing them enabled me to relax a bit, although I still took care to watch my back.

The homosexuality at CP was on a whole different level than what I had seen in Somers, where it was a small minority of brothers - mainly guys who were gay when they entered the pen and a few known perverts - having sex. But in CP there was so much homosexuality going on that I couldn't tell who was doing what. Brothers who you least expect to be with another man were flaming. Some of the hardest prisoners on the yard were participating in all types of perverted mess. During the day, they were the baddest brothers around, and if you had the misfortune of crossing them, they would fight to kill you. But at night, they were girls. We called them "switch out artists."

The sexual dynamics in prison, of course, are totally different than those in society. Acts that would get a brother labeled as a sissy on the outside are considered macho behind bars. A lot of the brothers justify their behavior by claiming to be "the man" of the relationship, thinking that their manhood is maintained and that their actions are somehow "less homosexual" because they give rather than receive during intercourse. The way some of the brothers talked about other inmates would be either disgusting or comical to men who have never been incarcerated. They used the same language they used to hit on women when they were out in the streets, talking about "Hey, baby...He fine...I'm gonna get me some of that..."

I think there was more violence and homosexuality at CP than at Somers because there were more "lifers" in North Carolina. There's a major difference in the mentality of an inmate serving three to four years and one serving 20 to life. In Somers, a lot of guys were going to be released in the foreseeable future, but in CP, that wasn't the case. So, whereas the brothers in Somers were trying to behave so they could get out, many of the brothers in CP had accepted the hard truth that prison was now their home. That acceptance changed their whole worldview, and they began pursuing happiness in prison, trying to be comfortable and live as if they were on the outside. In that scenario, issues like who runs the prison and who controls the cigarette trade become a big deal. In fact, they become matters of life and death. As a result, battles are waged, and blood is shed.

The entire system at CP was more conducive to long-term sentences. For instance, inmates were allowed to carry cash. You could take up to $15 per week off your books (the accounting system by which the prison kept track of the amount of money sent to inmates). This, of course, encouraged gambling, which turned into the prison's pastime. While gambling produced all sorts of negative side effects, such as loan sharks, indebtedness, robbery and violence, it also created excitement and made the time go by faster. I, for one, gambled around the clock. While I found it to be stressful on the outside, it proved to be relaxing in prison because I could only lose so much money. I viewed gambling in prison as purely recreational. With so little money involved, I really didn't care whether I won or lost.

CP also had a canteen, at which you could buy refreshments, and illegal after-hours stores run by enterprising inmates who bought items from the canteen and sold them at a high price. But the most lucrative business still was drugs. The trade in CP was five times as big as that in Somers. The sale and use of reefer and heroin were extremely widespread. Nearly everyone, it seemed, was hooked into the drug trade. Some guards were compliant, and an inmate organization that used Polaroid cameras to take pictures of the convicts and their guests, participated in the trafficking. The authorities were well aware of the drug trade, and the thinking among the inmates was that they let it go on to placate and control us. Whenever it got out of hand, the administration would do a "shakedown" and collect all the contraband. But before long, things would return to normal.

Thankfully, after three months in CP, I was transferred to a road camp in Currituck County, North Carolina. Road camps, also known as chain gangs, had been outlawed years earlier because the camp administrators were abusing the inmates profusely and privately profiting from their labor. But the prisons were beginning to bring them back on a limited basis. Though the idea of working on roads in the hot sun did not excite me, I would have preferred just about anything to CP. There were about 200 of us at the camp, crammed into tiny quarters that were built to hold about half as many men.

Once again, I was blessed to meet three guys who knew me, including one named Larry Hill who basically ran the camp. I met Larry while attending North Carolina A&T and ironically, we took the same shady path. As was the case with me, his school days didn't last long, and he ended up hustling in New York and North Carolina. It was sad to see him in prison because he had been so close to doing something positive with his life. A tremendous basketball player, Larry had a tryout with the Carolina Cougars of the American Basketball Association. When things didn't work out, he resorted to making a living off the streets.

Compared to CP, Currituck was heavenly. One of the greatest things about it was the relaxed visitation policy. I had told my parents not to visit me in CP because I did not want them to see the ghastly conditions I was living under. But once I got to Currituck, they became regular guests. It was great to see my folks. They never condemned me, and my mother constantly reminded me that she was praying for me. I did not truly appreciate her prayers then but now I know they played a large role in how my life has panned out. The loose visitation rules also enabled you to have real, quality visits with female friends, which, next to freedom, was the greatest gift the inmates could have asked for.

Currituck also had traveling athletic teams. After being allotted just 30 minutes of outdoor recreation a day at CP, that was like a dream. I had now been locked up for about three years so the thought of traveling, even if it was only to other prison yards, was exhilarating. I won a spot on the basketball team where I played shooting guard and took the title of my position literally. No fan of passing, I attempted a shot just about every time I touched the ball. I actually had pretty good skills. Back in New York, I had played with Robert Moore on a team full of hustlers in a playground league and became a decent player. I was fast and quick so my defense was good and I could get to the basket on just about anybody. I played like I thought I was Tiny Archibald, minus the assists.

As one might imagine, the league was no joke, as every institution had a core of talented and competitive players. Some of the guys undoubtedly had the ability to play at the major college level, if not the pros, but some form of drug abuse had screwed them up. The best player I ever saw was a guy called "Pulpwood" Charlie. He got his nickname from working in pulpwood factories as a kid. Six-foot-eight-inches tall and built like a defensive end, he was incredible. He looked like he could bench press the building. Watching him play, you would have thought he had patterned his game after Dr. J. His moves were that dazzling.

Since we had nothing of substance going on in our lives, the games were taken more seriously than those I had participated in on the playgrounds. Guys treated the competition like the NCAA Final Four, yelling at teammates who made mistakes and employing various offensive and defensive strategies to confuse the opponent. Not surprisingly, just about everyone was a sore loser and defeats often resulted in heated arguments and near fights. When basketball season ended, we went straight into softball, and even though I didn't have much experience, the guys put me on the team because I was so well liked. I also grew fond of chess, which I still love to play today.

Though it was easy to get caught up in the fun of the games, I did not let them distract me from my ultimate mission of recruiting entry-level salesman for my pharmaceutical business. Dope dealers often described their mischief in such high-sounding language; I guess it made us feel like we were doing something legitimate. Even so, the idiocy of it all was not lost on us, and sometimes, when using those lofty words, we would glance at each other in mid-sentence and bust out laughing.

One of my recruits was a brother called "Tramp." I won't call him a prized recruit because he certainly had his shortcomings, but he seemed like a brother I could trust. That might sound strange, saying I could trust a criminal, but convicts can be extremely loyal to one another. This is especially true on the outside because, for the most part, ex-cons are looked down upon by the rest of society. That common rejection sometimes binds them together tighter than the bonds that sustain most human relationships. I'll never forget how, shortly after I had escaped in 1977, a brother I had met in Somers bought me a cashmere coat worth hundreds of dollars simply because he saw me wearing a light jacket during a cold New Haven winter. I really didn't even know the brother all that well, but because we had

105

endured something that most people never have or will, he looked out for me.

Tramp wasn't the wittiest guy in the world but he was good company, at least as good as a guy with 63 assault cases can be. He used to peddle folks and then take them to work on a migrant farm. In prison, he became one of the underground wine makers, mainly so he could have an endless supply of intoxicant. He could have made a killing if he hadn't been addicted to the stuff himself. He would buy yeast from the brothers who worked in the kitchen, put together his concoction and then sit alone on his bunk and drink most of it. He would always save a little for me and I usually gave my share to some of the guys I viewed as potential recruits. I drank the wine myself once, but after seeing Tramp put old radio batteries in his brew to make it cook faster, I never made that mistake again. It was also rumored that Tramp would put his dirty socks in the mix to darken the wine. I never witnessed that, but knowing Tramp, I wouldn't put it past him.

Besides Tramp, I was also planning to take a young kid named "Bull" along with me. But no one else seemed to measure up to the standards I had learned from my mentors in Somers.

Shortly after settling on Tramp and Bull, I met Jack Best. We hit it off immediately and even though Jack has never converted to Christianity, to this day, we are the best of friends. Jack arrived at Currituck for the second time in 1975. Busted for possession of heroin in Greensboro, he had begun serving his original sentence two years earlier. Within a year's time, he had escaped and run free for nine months before being captured and returned to the road camp. Though a career criminal, Jack wasn't as wild as I was. He never carried a gun and, in terms of crime, never went beyond dealing drugs and pimping women. In his ideal world, he would have done neither. As a Black kid growing up in Goldsboro, North Carolina, Jack Best dreamed of becoming a professional golfer.

Jack's passion for golf began at the age of 13, when he began working as a caddy at a posh, all-White country club near Goldsboro. The fact that they wouldn't let Blacks become members was no big deal in 1958, and the club owners probably thought they were being progressive by letting Jack play on the course. Taking advantage of the opportunity, Jack played once a week. While other brothers worked on their jump shot or curveball, Jack fine-tuned his putting and chipping. He became so good that by the time he left high school for New York City in 1962, he was almost a scratch golfer, meaning he could nearly shoot par on any course around.

106

Jack stayed with his older brother in New York and, following the path of many Southern boys in the big city, got involved in crime. A prime-time womanizer, he became a pimp and before long was able to afford a Cadillac. Still in love with golf, he saved his money and began driving toward Florida to take professional golf lessons and hopefully, become good enough to join the pro tour. But an overnight stop in Greensboro changed his life forever. Meeting up with some old friends, he started gambling and lost all of the money he had saved for his lessons. Hoping to rebuild his savings, he hooked up with a drug dealer who gave him a package and instructions on how to sell it. The money came so quickly and easily that Jack forgot all about taking golf lessons and started dealing full-time between North Carolina and New York.

Jack and I met over a game of Black Jack when he loaned me some money to continue gambling. Later that day, we started talking, and I found that he was well connected in the narcotics game in New York. A level above the professionals I had met in Somers, he knew Black guys who received product directly from Thailand. Ever since the Vietnam War, brothers had been setting up their own drug routes from the Far East. No longer getting dope third or fourth hand from the Italians, they changed the racial makeup of drug trafficking in the inner city. I started dropping the names of some of the suppliers I knew and suddenly we realized that we had enough ties to set up an international drug route along the Eastern Coast of the United States.

Our goal determined, we began sharpening our strategy during daily walks around the yard. We talked about putting all of the pieces in place that I had been taught about in Somers - educated women, business fronts, street dealers. With my plan materializing before my eyes, I began to doubt the abilities of Bull and especially Tramp. Tramp would be useful to make hits, but his addiction to alcohol made him suspect. I liked Bull, but he was inexperienced. I figured with the right coaching, though, he could do well. Refusing to let anyone screw up my future, I cut off Tramp and continued to scrutinize Bull and a few others who had emerged as potentials.

The final part of my plan was escape. Eager to build my route, I couldn't bare the thought of staying behind bars until the early 1980s. Even if I did wait for my release date, going on parole was not a viable option because I refused to get a job or stay in North Carolina. So I began looking for chances to run. Though I was antsy, I realized that attempting to leave at the wrong time and getting caught would ruin all the plans I had made, so I waited for the perfect opportunity. It would be a couple of years before it came.

I passed the time by perfecting the plan Jack and I had formulated, playing ball and chess and writing poetry. I was a relatively gifted writer whom all of the inmates thought was Currituck's answer to William Shakespeare. My ability to use big words that are rarely found in everyday language impressed the convicts who, believe it or not, were very much into poetry. Some brothers would even have traded their hook shot for the ability to flatter through prose. This poetic interest was not due to anything academic, such as the love of the meter or the rhyme. It was a rap, a scam, as brothers, desperately trying to stay in the minds and hearts of their girlfriends back home, discovered that poetry did the trick. That made me a widely sought-after ghost writer, and a highly successful one too. I must have poetically romanced five or six girls for Jack Best alone. Jack and I got great kicks out of the way women responded to my writings. Once, a young lady visited Jack shortly after receiving one of my letters with Jack's signature on it and said, "Baby, say some of those things to me that you said in your letter." Jack, caught with a blank stare, almost lost his balance. Gathering his wits, he replied, "Oh, girl. I'm so glad to see you that I just want to hold you right now."

In the spring of 1977, I made the honor grade and was shipped to a minimum security facility in Raleigh called the Triangle Correctional Center, located in the shadow of the walls of Central Prison. Soon after arriving at Triangle, my 28th birthday came and went, creating a growing sense of desperation within me. Comparing myself to my cousins, I started to feel like a failure. They were all holding down steady jobs, buying homes and beginning to raise families, and I was rotting away in the prison system. The desire to achieve some degree of success began to well up inside of me, but unfortunately, it was not accompanied by the desire to clean myself up. I wanted to prosper but not through conventional means. I was not interested in returning to school or to the work force. I did not want to pay taxes or deal with White folks. I just wanted to be rich and free. Of course, I knew that being a wealthy thief would not please my mother but I figured that as long as I stayed out of prison, she wouldn't know where my money had come from. She might have even assumed it had been made honestly.

Shortly after arriving at Triangle, I met one of the wildest brothers I have ever known, a crazy character named Virgil Gaines. Because he was from Tyler, Texas, we called him Terrible Tex. Tex was a tall, handsome man who lived for the thrill of crossing the boundaries of human decency. To break every law imposed on him seemed to be his life's ambition. Even among criminals, he was considered a madman. Once, he disrupted an entire funeral procession just for fun.

A guy who owed him a few thousand dollars had been killed, and Tex, seething because the source of his money was about to be buried six feet underground, didn't like the fact that he hadn't enjoyed the pleasure of putting him there himself. So as the caravan drove to the burial site, Tex parked on a side street and waited for the mourners to come his way. When all of the cars had passed him, Tex flew by them in his Oldsmobile Toronado and made the hearse, dead body and all, pull over. He got out of his car, sprinted to the family vehicle and snatched open the door with the dramatics of a superhero. Then, with eyes beaming, lips curled and pistol waving in his hand, he screamed at the guy's mother, "Your boy owed me a lot of money. I want my money." The woman fainted in an instant, and Tex, laughing and feeling vindicated, got back in his car and drove off into the sunset as if some sort of hero in an action flick. All along, he knew the woman wouldn't be able to pay him; he just got a kick out of doing stuff like that.

Tex and I grew to be tight, and the more I got to know him, the more I realized how shrewd he was. He was flamboyant, to be sure, but everything he did was very calculated. For instance, he intended to get more than a rush out of disrupting that funeral procession. He also wanted to send a message to anyone who might think about crossing him in the future.

One of Tex's greatest strengths, albeit a misguided one, was his ability to focus all of his attention on achieving one particular goal. He could sit in the joint for years and lend all of his concentration to fulfilling a promise or threat he had made to someone on the outside. Once, after a White judge in Fayetteville, North Carolina sentenced him to two years in prison, Tex told him to beware because "I'm going to get your daughter when I get out," meaning that he would make her his lover. Sure enough, two years later, Tex was dating the judge's daughter. Word of their relationship spread all over town and when the judge found out, he was irate. He tried to make Tex leave the county, but Tex used his daughter for protection since no officers wanted to be the ones to bust Tex with the judge's daughter. Clearly, Tex had more than revenge on his mind when he set out to get the judge's daughter.

Since Triangle was a minimum-security prison, inmates were able to hold work-release jobs that allowed them to leave the prison during the day and return in the evening. That created a lot of cash flow in the prison and turned the bribing of guards into a daily occurrence. With guards receiving hush money for drugs and other favors, the prison population began to resemble free America in the amount of disparity between the haves and the have-nots. I was in a road gang of about 30 inmates that was taken to a highway every day to do landscaping and other chores. Between my job and my gambling, I made enough money to pay the Black guard who ran our group $5 a day to skip my name in the morning roll call. That enabled me to relax all day and work on my plan of escape.

While both Black and White guards could be bought, Black guards were sometimes more sympathetic to inmates because of the lingering effects of the Black Power movement. Looking for every advantage possible, convicts would make themselves out to be the victims of an unjust system and try to put the Black guards on a guilt trip for working for "The Man." Among themselves, the Black guards would display their racial consciousness by calling each other "Brother" or sometimes "Soul Brother." The White guards reacted by referring to one another as "Cousin." It was funny.

Though the period of racial rebellion and consciousness had given way to the "Superfly" era in the Black community, there was still plenty of tension between Blacks and Whites in the joint; tension that was only exacerbated by the airing of Alex Haley's "Roots" on television. I'm surprised the prison let the inmates watch something so inflammatory. If "Roots" angered many average, law-abiding Black men, imagine what it did to violent criminals. Predictably, the number of racially-motivated attacks increased, and the White guards were on the defensive. Knowing they were in the position of the slave masters and overseers in "Roots," the guards made sure not to be as harsh and as confrontational with the Black inmates.

I chose not to watch "Roots" because I knew it would lead me to attack a White inmate. I was already overly aggressive when interacting with Whites because that brother's words in Somers - about me having a slave mentality - still sat in my soul. An incident that illustrates how incensed I became when dealing with White folks occurred when the Black guard I had been paying off took a two-week vacation. A White man replaced him and naturally, read my name from the roll and sent me to work. It had been a long time since I had done road work, and I wasn't about to be forced into it by anybody; so I lollygagged all morning. When the guard discovered during his afternoon inspection that I hadn't lifted a finger, he started yelling at me as if I was a rebellious child. Not the least bit afraid, I

110

got in his face and started cursing at him, which landed me in the hole and cost me my visiting privileges. I never got to him while in prison, but I was so angry that, after escaping, I drove to the prison twice and waited outside of the gates for him to get off work. If I had seen him, I probably would have killed him. Fortunately, he never appeared.

In the area our road gang worked, the laundry room was the only building around. A fence surrounded it, but you could clear the fence by leaping off the roof of the laundry room. We were still within the city limits of Raleigh so the fence was the only obstacle between freedom and us. I remember saying to Tex, "If the cats back in New York knew that the only thing keeping me in custody was this little fence, they would laugh at me to no end." So I decided that when the time was right, I would jump.

I had two accomplices to my plan. The first was a free sister who lived in Raleigh. Her brother was an inmate and I met her during one of her visits to him. We began rapping, hit it off and soon she began visiting me. After gaining her trust, I told her of my plans for escape and she said I could stay with her once I broke free. My second co-conspirator was a fellow inmate who was familiar with Raleigh. He was afraid of being sent back to Currituck and was looking to escape. I told him I would get him out of prison if he would lead me around the city. He said it was a deal.

The laundry building was two stories high, and there was a railroad track just beyond the fence. Our plan was to run off the roof, jump the fence and land on the tracks. What we didn't know was that they had dug down another story behind the fence, so if we didn't reach the railroad tracks we would fall three stories instead of two. Eager to go, we slipped anxiously into the laundry room one November afternoon before the guards locked the building and hid until dark. The evening roll call was at 6 p.m., so we planned to jump at about 5:45. That would give us 15 minutes, plus the 15 or 20 minutes it took them to figure out who was gone, for a head start.

When darkness arrived, we climbed up to the roof and leapt like Olympic long jumpers over the fence. To make sure I cleared the fence, I jumped vertically rather than horizontally and as a result, never made it to the tracks. The sudden realization that I was dropping more than two stories, combined with my inability to see in the darkness, forced me to panic and begin turning sideways in the air. I was able to right myself and land on my feet, but on impact, my chin slammed against my knee, dazing me and leaving me disoriented for close to a minute. When I gathered my senses, my partner was gone, my chin was busted and I was in a strange city wearing bloodstained prison clothes.

I walked two or three blocks and found myself in a Black neighborhood. That made me feel better because I thought a friendly face might not be that hard to come by. My instincts proved correct when I ran across a young woman and two little girls. Though my appearance would almost certainly frighten the girls, I had no choice but to approach the sister. I asked if I could use her telephone and to be honest, was a bit surprised when she said yes. She didn't act out of ignorance because anyone could see that I had escaped from the penitentiary. Neither did she act out of fear. "Come on," she said. "I've got some brothers out there doing wrong, and they might need help one day." As it turned out, she didn't even have a phone, but she took me into her home and stopped my chin from bleeding with some towels. Then, she went outside and hailed a cab for me.

The cab driver had to notice my prison garb but like the sister, he was unfazed. Driving in silence, he simply took me to the home of the sister I had met in prison. There, I showered and changed clothes. Three days later, I left Raleigh and spent idle time in Smithfield, North Carolina and Warrenton, Georgia while waiting for things to cool down. I returned to New York City early in 1978.

1978 29th birthday party in Brooklyn, NY, for Mark Olds that lasted 3 days.

1979 Just returned from hair salon.

1979 - Resort International Casino. Only one casino in Atlantic City at that time.

1978 Camak, Georgia - A place of refuge. Mark Olds and Patricia "Boss" Hill.

Mr. Willie Grey Olds, father

Mrs. Ida Mae Olds, mother

Late sister Julia M. Olds &
cousin Velma.

Brother Rufus Olds with cigar,
and unidentified friend.

Brother Aaron Olds

Sister Christine Olds

Mark Olds 1980's penitentiary recreation yard in Lewisburg, PA.

June 1969 Mark Olds in the military - Fort Dix, New Jersey, Basic Training graduation.

Unidentified female; eldest brother Earl Freeman; cousin Sheila; late nephew Willie David Olds, Jr., known as "Smokey."

1978 Mark C. Olds - Brooklyn, N.Y.

1971 - After hour's spot in Long Island, NY - top standing - Mark Olds. Center - Willie D. Olds, Sr., the late Levi Pearson. Kneeling unidentified female; my late brother James Olds; friend Levonia Nelom.

Rev. Mark C. Olds at New Shiloh Baptist Church in Baltimore, Maryland, in the office of Pastor Harold A. Carter, Sr., my father in the ministry.

Rev. Milton S. Brown, my friend who was in prison with me. Deacon Howard Lyles; retired warden for Maryland Department of Corrections & Rev. Mark Olds taken in prayer room of New Shiloh. Deacon Lyle leads 6:00 AM prayer service each day.

May 1997 - commencement at Case Western Reserve University; Drema, Brittany, and Jacquelyn; Mark Olds & brother Douglas Olds.

Rev. Mark C. Olds exiting Women's Prison in Ohio after having led worship service.

Arnold Pinkney, campaign manager for Jesse Jackson's 1984 Democratic Presidential Campaign; Rev. Mark C. Olds, Rev. Jesse Jackson; Leonard Jackson, superintendent of recreation for Cleveland Public Schools; my pastor, the Reverend Dr. Otis Moss, Jr., Olivet Institutional Baptist Church, Cleveland, Ohio.

Rev. Mark C. Olds; Alan Boesak, Mrs. Boesak; ex-wife Linda.

Former Congressman Louis Stokes & Rev. Mark Olds, Cleveland Clergy Welcome First Lady Hillary Rodham Clinton to Cleveland.

Rev. Mark Olds and Shirley Haynes, Cleveland Clergy Welcome First Lady Hillary Rodham Clinton to Cleveland.

Daughter of Bishop Desmond Tutu's, Naomi Tutu & Rev. Mark C. Olds.

Attorney General for State of Ohio, Betty Montgomery & Rev. Mark Olds.

Wedding scene - August 1, 1998. Left: Best man and friend, Jack Best, Mark Olds, Jacquelyn and maid of honor Felicia.

Wedding photo - Front row: daughters Brittany and Drema; Granddaughter Jasmyne. Second row: Felicia, Jacquelyn, Rev. Olds, daughter LaShon, & brother-in-law Rashawn.

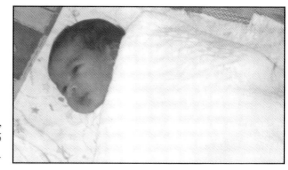

Madison Marie Ida Olds, born April 11, 2000, at 1:15 AM, 6 lbs. 15 oz., 17³/⁴" long.

Chapter *VI*

FREE TO CHASE A DREAM

Though one might think it is difficult to survive as a fugitive, it really is very simple. Being tracked down by the authorities was the last thing on my mind because I knew how easy it was to stay free. Police typically have only one address for convicts, so as long as you don't stay at that residence, you're fine. As far as they knew, my home was my mother's house in North Carolina, a place I hadn't lived at consistently for 12 years. When it comes to catching escapees, police basically have two chances: get one of the convict's friends or partners to talk, or arrest him after he commits another crime. If an inmate escapes and goes legit, giving up his life of crime and obeying the law, he can stay free forever. His only obstacle would be his identity, but obtaining aliases is an entry-level course in prison.

I actually learned to attain multiple identities before I went to prison. Sometime in the late 1960s or early 1970s, I watched a 60 Minutes broadcast about how simple it was to change your identity. The piece reported that the birth certificates of dead people are kept on file along with those of living people, and that procuring one of those birth certificates allows a person to get a social security card, driver's license and passport in the name of that dead person. Nowadays, it is not that easy because people receive social security numbers at a young age, but back then you could show up at 25 or 30 years of age and get a social security card with no questions asked. Of course, at that time, records were kept by hand rather than by computer, so obtaining someone's birth certificate was as simple as going to a courthouse and giving the person's birth date and parents' names.

As a Black Southerner, I was aware that the infant mortality rate in Black America was extremely high because I had seen scores of women lose one or two babies before the infants' first birthday. All of my aunts had babies die, and I capitalized on their misfortune by securing the birth certificates of my dead cousins. Following the strategy outlined in that 60 Minutes telecast, I soon obtained two other identities besides Mark Olds: Thomas Randolph, and my favorite and most traveled name, Billy Dee Hill.

One of the positive things I learned from my prison experience was how to interact with people from different regions of the country. As I said earlier, the majority of my previous friends and acquaintances, even those living up North, had originally been from the rural South. In the penitentiary, I began to see how restrictive that was, particularly in the drug business, so I made a point of interacting with guys from different areas, as well as Colombians and Hispanics. Leaving my comfort zone of Southerners had immediate advantages upon my return to New York.

Within weeks, I met a group of dealers from Harlem who supplied me with nine ounces of heroin. I took the drugs down to Raleigh and made a killing, selling them for five times the price I would have gotten in New York. Still not a saver, I went out and purchased a brand new Lincoln Towncar. I did this not only because the car was sharp, but because it was time for me to shape my image. If I was going to be an international drug dealer, I had to look the part. As I drove back to New York, playing eight-track tapes of Rick James and Parliament/Funkadelic, I remember thinking to myself, "M.C., you're finally on your way." My joy subsided quickly, though, as I returned to Harlem to find that my newfound suppliers had been busted and sent to jail.

That sort of thing was becoming a problem and threatening to ruin the plans that Jack Best and I had designed at Currituck. Jack was scheduled to be released roughly six months after my escape, and I was supposed to greet him with a reliable group of runners for our international drug trade. But I was having trouble solidifying a staff because many of the guys I had planned to incorporate into our route were either dead, locked up or drug-addicted themselves. My homeboy M.B. was a junkie. Another brother from New Haven named Jack was nowhere to be found. A partner from Brooklyn called Minnesota Fats, whom we were relying heavily upon for our heroin supply, had dropped dead of a heart attack while playing a round of golf. And most of the cats I had gambled with back in the day were doing bids in prison. Frank "Pee Wee" Matthews, the brother whom the hit 1970s movie Superfly was based on, had disappeared. He was an old acquaintance from Durham, North Carolina.

Hooking up with Frank would have been quite an experience. Though Gordon Parks, the director of Superfly, modeled his star character, Priest, after Frank, there were a lot of differences between the real version and the Hollywood version. First, the light-skinned, straight-haired Ron O'Neal looked nothing like Frank, who was a big, dark-skinned brother with an afro. Second, Frank was a lot wilder and much more treacherous than the character in the movie. I never really hung out with Frank, but one of the legends surrounding him was that he once returned to Durham and bought seven Cadillacs in the names of his old partners. Then, as if having a procession, they drove through Durham real slow. When Frank got downtown, he jumped out of the lead car and shouted, "White folks, I'm rich!" Frank's homeboys were laughing hysterically, and not just because they thought his act was funny: they thought they were going to get to keep those Cadillacs. Instead, Frank brought every last one of the cars to New York and stashed them around the city so he would have different rides under different names wherever he went. In the movie, Priest was somewhat mellow, but Frank was such a madman that when he drove, he rarely stopped for lights. He was crazy. One of the few things Frank and Priest truly had in common was Sheila Frazier, Frank's real-life girlfriend who played Superfly's love interest in the movie.

With my chief suppliers out of the picture, I began searching for a new connection. My cousin, Elvin Bryant, hooked me up with one of his contacts in Harlem, and we planned to meet in an apartment building uptown on 110th Street. But instead of showing up himself, he sent one of his cronies, which infuriated me. Having set my sights on sophisticated crime while in prison, I was losing my tolerance for street-level foolishness. So, hardened after my stint in the joint, I shot the guy in the leg right there in the 14th floor hallway. There were plenty of eyewitnesses, but their presence only emboldened me. I could have killed him if I had wanted to, but my intention was merely to send this message loud and clear: Mark Olds was done fooling around with trifling brothers.

Six months passed quickly, but Jack's release date was pushed back until December of 1978. That wasn't all bad because it gave me more time to lay a foundation for our drug route. I kept my cash flow high by gambling and employing young recruits to sell dope in New York and North Carolina. If they did well, I told them, I might include them when Jack and I went international.

I spent my money almost as fast as I made it. I would drop tens of thousands of dollars at a time by throwing lavish, marathon parties that boosted my image as a high roller. I would spend hundreds of dollars on alcohol and reefer and thousands on heroin and cocaine. Once, I had a birthday party in Brooklyn that started on Friday afternoon and ended on Sunday night. That Saturday morning, I went out and robbed a supermarket in Harlem, then used the money to buy more drugs for the party. The next morning, I flew to Raleigh to drop off some drugs and returned to the party that afternoon. Half of the people there didn't even know I had left.

One of the liveliest aspects of the parties I threw and attended was something we called "toasting." Toasting was the precursor to today's rap music. To see how huge rap has become is incredible because we used to do it all the time and think nothing of it. The Jamaicans, with their tradition of giving colorful toasts before taking a swig of alcohol, were the first ones I saw do it in New York. But my father, uncles and their friends used to toast down South. It was sort of a rite of passage for a young boy to be allowed to stay under the shade tree while the men drank and told toasts. When we toasted in New York, every brother had a nickname and told rhyming tales of power, criminal activity or sexual prowess. Each toast was either highly exaggerated or completely untrue. It was exactly like rapping is today except that we didn't do it over a rhythm track. Our toasting also borrowed from the age old art of "the dozens" because brothers usually compared themselves to one another and put each other down in jest.

When we first started toasting, brothers would just say something wild off the top of their head, what they now call "freestyling." But after it got competitive and everyone started trying to outdo one another, we started writing stuff down in advance. Cats would prepare all week long for that weekend's party. It became such an art form that rookies kept quiet and studied the work of the others before attempting to compete. Once, an extremely ugly brother who somehow got the nickname "Pretty Willie" gave a toast that no one could top. My brother Douglas, who was a masterful storyteller, couldn't believe he had been bested. Intense about his toasts, Douglas would sometimes avoid a hangout for weeks until he came up with the right story. Eventually, he returned to the site of Pretty Willie's piece and told a tale that became legendary in the Bronx.

I toasted under the name of "Slim Gator" because of my thin frame. Since I traveled a lot, I gathered stuff from all over the country, sometimes using material I had heard down South in New York, and vice versa. Most of my stuff was original, though, and I had a whole notebook full of toasts. I don't remember most of them but I do recall having one in which I bragged about being "wanted by The Man in 48 states and on two planets." It would have been categorized as a "gangsta" rap nowadays. The significant thing about that is that I was simply toasting about my reality. Even though my rhymes were overblown, they were rooted in true-life experiences and served as a window to my mentality at the time. If I had been a Black Nationalist, my rhymes probably would have reflected militancy and Black pride. If I had been a star athlete, I probably would have boasted about my athletic feats. Whatever my personality and worldview was would have come out in my toasts.

That is what today's critics of rap music must understand. I agree with them that much of the music is negative and portrays Black youth as being nihilistic, but the question that must be asked is, "Why are our children producing such vile material?" From my experiences and observations, I believe it's because that's either their reality or their mentality. Today's gangsta rappers are either real-life gangstas, just as I was a real-life hustler, or admirers of that type of lifestyle. The rap itself is a symptom first and a problem second, so those who want to ban obscene rap music should also concentrate on eliminating the factors that create such destructive mindsets in Black youth. I'm not saying that delinquent or pornographic rap music should not be censored; it should, along with lust-driven Rhythm & Blues songs.

The noxious lyrics of rappers glorify the depraved thinking of the rapper and are inserted into the mind of the listener. Consequently, Black youth whose outlook is not so bleak begin to think like they were raised in dysfunctional ghetto environments. That's why we have young people all over America wearing their pants sagging down on their behinds. Even so, negative rap music is merely an expression of the rapper's negative outlook on life. So just as much time and energy should be spent trying to change the youth's thought patterns and experiences as is spent trying to ban their music.

Of course, another key component of the hip-hop culture is deejaying. I think party deejays like "Kool Herc," "Grand Wizard Theodore" and "Grandmaster Flash," showed remarkable creativity when they decided to use two turntables instead of one so they could mix records together and lengthen a song that had the people jamming. The first time I heard mixing was at an outdoor party in the Bronx. I was high on angel dust at the time, which made the experience a harrowing one.

I was dancing with this girl to a song called "Do What You Want To" by the Bar-Kays when the deejay started mixing. The art of mixing had been around for a couple of years, but I hadn't heard it because I had been in prison. Anyway, this particular deejay - I don't know who it was - started mixing back and forth from one turntable to the next so the chorus ""Do what you want to, Do it everyone" kept playing over and over again. To me, it sounded like the record was scratched, but everyone else seemed to be enjoying it. Before I had gone to prison, a scratched record would have stopped everything, but now it seemed to ignite the crowd. I thought, "This can't be right. I must be hallucinating." I thought I was going crazy. I started getting a headache and feeling dizzy and eventually had to stop dancing and go sit down.

Whatever money I didn't spend on throwing parties went toward enhancing my appearance. Intent on creating an image of wealth, I spent thousands of dollars on clothes, jewelry, hairdos, manicures and pedicures. My aim when buying clothes was to never wear the same outfit twice in the same city. I had dozens of outfits worth thousands of dollars apiece that were worn only once or twice. I was just as outlandish when it came to my hair. Sporting a perm, I would fly to Columbus, Georgia every two weeks to get my hair done. There was a woman at a shop there who did my hair better than anyone else. When she was done with me, my hair was as straight as a White person's. Long and flowing, it looked like Ron O'Neal's in Superfly.

A related incident that makes me look back and laugh took place in a beauty shop in Goldsboro, North Carolina. I was sprawled out in a chair with my freshly-fried hair underneath a dryer. My arms were stretched out while someone manicured my fingernails, and there were cotton balls between the toes of my feet as a young lady administered a pedicure. As I laid there looking like some kind of prince, an older woman walked by, looked me up and down and began shaking her head while sighing in a tone that said, "Honey, that boy thinks he's too cute!" I definitely did. I was very meticulous about my appearance, demanding that everything be done just right. Once, a young girl got so nervous about the prospect of giving me a manicure that she shook uncontrollably and was unable to grab my hand. The owner of the shop, unable to get the girl to calm down, had to come and do my nails. That really inflated my already sizeable ego.

Perhaps the only thing that equaled my love of clothing was my love of jewelry. I spent about $20,000 on handcrafted, custom-made jewelry that would probably be worth between 70 and 80 thousand dollars today. Among other items, I had an antelope pinky ring that had seven diamonds in each of the antelope's horns and two in its eyes, a gold bracelet that spelled out "Billy Dee" in diamonds, and a white gold watch. In the circles I ran in, my jewelry was always the finest. My stuff was so far beyond everyone else's that they started calling me "Billy Dee Player." I even had a name plate around my neck that hung from a wide gold chain and spelled out "Mr. Dee Player" in diamonds. A gold scorpion with rubies was fixed at the bottom. For all of the extravagant jewelry I had, the piece that meant the most to me was a sterling silver ring with an onyx stone that my sister Julia gave to me shortly after I escaped from the prison in Raleigh.

While my jewelry made me the envy of my crew, there were hustlers who had better. I discovered that after meeting a couple of Colombians on the gambling circuit. I got to know them fairly well and then let them in on my plans to establish an international drug route. Without much contemplation, they said they could help me and then set me up with some of their contacts in Miami. Feeling as though I had finally made a breakthrough, I flew to Miami in great spirits. Knowing I would have to make a good first impression, I wore the finest pieces I had. As I prepared for our meeting, my only concern was whether I would appear to be pouring it on too thick, with my elegant jewelry and all.

That concern quickly turned into embarrassment when I met my contacts in Miami's Liberty City section. Their jewelry was the best I had ever seen. While I spent $20,000 total, they spent $20,000 on one piece. It made the stuff I had on look tacky. My jewelry was street, like the gaudy gold chains the rappers used to wear in the mid-1980s. My "Billy Dee" name plate didn't impress them at all. In fact, they wondered what kind of a criminal would have his identity splashed across his chest. In contrast, their pieces were classy, not too pretentious and not too discreet. I was blown

119

away. When I finally caught my breath, I said, ""Man, that's some nice jewelry you have on." Aware that mine wasn't on the same level, I didn't anticipate the same type of enthusiastic compliment in return. But I did expect a polite comment, something along the lines of, "You're not doing too badly yourself." Instead, I got nothing. They looked at my stuff, glanced at each other and started laughing, as if to say that I had bought junk. I felt like I was wearing cubic zirconia. I endured the same type of humbling experience every time I saw those brothers. Sometimes, I just wanted to take my stuff off and put it in my pocket. Eventually, I stopped wearing my jewelry around them altogether.

Those brothers were big-time. They were receiving cocaine straight from Cuba. They used to sit on the dock and jokingly say, "I'm waiting for my ship to come in." It would be funny but true. They literally were waiting for a huge international ship to come in. It would always pull up a few hours after the Coast Guard made its rounds. Once it docked, a group of brothers would transport the cocaine to smaller, national ships that took the dope to Georgia, North Carolina and the rest of the Southern states.

"Waiting on a ship to come in" was not a boring assignment. Rolling in money, those guys would party hearty. They would give away 10 to 15 thousand dollars worth of cocaine without blinking. I used to go down there, and they'd hand me nine or 10 ounces just to play with that night. Witnessing their lavish lifestyle really made me hungry for my own route. Before I could start working with these guys, though, I had to pass a background check. While they inquired of others about my past, I would assist them in a task every now and then. The entire process took a few months. When they finally finished their check and told me I would need $150,000 to get started, I fought hard to contain my excitement and coolly said, "No problem."

The $150,000 I needed for a cocaine route through South Florida was only part one of my plan. I had a cousin, a lifetime military man, who lived in Fort Lewis, Washington and was married to a South Korean nurse. His Korean brothers-in-law had a heroin connection in Thailand, and agreed to let me exploit it along the West Coast. I would need $50,000 to get that route off the ground. With travel and front money thrown in, I figured I needed to get my hands on about $250,000 total.

As my dream began to materialize, my commitment soared. To save my money, I stopped gambling. To keep myself sharp, I stopped drinking

120

and using drugs. I had the attitude of a college football player preparing for the NFL combines, or a medical school graduate preparing for the board tests. Drug dealing was my profession, and I realized that I had to take it seriously.

After much contemplation, I concluded that the quickest way to get the $250,000 was to take it. So I started robbing banks. That might sound complicated but it actually was quite easy. I robbed four of them with no problem and would have taken a fifth if I hadn't gotten careless. The first bank I hit was in Goldsboro. I had flown to Atlanta and then driven to North Carolina in a Hertz rental car. I knew a few people at Hertz who would give me cars without a contract, so I would rob banks with the rental cars and not have to worry about leaving a scent, so to speak. I wore disguises when doing robberies but nothing like ski masks or panty hose. Considering myself to be a more cultured thief, I had a professional makeup artist from Washington, D.C. who would mask me in makeup. I would fly her to the city of my choice, and she would give me whatever look I wanted. I also wore wigs, usually afro-wigs that made me look much different than I did with my perm, and sometimes I sported fake beards.

The final piece to the puzzle was Ronald, my driver. In addition to driving my getaway cars, he picked me up from airports in various cities. Employing Ronald, whom I had recruited while in the North Carolina penal system, proved to be my downfall because ultimately he sold me out to the cops. Though he appeared to be loyal, I should have known he was a potential squealer because of his heroin addiction and lack of heart. He was impatient and restless, traits that are not conducive to big-time hustling.

On my first bank robbery, I made $20,000 in about 90 seconds. I went in, approached the manager and put my gun in his back. Unaware of what was happening, the customers, tellers and other employees kept going about their business. I instructed the manager to lead me behind the counter and give me all of the money. With him by my side, each teller filled my bag without a hassle. It was done so quietly and smoothly that the bank didn't even get a chance to turn on the cameras, and the customers didn't know a robbery was taking place.

Afterwards, I went back to Atlanta to celebrate at my man Big Tex's bar. I was there with a couple of girls from North Carolina and a brother named Shaft, whom I had met at a barbecue in Atlanta. Shaft and I had started talking because we were the only hustlers at the barbecue. With

121

everyone else talking about things like their jobs and families, we were a bit out of place. So we ended up talking to one another and found out we had a lot in common.

Shaft was a crazy brother, and his pet Doberman pinscher, Sly, bore the brunt of his wackiness. Shaft would give Sly cocaine and blow reefer smoke in his face. That dog was more strung out than half of the junkies on the East Coast. He would go absolutely bonkers when flies started bothering him. It was hilarious. I always used to anger Shaft by mixing him up with Sly. The names were so close that I couldn't remember who was who.

My weakness of spending rather than saving money manifested itself at Tex's, as I treated Shaft and the girls to a high time. We were partying and getting loud and Tex asked us to move into his private poolroom behind the bar, so we wouldn't run off his regular customers. When we got back there, a loudmouthed guy was hanging out in the room, and he got on my nerves. I felt like throwing him out, but I didn't want to spoil the festive mood, so I let it go. But eventually he crossed the line. Shaft and one of the girls with me were about to play a game of pool when this brother grabbed my stick and said he was going to play. Though upset because he had disrespected me at my own party, I was glad because it gave me an excuse to shut him up. I told one of the girls to hand me the 38 pistol in her purse and then began lecturing that dude like I was his father: "Look, I was going to let you stay, but since you think you're going to take over...." Before I finished my sentence, I had put a bullet in his calf. Afraid that I was going to kill him, the brother got humble and quiet real quick, sitting down in his chair and shivering. He was so scared to say another word that he didn't even allow himself to whimper; he just sat there holding in the pain.

Everyone was shocked, and the whole place got quiet. Tex ran in to see what had happened and when he saw the brother gripping his bloody calf, he just looked at me and started laughing and shaking his head. He knew right away what I had done. He said he wasn't going to call the police and would give us time to get away. As we were about to leave, my victim raised his hand tentatively and asked softly, "What about me? I'm bleeding to death." I laughed in his face because I thought his transformation from the big, bad bully selling wolf tickets to the meek, little lamb was hysterical.

We figured it would be best to get out of town for a while and decided to look up a friend of mine in Alabama called Redd Foxx. He wasn't the famous actor/comedian but he was prominent in his own right. The most prolific Black dope dealer in Alabama, Redd was known up and down the

East Coast. As a front for his drug activity, he ran a nightclub called The Redd Foxx Lounge in a small town called Dothan. The brother was so bad that he had White women running dope and serving as prostitutes and barmaids right there in the heart of Dixie. His outright defiance of the South's unwritten racial codes might have been his downfall as he disappeared one evening and was never seen again. Nobody would say a word about what happened to him. It was as if he had never existed. I'm all but certain that some White guys, furious about the way he shamelessly flaunted their women, got a hold of him.

When Shaft and I stopped by his nightclub, Redd was living the good life, driving a white Lincoln Mark III and pulling in enough money to buy seven more. We were hanging out, having a grand time, when Shaft and another guy became engrossed in a competitive, high-stakes game of pool. Midway through the game, Shaft took off his black leather coat and laid it on a chair. Just moments later, the guy he was playing with, who happened to be wearing a similar black leather coat, put his coat next to Shaft's. After another game or two, the brother gave up, saying that Shaft was too good, and left the bar. Another guy, noticing that Shaft's play was starting to slip because of the alcohol, eagerly stepped up and challenged Shaft to a game. We didn't think anything of it at the time, but later that evening, after Shaft had lost, he dug into his coat pockets to get his money and realized that the guy had switched coats on him.

Shaft was steaming. We took the second brother outside and made him tell us where the first guy might have gone. Before long, we found him at a nearby nightclub. By this time, Shaft's high had worn off but his rage had only increased. We dragged the brother out of the club, pistol-whipped him and threw him in the trunk of our car. Not sure whether we would kill the guy or just maim him, we drove across the state line and into a secluded, wooded area of Georgia, where we stripped him naked and beat him from 12:30 to 6 a.m. We scared him nearly to death by putting his head underneath the back tire of our car. He begged us to let up, but we showed him no mercy. In an effort to stop the flogging, he told us he had a wife and two kids and made all sorts of confessions; but to no avail. By the time we were done with him, he was covered in blood and all but lifeless, as we left him there to die in the woods. Of all the evil I did, that is one of the acts of which I am most ashamed. My only consolation is that the brother survived and, from what I hear, swore off hustling that very night.

Incidents like that earned me a reputation as a ruthless killer. It got to the point where people wouldn't even think about challenging me. I would walk into a room and see guys look the other way. I realized the magnitude of my notoriety in the Bronx one night when I overheard a bunch of brothers talking about the cruelest cats they knew. I had walked in unannounced and unnoticed, and after a number of guys had been discussed, my brother Willie said, "M.C. is badder than all of them. He don't care about nobody. He'd kill me if I crossed him." Though his comments enhanced my reputation, I actually was hurt by his words. I couldn't believe he said I would kill him. I didn't mind others thinking of me in that way - in fact, I liked it - but my own brother? I thought he knew the real Mark, the guy who had given away thousands of dollars to family and friends. When I asked him about it later, he just looked me in the eye and said, "It's the truth."

As I got closer to securing my drug routes, my traveling increased substantially. By car and by plane, I trekked up and down the East Coast, from New Haven to New York to Maryland to North Carolina to Georgia to Alabama to Florida, and just about all spots in between. I did three things everywhere I went: met women, set up apartments, and recruited for my route. I had contacts from prison in all of these places, so recruiting runners was easy. Even if the guy I knew was still behind bars, I had the names of three or four of his partners. I would buy relatively small amounts of cocaine, just enough to keep the brothers interested, and divvy it out among my runners, always with the promise that this was only the beginning. I was tireless, spending 16 to 18 hours a day on the job. It was not unusual for me to fly into one city and then fly somewhere else the next morning. I'd put down hundreds of dollars for a plane ticket in a heartbeat.

Setting up the apartments took a little longer but it was just as simple. My goal was to have apartments scattered all along the East Coast so that no matter where I was, I would always be within a three or four hour drive of home. Of course, with no job, no credit and dozens of cops in North Carolina looking for me, I couldn't put an apartment in my name, even though I was going by Billy Dee Hill. That's where the women came in.

I must have had about 20 girlfriends at that time and all of them were used to set up apartments. Every pad I had was in the name of an educated and reputable woman. Putting into practice what I had learned from the professionals at Somers, I nixed my previous custom of fooling around with married women and prostitutes and began dating nothing but single women with good jobs and established credit. It wasn't long before I was buying cars and obtaining credit cards in their names. I never told any of them what I did for a living and as long as the money kept flowing, none of them cared. I promised them that I would soon introduce them to a lifestyle they had only dreamed about, that "when my ship came in" they would have all the best clothes, furs and jewelry. Some of the women were so excited about the prospects that they gave me access to their bank accounts to expedite the process. If they ever had any questions, concerns or suspicions, they never voiced them to me. Occasionally, I would have one of my most trustworthy girls unwittingly carry drugs across the country. I used to use a woman named Sandy, an upstanding citizen by anyone's standards, to lug packages of dope throughout the Eastern states. I tricked her into thinking she was hauling money by opening a package of greenbacks I had received from Jack Best before her eyes. Awed by the amount of money and delighted about what it could bring her, she became a more than willing interstate carrier.

During the course of my travels, I would periodically visit my parents at their house. They knew I had escaped from prison and that the police were looking for me because it had been all over the news. Plus, the cops had been harassing them and my cousins about my whereabouts. They had no idea of where I was staying, though. They would not have told the police anyway, but I felt like I was protecting them by telling them as little as possible. My visits to my parents would always be unannounced and usually at odd hours of the night or early in the morning. Sometimes, I would get a burning desire to go to my parents' home and sleep in my old bed. I believe now that those strong urges were inspired by my mother's prayers of concern about how her baby boy was doing. Every time my mother saw me, she laid hands on me and prayed before I left. Because my heart was hardened and I was very cynical, I mocked her prayers. I told her and my aunts that they didn't know how to pray, that instead of praying for me to stop doing wrong, they should pray that I get rich. Then, once I got rich, I would stop doing wrong.

I also took time to visit my daughter, Lashon. In much the same way that I went to see my parents, I would pop in out of the blue and shower her with clothes, candy and money. Though I didn't know how to express it, I genuinely loved Lashon. She made me feel human. Because of the dark subculture in which I roamed, I rarely was able to relax. Even when I slept, my pillow was uncomfortable because I had a pistol underneath it.

125

For some inexplicable reason, I would also visit two preachers who lived near Columbus, Georgia: Dr. Dallas Moore and Reverend Eugene Moore. They had struck it rich off of peanut farming and, since work and money were no longer issues in their lives, they held church services every single day. Sincere men of God, they could preach the walls down. I can recall almost word-for-word a message Reverend Eugene preached entitled "The World Has What You Want, But God Has What You Need." His words gave me so much peace that I stayed with the preachers for two days after that sermon. They knew I was not a Christian and that I was up to no good but they had no idea that I was an escaped convict. In fact, as far as they knew, my name was Billy Dee Hill.

When I was not robbing banks and roaming around down South, I was holding up supermarkets in the North. Supermarkets in New York were open on Sundays so I robbed banks during the week and supermarkets on the weekends. Supermarkets were much easier to rob than banks and almost as rewarding. They always had limited operating capital available, but I could count on bagging about $5,000 a pop. A guy named Phil and I hit about 15 supermarkets in New York City, and I robbed another 20 or so by myself.

I would stake out the store early in the morning and wait for the manager to open up. It was comical because he would go through all of these elaborate precautions, undoing what seemed like 15 or 20 different locks before opening the doors. Then, once the doors were open, he'd leave them open. So I just strolled in behind him and made him lead me to the safe. I treated supermarkets like ATM machines, making withdrawals whenever I was low on cash. Sometimes, I would wait for the security truck to come so I could get more than the $5,000 the supermarket had. Once, Phil and I hit an armored truck. It was the most lucrative heist of my career. We netted $75,000 and still didn't get all of the money. We caught the unsuspecting driver and his partner as they were exiting a supermarket, money in tow. Before they got to the truck, we took the 75 grand and were off within a matter of minutes.

After ripping off the armored truck, dozens of supermarkets and a couple of banks, I began to slip. I had so much success that I began taking it for granted. I no longer spent time before the robbery rehearsing how I would react to every possible scenario the situation could present. I started thinking I could just roll into any place I wanted to, prepared or not, and leave with thousands of dollars.

That attitude caused me to blow a bank robbery in Atlanta shortly after one of my visits with the preachers. I don't discount the notion that subconsciously their preaching was starting to sink in, perhaps making me a little less enthusiastic about my lifestyle. Hitting the bank in Atlanta without total concentration, I let the tellers give me the money in a briefcase for the first time ever. I knew I had screwed up as soon as I left the bank. I hopped in the getaway car driven by Ronald and within seconds, red dye was all over the place. It was coming out of the briefcase and burning the money all at once. That was a tactic banks used to foil robbery attempts and the reason I usually put the money from the tellers into my own bag. The police put a helicopter on our trail, and we stopped and tossed the briefcase out of the window. We didn't get caught but I almost felt as if we had since we left Atlanta with no money. In a perverted sense, I felt like I deserved the money in that bank, like it was mine.

A few days later in Goldsboro, I picked up a local newspaper and read that a Black man had been sentenced to 40 years in prison for robbing a bank in Goldsboro. After checking the date and details of the robbery, I realized that he had been sentenced for my crime. Usually, something like that would have made me laugh and then beam with pride about pulling one over on the law. It would have been great material for a "toast." But this time, I didn't find it amusing or pleasing in the least bit. Rather, it disturbed me. That man had a wife and children. He needed to be home with them, not behind bars struggling to survive.

Those weren't the only peculiar feelings I was having. Suddenly, nothing was satisfying me: not my dream of a drug route, not my thousands of dollars, not my new clothing and expensive jewelry, not my 20 some odd women. Seemingly overnight I went from enjoying those things to being bored with them. Now, I know it was the Holy Spirit working toward my redemption, but at that time, I didn't know what was going on. I certainly didn't think it was the beginning of an entire change of lifestyle.

Distracted and somewhat confused, I prepared to rob another bank in North Carolina. The banks in Goldsboro had been good to me, supplying me with some of the most lucrative paydays of my career, so without the typical fear, anxiety and excitement that had accompanied my previous robberies, I set out to make another 20 to 25 grand. The robbery itself went off without a glitch, but my inattentiveness afterwards proved to be my undoing.

My plan was to switch getaway cars after five minutes, so Jack Best met Ronald and me at the designated spot and I switched cars, money in tow. In the past, I had always taken great pains to carefully dispose of my wig, clothing, gloves and other possible evidence. But that day, for some strange reason, I just tossed the wig out of the window and watched through the mirror as it landed in the middle of the highway. With my experience, I should have known better. I knew that whenever a bank was robbed, the highway patrol was contacted and summoned to do sweeps of the local highways. They couldn't just randomly stop people, so without an accurate description of the getaway car there wasn't much they could do. I would have been fine if I hadn't absent-mindedly thrown out my wig.

Moments later, a state trooper passed us, saw the wig, made a U-turn and started following us. Ours was the only car he had passed so he knew the wig was ours. To make sure he was trailing us, I told Jack to speed up. Sure enough, the state trooper sped up. Then, I told him to slow down. Sure enough, the trooper slowed down. I knew the highway and was aware that a long curve was coming up ahead. Figuring that a police roadblock would be waiting on the other side of the curve, I pulled out two pistols. Jack, knowing I would not hesitate to start a shootout, started tripping. Without a hint of doubt, I told him I'd rather die than go back to prison. But Jack's silence kept pleading with my spirit so finally, because he was such a good friend, I put down the guns. We took the curve and as expected, were met by a roadblock of state troopers. Jack got out of the car immediately, but I remained in the passenger's seat. To my surprise, they knew who I was. It turned out that Ronald had been squealing, giving the cops information about me. He had been arrested in Goldsboro on a petty burglary charge, so to get the heat off his back, he gave up the phone numbers and addresses to all of my apartments.

Aware that I was an escaped convict, the police were prepared to blow me away. Knowing my reputation, they figured I'd go for my gun, so about five of them had their shotguns aimed at me. As I was contemplating what to do, a trooper slid behind me and pulled me out of the car while telling me "I'm a Christian and I'm not going to let you die." I noticed that the name on his badge was Albritton. Oddly enough, I felt a sense of relief. With nothing left to do but surrender, I put up my hands and got in the backseat of Trooper Albritton's car. To this day, I believe God used that man to save my life.

Chapter *VII*

REDEEMED

The ride to the Cumberland County Jail in Fayetteville, North Carolina was the most peaceful trip I had ever taken to a penitentiary. Though I knew I was going to prison for a good long time, there was a part of me that was glad I had been caught. I was not yet a Christian but I felt some sense of divine providence over my life because of the way Trooper Albritton had stepped in and saved me at the last possible moment. I felt like my life had a purpose. I had a purpose before, of course, but it had always been criminal in nature. Never, or at least not since my one quarter of college 12 years earlier, had I felt destined to make a positive contribution to society. What I was supposed to contribute and how I was to do it, I did not know. But I remembered that sermon preached by Reverend Eugene Moore – "The World Has What You Want, But God Has What You Need" – and decided to start reading the Bible.

My interest in the Bible did not make me unique. Behind bars, Bible reading is as prevalent as weight lifting. All types of inmates - devout Christians, Muslims, killers, lunatics - read the Bible, pray, wear crosses around their necks, or display other outward forms of religiosity. This is understandable since prison forces a man to take inventory of his life and begin a search for deeper meaning. Those prisoners who can read typically devour anything they get their hands on. Malcolm X, who memorized thousands of words from the dictionary, was the greatest example of this. Whether an inmate learns his lesson or not, being jailed is an incredibly educational experience. Previously, I had spent my period of incarceration advancing my education in crime, but this time I was on a completely different plane.

I started reading one of those Gideon' s Bibles, the pocket-sized, colored Bibles that include the New Testament and the Psalms. Though I had no idea of how to study the Bible, I actually got something out of it, feeling peace and comfort whenever I read it. Having grown up in the church, I knew that a person gave his life to God by getting "saved" but I did not know how to go about doing that. I did not know if I had to be in church or if a preacher had to be present or if I had to be baptized or if I had to swear off wrongdoing or what. That was really a shame considering I had spent the first 14 years of my life in church. I had either forgotten the process or never been taught it in the first place. I have been in numerous churches that have "opened the doors of the church," allowing folks to become members, without fully explaining to them the meaning of Christian salvation. It is a sad but true fact that many people walk around thinking they are saved, regardless of how immoral their lifestyle may be, simply because they have been baptized or because their name appears on the role of some church. As was the case with me when I was 10 years old, many of these people probably joined the church as youngsters without truly understanding what they were doing. In fact, I would not have been an anomaly had I claimed to be saved while involved in my most detestable criminal activities. My search for salvation continued for three months until God used a most unlikely individual - a White man - to explain to me the process of salvation.

It was a Sunday afternoon in December of 1979, and I was one of the many inmates at the Wake County Jail in Raleigh (I had been transferred) whose mind was on football, not God. One of the more humane things about penitentiaries is that they allow you to watch television, so all 16 guys in my cell block were huddled around the TV set, waiting to see the Tampa Bay Buccaneers face the Los Angeles Rams in the National Football Conference championship game. Tampa Bay's quarterback, Doug Williams, was one of the few Black quarterbacks in the league at that time, so every brother in the joint was pulling for him. A Black man would have been crazy to root for the Rams in that jail. Even if you had been born and raised in Los Angeles, you had to be on Williams's side. Brothers had put Williams in the role of Black savior, so the loud-talking and jiving was at a maximum when this White man, Bible in tow, walked up to the gate and started preaching.

Even though the game had not yet started, no one paid him any mind, and I actually felt sorry for the guy. He looked so pitiful, sitting there talking into thin air, that I decided to go over and give him an audience of one. So there I was, alone in the back of the Wake County Jail recreation room, listening to this White man tell me about John 3:16 - "For God so loved the world that he gave his only begotten Son, that whosoever believeth in him should not perish but have everlasting life."

For three hours, he preached that verse from the King James Version of the Bible. I know it was three hours because I missed the entire football game. This man, who appeared to be in his early 50s, made the plan of salvation crystal clear: he explained that every person on the face of the earth was a sinner; that God had sent Jesus Christ, His only begotten son, to die on the cross as payment for man's sins; that the penalty of sin was separation from God and eternal damnation; and that the only way to avoid that penalty was to repent and sincerely believe that Jesus Christ had died on the cross and risen from the dead as a sacrifice for our sins.

After occasionally going off on some spiritual tangent, he would always return to John 3:16 and tie it into Romans 10:9 - "That if thou shalt confess with thy mouth the Lord Jesus, and shalt believe in thine heart that God hath raised him from the dead, thou shalt be saved." He did not stop until the game ended and the rest of the inmates, depressed because Williams and the Buccaneers had been beaten, started filing slowly out of the room. Before I left, he asked me to accept Jesus Christ as my personal Lord and Savior. Even though I had been reading the Bible for weeks and was intrigued by what he was saying, I declined, leaving him with a shattered, befuddled look on his face.

I don't know why I listened to that man for so long and then subsequently rejected his call to salvation, but that night, I couldn't sleep. His constant talk about sin and the price that must be paid for it had sunk deeply into my psyche. As I lay in my bed, trying to force my eyelids shut, I was tormented by thoughts of the wretched crimes I had committed. The senseless acts of brutality I had once flaunted with great pride now made me sick of myself. The selfish and deceitful ways I had treated women made me feel ashamed and filthy. The incessant plotting, lying, scheming and conniving that had come to dominate my thinking and conversation made me feel small and rotten, almost inhuman. Overcome by guilt, I realized that I had become everything my parents did not want me to be; everything that humble, honest, hard-working people like my folks, my Uncle and Aunt Williams, Mr. Willie Morris and my Reverend friends in Georgia abhorred. I knew that prison was where I belonged, and even worse, that if I died in my unredeemed state I deserved hell.

I tossed and turned, fighting against my invisible enemies, hoping that morning would come and that the clamorous bustle of jail life would free me from my thoughts; that I would be able to hide from myself amidst the commotion and activities of the day. But time moved slowly, even slower than usual in jail, and the maddening hours on my bunk seemed like days. Finally, I gained enough composure to send my mind elsewhere. I began to picture the many times my mother prayed over me by laying her hands on my head and asking God to soften my heart that I might one day serve Him. I thought about the Reverends Dallas and Eugene Moore, who seemed to have the peace and contentment that I could never find in money, partying and drugs. And I remembered what the evangelist had said about Jesus Christ: that faith in him could remove the sting of sin from our lives and make us new creations. That final thought – that I could become new, that my previous wrongs could be erased from the scroll of my life – made me feel especially good. I settled on that notion, and ultimately peace came. It was as if a barricade had been set up around my mind, one that blocked the thoughts of my past sins from reentering my thinking. The feeling was divine, and so without even thinking about it, I dropped to my knees, repented for my sins and asked Jesus Christ to come into my life as Lord and Savior.

Overjoyed, I telephoned my mother a few days later. I told her that I had been having this recurring dream in which she and I were praying in her living room in Maury, North Carolina. Excited, she shouted into the telephone, "I know it's real because everyday at noon, your aunt and I have been in the living room, praying for your salvation." That blew my mind because I had no idea they had been doing that. She said it was confirmation that I truly was saved, that God had answered their prayers.

I truly felt saved. The morning after my conversion, I could already understand the Bible better. Before, it was just a bunch of soothing words but now it made sense. I could follow the gospels as stories and the epistles as instructions. I could identify with the words of the Apostle Paul, feeling at times as if he were reading my mind. I understood that true Biblical Christianity was a relationship with Jesus Christ rather than a stodgy religion; that it was not about rituals, Roman collars, rules and regulations. To me, Jesus Christ had become an ever-present and totally trustworthy friend and guide, someone whose presence I felt during every waking moment.

Though I realized there was a definite code of morality I had to live by, I knew that Christianity was not about do's and don'ts. Instead, it was about me living to please someone whom I was thankful to and in love with.

The Biblical verse I kept focusing on was 2 Corinthians 5:17 - "Therefore if any man be in Christ, he is a new creature: old things are passed away; behold, all things are become new." With the background I had, that scripture really inspired me. I read and reread it, memorized it and quoted it throughout the day. It made me feel like I was no longer a criminal, like I no longer had this burdensome, pages-long rap sheet hanging over my head, announcing to the world that I was a crook. That scripture told me I could start over, which was something I desperately wanted to do.

Once again, my location was changed and I was sent back to the Cumberland County Jail in Fayetteville. Though I had been reading the Bible at Cumberland, I had not been converted until going to Raleigh, so my reputation as a hustler was still well intact. Because I had spent a lot of time pimping women on Fayetteville's Hay Street, there were numerous brothers in Cumberland who knew me. When I returned from Raleigh with a Bible in my hand and a smile on my face, most of them thought I had gone crazy. And I'm not using that merely as a figure of speech.

Going off in prison is a common occurrence. Many guys who are tough on the streets can't stand being locked up. Being confined with other brothers in the small quarters of the county jail causes some to become claustrophobic, while others bug out simply because they have lost so much. These brothers knew I had been living well on the outside and figured that the loss of my cars, jewelry, money and women had pushed me over the edge. As a result, they watched me closely. But the fact that I was coherent and speaking in complete sentences confused them. Though my conversation was completely different, I clearly had my wits about me, which caused them to pay attention to what I was saying.

I felt no apprehension whatsoever in sharing the gospel. Full of boldness and zeal, I started a Bible study within two weeks of my salvation. It is amazing how God immediately opened up the scriptures to me. I had no knowledge of deep theological principles but I knew how to lead a person to Christ. Through my simple approach to the Bible, many men were comforted and saved. We saw drug dealers and robbers break down and cry and we experienced a true feeling of brotherhood at our meetings. I was fanatical, preaching Jesus Christ all day to all people. Anytime a brother had a problem, no matter how big or small, my answer was the same: give your life to Christ and He will fix it. Some guys found my attitude refreshing, while others thought I was a pain in the rear.

Once, a young guy about 18 or 19 years old grew annoyed with me. We were in a four-man cell, and he had been charged with murder. His victim was an older man who had been something of a mentor to him, giving him a job in an effort to help him turn his life around. Instead of being thankful, the youngster attempted to rob the man and ended up killing him. Before dying, the old man said he forgave him and that he should also seek the Lord's forgiveness. That seemed to spark a fire in the young man that was set ablaze by the mere mention of religion; so naturally, he had a problem with me.

I had been preaching to him ever since he arrived, telling him that Jesus loved him and wanted to set him free. One day, I was about to go to Bible study and invited him to attend. Fed up, he jumped off his bunk, grabbed me by the collar and threw me against the wall. I hadn't been in a situation like this since becoming a Christian and I was really stunned; not scared but stunned. All that was going through my head was "turn the other cheek, turn the other cheek," so I didn't attempt to get him off me. I didn' t curse or say anything. He uttered plenty of threats but never hit me. After realizing that I wasn't going to defend myself, our two cellmates snatched the guy and made him release me.

That was a tremendous witness for me because many of the inmates knew about my reputation for violence. They had heard so many fake penitentiary preachers before that they were having trouble taking my salvation seriously. But after seeing or hearing about the way I responded to that young cat, they knew I had changed. Truthfully, even I was surprised by my reaction. In the past, I would have tried to kill that kid just for having the gall to challenge me as a teenager.

Since my conversion, I had not thought about what I would do if someone physically threatened me. I just figured that I would cross that bridge when I came to it. While I was glad I reacted in the "Christian" way, I was also faced with the realization that I wasn't going to be able to skip and whistle my way through penitentiary life just because I was saved. When I lay down on my bunk that night, I remember thinking that maybe this Christian thing was a little too unrealistic for a convict. With turning the other cheek being a requirement, I began to understand why more inmates didn't become Christians. I decided to read more on the subject because I knew that being a pacifist could be a problem if I was sent to a maximum security prison, where Christians were automatically viewed as weak. I eventually concluded that I would trust the Lord first and foremost but be prepared to throw punches if necessary.

Of course, the other convicts were not aware of my doubts, so after that incident, they started calling me "Rev," short for Reverend, and my Bible study grew to the point that 10 or 12 of the 16 guys in my cellblock would attend. Many of them were not practicing Christians, just guys who wanted prayer. Interestingly enough, most of the guys we prayed for were released from the joint. In my spiritual immaturity, that led me to believe that freedom from prison was a part of the package one received with Christ. So even though I had been caught on escape while robbing a bank, I thought I would somehow avoid doing hard time.

Thinking my freedom was secure, I set my sights on trying to free Jack Best. He had been arrested along with me for bank robbery but actually had little to do with the crime. He had simply picked me up after I had driven from the bank. I knew that didn't make him exempt from responsibility but I didn't want him to get convicted for bank robbery, which would have resulted in a much harsher sentence than he deserved.

By this time, Jack knew I had become a born-again Christian, but he didn't believe it was genuine. He had spent enough time behind bars to know that prison conversions were oftentimes no more sincere than the lines brothers used to pick up women. He even read the Bible himself whenever he was locked up. When I told him I had gotten saved, his response was, "Yeah, right." Out on bond, he had visited me the week before my conversion, and all I had talked about was escaping and paying back Ronald for dropping dime on me. Now, seven days later, every word out of my mouth was about the gospel of Jesus Christ. Sometimes, Jack would bring my mother to the jail to visit me, and on the drives to and from the penitentiary, she would preach to him about how blessed I was. While she lectured him on the glory of my salvation, he would sit their wearing a sly grin and thinking, "Ole' Mark done found another scam." Indeed, my transformation was so quick and dramatic that I couldn't blame Jack for questioning my sincerity.

While Christianity did not appeal to him, Jack nevertheless believed in the supernatural, so in an effort to avoid a return to prison, he put his trust in a root doctor, paying a man $600 to work some magic. The guy gave Jack some powder, six bones of some sort, and some Bible verses to read. He told Jack that if he put the bones and the powder in his shoes when he went to court, he would not get any time. Fully persuaded, Jack refused to cop a plea that would have gotten him seven years in the joint and instead decided to fight the charge. When the judge sentenced him to 15 years, he was shocked.

Jack and I have remained good friends but he has never followed me to Christ. He has heard me preach some of my most powerful messages and seen me lead dozens of people at a time to Christ but never come forward himself. His stubbornness has cost him, as he's been back to prison three times since being released from his sentence for aiding and abetting a bank robber after four years and eight months. Finally, after a seven-month jail stint in 1997, Jack seems to have learned his lesson. Now 54 years old, he runs a legitimate grille and pool hall in Goldsboro. More importantly, he has begun to explore what personal faith can do.

Though the scope of our relationship obviously has changed, Jack and I are as close as ever. Even though crime is what brought us together, we have realized that we are true friends, guys who would have been tight even if we had never been criminals. Even when Jack and I were in different jails, we always found ways to communicate through a third party. Though Jack continued in his wrongdoing, he never once tried to recruit me back into the world of crime. He was actually very protective of me. Whenever he was involved in mischief, he always made sure that my freedom or good name was never put in jeopardy. Nowadays, we talk to each other on the telephone every week and play golf together whenever possible. His is the only friendship from my days as a hustler that has lasted. I have remained close with childhood friends who were never involved in my criminal activities, like Jasper Ormond, but I have not kept in touch with any of my other hustling partners.

Helping Jack avoid being sentenced for bank robbery wasn't the only thing weighing heavily on my mind back in 1980. Even before my conversion, the sentencing of an innocent man to 40 years in prison for a bank robbery I committed had gnawed at my conscience. When I became a Christian, it really began to disturb me. So when an FBI agent came to question me about the robbery for which I had been arrested, I told him I had also robbed a bank in Goldsboro, and that an innocent man had been convicted. They hadn't the slightest idea that I was involved in that crime and in fact, did not believe me. I had to go into great detail about the holdup just for them to take me seriously. Still not totally convinced of my guilt, they put that crime on the back burner and continued prosecuting me for the one they knew I committed.

Though I was now in danger of being sentenced to more than half a century in prison, I still believed God would set me free. Most of the other brothers in the Bible study had been getting released, so why not me? When the time finally came around for my sentencing, I went before the judge in good spirits. His name was Judge Franklin T. Dupree and like most Federal Court judges, he didn't like having his authority questioned. But in my naiveté, I did just that.

Before being sentenced, I was asked if I had anything to say. Thankful for the opportunity, I boldly declared, "Go ahead and do what you have to do. I have committed my part and taken my case to a higher authority. It doesn't matter if man gives me 200 years because when it's time for me to get out, God will open the door." Wondering who besides the Supreme Court had more authority than him, Judge Dupree looked at me like I had gone mad; so did the FBI agents. Everyone in that courtroom thought I was crazy. Doing what he had to do, so to speak, the judge sentenced me to 30 years at the United States Penitentiary at Lewisburg, Pennsylvania and then ordered the U.S. Attorney to send me out for a psychiatric evaluation. I later realized how offended Judge Dupree was when he established an order that prohibited me from being transferred from Lewisburg without his permission.

Soon after being shipped to Lewisburg, I was called to Goldsboro for a hearing concerning the man who had been convicted of my bank robbery. Knowing that I had been in Atlanta on the day of the robbery, the state district attorney said there was no way I could have gotten to that bank in Goldsboro. I scoffed and said, "Man, I can get from Atlanta to Goldsboro in six hours." When I said that the judge smiled and to my surprise, moved on to another case, one I had forgotten about.

The authorities had studied the similarities between this robbery in Atlanta and my first heist there - the one I had botched and ended up covered in red dye - and concluded that I had also hit that bank. I did not intend to lie but when they asked me to plead guilty and receive another 25 years, I said, "No way." I had already received 30 years; I wasn't about to stand by and watch them give me 55. In fact, it would have been closer to 70 since after serving my time in the Federal pen, I would have to return to North Carolina to complete my 6- to 8-year sentence for involuntary manslaughter and then do more time after that for escape. Sure, I was saved, sanctified, born-again and all of that, but that didn't mean I wanted to spend the rest of my life in prison. So I went to trial, not to deny my crime, but to fight for the 25-year sentence to run concurrently with my 30 years rather than consecutively.

For nine months, I sat in the United States Penitentiary in Atlanta, waiting to go to trial. Spiritually confused, I wondered what had gone wrong. I had given my life to Christ, done away with my plans of escape, sworn off violent behavior, taught Bible study and preached the gospel throughout the jail, and still I was receiving more and more time. It seemed like God wanted me to die in prison. I was too young in the Lord to understand trials and tribulations or even reaping what I had sown. I just believed that if I prayed everything would work out the way I planned. When it didn't, I backslid.

Of course, if you don't do drugs or have sex, you can only backslide so far in prison. My problem was not what I was doing, but what I was thinking and planning to do. Since I had a lot of connections in Atlanta, I started receiving visits from old partners. Dead set against doing 30 years, let alone 55, I began plotting an escape. I also started making moves toward setting up another drug route. During that time, I didn't read the Bible or preach but I couldn't help but pray. Even the most hardened convicts pray on occasion just to make it through the prison experience. And at that time, this particular prison offered quite an experience.

The pen in Atlanta had become a holding facility for deported Cubans who had come over on the infamous Freedom Flotilla, that well-intentioned attempt by President Jimmy Carter to get the Cuban President, Fidel Castro, to release the country's political prisoners and allow them to immigrate to America on boats. Carter thought he had negotiated a great peace treaty, but Castro tricked him by emptying his jails and mental institutions and thus sending over thousands of madmen and villains. After supplying them with boats for their journey, Castro told them that if they ever returned to Cuba they would be killed on the spot, a decry that made them even more lawless. Aware of what awaited them in Cuba, they would kill somebody in prison just to get a life sentence and remain in America. When other convicts realized how crazy the Cubans were, they began hiring them as hit men for two or three packs of cigarettes. Since they didn't mind getting caught, the Cubans would walk into the mess hall and stab someone in front of four guards. Fortunately, I was separated from most of them, but their presence nearby made for harrowing times.

Even though I continued to pray, I knew my prayer life wasn't right. Before, I had talked to God like a friend, totally opening myself up to Him, laying all of my thoughts, fears and aspirations before Him. But now I was hiding from Him. It was like I couldn't look Him in the face because I was too ashamed of what was in my heart. My talks with Him were superficial and one-sided as I refused to entertain or listen to what He was telling me through the Holy Spirit. As the trial neared and it became time to select the jury, I reverted back to one of my old strategies. Though I hate to give any credence to my former way of thinking, this plan actually worked to my benefit. In picking the members of the jury, I knew to choose as many grandmothers as possible. If there is any doubt whatsoever, a grandmother will always vote not guilty because when they see you, they see their grandson; whether Black or White, they see their grandson. I ended up receiving a favorable jury, but that small victory did little to relieve my frustration. After all, even if I won this trial, I still had to serve 30 years for the Federal authorities, plus the state time that I owed. Back to being a smart aleck, I told the judge, "Just send the time over to the jail. I don't feel like going through another trial." He didn't like that and made me appear in court every single day. Deadlocked at six, the trial ended in a hung jury.

A strange thing happened on the way back to the prison. As usual, we rode through the shopping district in downtown Atlanta, but this time I paid special attention to the people on the streets. I wasn't doing it on purpose; it just seemed like I was more observant than usual, like I was seeing things I had not seen before. The people were of different races, but most of them looked to be middle-class. As they walked along the sidewalk, carrying bags full of new clothing and other items, I noticed that all of them had the same bland expression on their face. Although it was the Christmas season, none of them looked happy or excited. They just seemed to be going through the motions. For the rest of the ride, those lifeless faces, dozens of them, flashed through my head like slides in a projector.

Then, shortly after we arrived at the jail, about 20 hustlers that I knew from the old days were captured and booked after a drug raid. I sat there in the cell, staring at them and thinking, "Do I really want to go back out there and have the same stuff happen to me." That night, I said the first real prayers I had said in nine months. I repented for leaving the Lord, asked Him for forgiveness and rededicated my life to Him. Reflecting back on the somber looks on the faces of the shoppers in downtown Atlanta, I concluded that being in prison with the Lord was better than being in society without Him.

Despite my revelation, things continued to get worse before they got better. Almost immediately, my faith was tested once again as precious family members began dying. My sister, Julia, died of lupus in January of 1981. My father died of cancer in February, and my father's sister died of cancer in March. My cousin, Mel Bryant, whom I loved like a brother, died in May. I started thinking, "Man, if I don't get out of here soon, I'm not going to have any family to return to." Sad as I was, though, I refused to backslide. I was totally committed to the Lord and would stay that way throughout the remainder of my incarceration.

My zeal restored, I began telling my fellow inmates that God had called me to bring the gospel to America. Knowing that I had 30 years, the other inmates joked, "You mean God has called you to bring it to America's prisons." It turned out that they were right, at least to a degree. Unable to attend seminary or learn at the feet of an established pastor, I underwent nine years of spiritual training in one of the country's most barbarous penitentiaries.

After spending a brief time in the Wake County Jail in Raleigh, North Carolina, I was moved to the maximum-security facility in Lewisburg. As a street hustler, I was well aware of Lewisburg's reputation, which only made the 36-hour bus ride all the more dreadful. We made stops in Butner, North Carolina, Petersburg, Virginia and Morgantown, West Virginia, where, because of a snow and ice storm, we spent the night in the county jail. I later learned that transfer trips such as these were the only traveling experiences that many inmates had ever had outside of their respective cities.

Chained at my wrists and ankles, I sat in my seat, trying to maintain my optimism in the Lord. In what seemed like a cruel joke, the bus driver played a cassette tape that included a hit single by the group Shalamar called "The Second Time Around." I'm sure there were other songs on the tape, but it seemed like that one played repeatedly. I liked the song, but under the circumstances, it was getting on my nerves. When we finally arrived, I was checked in, given my bed linens and sent into the cellblock. That terrible first walk through the sea of inmates that shook me up so much at Raleigh was once again upon me, but this time in a more brutal environment.

Lewisburg was the most violent prison I have ever been in. Easily. Raleigh was dirtier, but the brothers in Lewisburg were more vicious. Besides Marion, Illinois, where only convicts who had been a threat to national security were sent, Lewisburg was probably the most treacherous prison in the entire Federal system. I met some of the most ruthless men imaginable there. The Mafia was in full force, and inner-city gangs, as well as those that were international in scope, were all merged into this hellish walled city.

Knife fights, many of them to the death, were a constant, and they often resulted from ordered hits rather than random disputes. Occasionally, you would walk out of your cell and see blood splattered on the walls. And among the guards were a significant number of unflinching racists. One such guard would physically attack any Black inmate he caught alone in the rec room. That same guard carried a deep hatred for Christians and would break up any type of Christian gathering he came across.

Illegal activities never ceased. Naturally, the typical prison trades involving drugs and alcohol were prevalent, but Lewisburg also featured a vice I had never seen behind bars: female prostitution. Two or three times a month, on a Saturday or a Sunday, a chapel service would be held with Islamic visitors from the outside. The visitors usually came for a workshop or seminar for one of the Islamic sects, and the inmate Imam (Muslim teacher) made sure that the group always included a few prostitutes. These were real prostitutes so only the inmates with money were allowed to have sex with them. It was a lucrative moneymaking scam for the Imam, which is why so much blood was shed over who would control the different sects. It wasn't about who the holiest man was. It was about who was going to control the prostitution, the drugs, the loan sharking, all of which enabled a convict to raise enough money to hire a good lawyer and get out.

If an inmate could pay enough and was brave enough, he could smuggle his wife inside. But usually the only brothers who dared do that were those who were well respected within the Islamic community or those who were strong and rugged enough in their own right to deal with anybody who tried to act up. I recall one inmate who was neither a Muslim nor a reputed hustler regretfully paying to have his wife come in for a weekend. To his surprise, before he was permitted to go into the mop closet with her, the inmate Imam had sex with her first. He was taken advantage of because he

141

was not connected to the Islamic community and he was not a gangster who could get on the phone and have somebody killed. It goes without saying that his wife divorced him. In addition to giving sex, these weekend visitors also transported drugs, cash and information. For instance, an inmate who made money from drug dealing could not walk around with it in prison, so he would give it to a visitor to stash away until he was released.

These types of activities were an institution within the prison walls, so later, when I became the Christian inmate leader, I was approached by numerous individuals and factions that wanted me to perform such activities for pay. I refused them all and because of it, received great respect within the pen. My stance showed that I was not for sale, that I was really saved and really into practicing what I read in the Bible. Eventually, brothers stopped asking me to partake in their wicked schemes because they knew I would not budge. I was never threatened because of my position. The longer you stay in the penitentiary, the more aware people become of your toughness or weakness. Besides, all but one of the 40 or 50 members of my Christian fellowship had killed at least one man, which gave me, as the leader, lots of clout. Brothers wondered how vicious I must have been to be able to control 40 some odd murderers.

In such an atmosphere, one might imagine how unpleasant my initial walk through the cellblock was. As the convicts whooped and hollered, I had to call to mind every comforting Bible verse I knew just to maintain my sanity. By the time I reached G Block, the orientation block, I felt like I had walked two miles beneath burning sun.

Lunch was served a few hours later, and as I joined the line to file into the cafeteria, I heard someone yell, "Hey, Baby!" While I was known as M.C. or "The Bronx Star" in the New York, I had two other nicknames in New Haven. One was "SupaNigga" because I gambled so well, and the other was "Baby," because even though I was in my 20s, I looked like I was about 16 years old. Most of the guys called me "Baby." I think at one time I even had a bracelet with "Baby" spelled out in diamonds.

Even so, I wasn't about to turn around in prison because someone yelled "Hey Baby." So I kept facing forward and soon saw a behemoth of a man, about 6-foot-5-inches, approaching me. He was the one yelling "Hey Baby." I couldn't place him at first but as he got closer, I realized it was Frank Atkinson, a brother I had met back in 1974 in the Whalley Avenue Jail. The last time I had seen him was in Somers Prison in Connecticut.

Though we were not especially close, I felt like I was being reunited with a long lost brother. Genuinely glad to see each other, we hugged, and then Frank began telling me about all my homeboys in Lewisburg.

Pudgy, a bank robber from Bridgeport, Connecticut, was there. So was Jake the Snake, a drug dealer from New Haven who got his nickname by poisoning informers. I later found Richard Thrasher, a drug dealer from New York who was a personal friend of Jack Best's. And O.J. Johnson and his younger brother, Doc, whom I had met through our Miami drug connection, were also there. I saw guys from North Carolina I had not seen in years. My cellblock was full of hustlers I knew from Somers Prison or from the streets of New Haven. What was funny was that they were all calling me by a different name. The cats from Connecticut and my homeboys from way back knew me as "Baby." The Florida boys referred to me as "Slim Gator." The dudes from the deep South knew me as Billy Dee Hill; and still others were calling me "Tommy," short for Thomas Randolph, another one of my aliases. All the various names got really confusing, especially when a prison official would call me "Olds," a name that none of my partners knew me by.

Within three weeks, I was transferred to C Block, which put me in contact with even more of my old running mates. All told, I was reintroduced to more than 40 guys who I had known from back in the day. The number was even higher when you factor in all the guys who knew me by reputation. That's how it is in the street life: people disappear for a period and then show up again. And in most cases, their predicament grows worse with each successive reunion.

Most of these guys had not been rehabilitated in any way and were planning to return to crime as soon as they were released. They were running down the typical plots and schemes to one another and naturally, expected me to join in. When I told them I had become a Christian, their jaws dropped. But after getting over the initial jolt, they were supportive. They told me that what I had done was great, that they were happy for me; but none of them were about to take the same step. They said, "That's cool for you, but I'm a hustler 'till I die."

Their response was not baffling. Most of them had grown up in a church down South and knew they had a mother, aunt, sister, grandparent or cousin praying for them. They had been raised by a spiritual mother and taught about Jesus and "being saved." They had seen their mothers pray the family out of seemingly impossible situations, heard her cry out to the Lord for hours when they were sick as youngsters and unable to afford a visit to the doctor, and witnessed the unshakable peace God had given her in the midst of poverty, racism and unfaithful and rebellious men. And because they respected their mothers so much, they could not help but respect her Jesus, even if they never would submit to Him themselves.

That's still the case with many young Black men today, particularly in inner-city and rural areas. You would be hard pressed to find a Black convict, gang banger, professional athlete, entertainer or college student who does not have a close relative who is saved and praying for them. I believe that's why many Black men end up in prison rather than the grave; because God, in answering a loved one's prayers, gives them an opportunity to clearly see their mistakes and turn to Him for salvation.

My former running buddies and I retained a healthy respect for one another, but for the most part, I didn't hang out with them. They still looked out for me, which was nice, and I never condemned them, but there was no way I could remain in their clique when crime continued to be their main focus. I wanted to be around like-minded men who would strengthen my faith, so I started hanging with the other Christians.

Raymond Carter, an inmate from Washington, D.C., was my first Christian mentor. Raymond had been a malicious street hustler and bank robber. Many of the other convicts from D.C. remembered him for being the most callous man they had known, one who was extremely demeaning toward women. He had been a Christian for about six years – all in prison – when I met him, and I found him to be the most humble man I had ever met. He was full of the Word of God. He memorized whole chapters of the Bible and also had great wisdom interpreting the passages. He always said, "If you can't explain the Bible to other people, what you know will never impact their lives." I learned from Raymond to always tell the gospel story in ways that people can relate to and understand. Raymond is out of prison now and doing well. Upon release, he returned to D.C. and married the mother of his children.

I later met Milton Brown, a Christian inmate from Harrisburg, Pennsylvania. Milton was a lot like Raymond in that he was very humble. He was already a Christian when he arrived at Lewisburg in 1982. As had been the case with Jack, we hit it off immediately. Our relationship was like a spiritual version of the bond I had with Jack. Whereas Jack and I had been drawn together by the same vision of crime, Milton and I had been united by similar aspirations in the Lord. The first day I met Jack, we began talking about setting up an international drug trade. The first day I met Milton, we began talking about creating a Christian organization inside the prison walls. Our backgrounds were comparable as well.

Like me, Milton grew up in the church; the difference being that he sat under solid, Bible-believing pastors. He was active in his church in Harrisburg, Pennsylvania as a youth and honed his musical skills in the choir. After graduating from high school, he began playing the piano and writing music for a secular group called The Imperials. They had two big national hits, "Karate" and a smash single called "Everything is Everything." The group began touring the country, and Milton began partaking in all the fruits of stardom, mainly women and drugs. Soon, he found himself hooked on heroin. Willing to do whatever was necessary to get a fix, he started robbing banks, stealing and brutalizing people.

Because Milton moved very slowly and never appeared to be in a hurry, his friends referred to him as "The Last Rose of Summer." But Milton was hardly delicate by nature. His temperament while on the streets was similar to mine in that it was extremely violent. Short but powerfully built, he was incredibly dangerous with his hands. He was capable of doing with his hands what most men could do only with a weapon. Eventually, Milton's lifestyle caught up with him, and he was arrested and sent to Pennsylvania's Huntington State Prison, where he made a half-hearted commitment to the Lord. After being released, he went back to the women, heroin and crime and ended up in Lewisburg. Chastened by the Lord, he repented and finally grew serious about his faith.

On an average day in Lewisburg, Milton and I would wake up at about 4:30 in the morning to pray. We were not cellmates; we were not even in the same part of the prison. But we challenged each other to rise for early-morning prayer. We became so close that we could tell without a word when the other had cheated and slept in. We also fasted quite a bit, and since the prison food was so repulsive, it was much easier than one might expect. We fasted so frequently that going one to three days without food was nothing; it was like skipping a meal. It got to the point where we were going on 7- to 10-day water-only fasts two and three times a year. My longest such fast was 10 days. However, I would do 40-day fasts of one light meal after 6 p.m. a few times a year.

A healthy competition existed between Milton and me; not something prideful like who knew more Bible verses, but a pure desire to help one another become as strong as we could in Christ. Praying for about two hours each morning did wonders for both of us, cleansing us of various lusts and thought patterns that we had developed in the streets. I am convinced that I could not have experienced such dramatic spiritual growth outside of prison. My other responsibilities would have taken away from my time with the Lord. In the penitentiary, my entire focus was on Jesus. I had nothing else of significance to do, so I spent hours upon hours each day studying my Bible, praying and taking part in spiritual conversations with the other inmates.

The prison chaplain, Bryn Carlson, noticed how dedicated Milton and I were to our walk of faith and gave us positions of responsibility in his ministry. I started as the orderly in the chapel and later became the clerk. Milton worked in the prison factory but committed his musical talent to playing the piano and leading the music ministry during service. Every couple of months, Reverend Louis Correa, a Puerto Rican minister from the Youth Challenge Ministry, would let me preach on a Wednesday night. I prepared for those messages as if I was a law student about to take an oral exam. I did not preach cursory, emotional sermons that were nothing more than rehashed versions of my personal testimony. I actually tried to expound on the Biblical text and teach how we could apply it to our daily lives behind bars. While I would be embarrassed today if I still preached like I did back then, for a convict who was young in the Lord and lacking official Bible training, I did pretty well. Having the opportunity to preach not only encouraged me to continue growing, but also gave me a measure of respect among the inmates, saved and unsaved alike.

Though the chaplain was a Protestant minister, the chapel was available to every religious group in the prison, and just about every religion known to Western civilization was represented in Lewisburg. There were Catholics, Jews, Black Hebrew Israelites, Rastafarians, Buddhists, Hindus, Hare Krishna's, White supremacist groups based on twisted interpretations of the Bible, and about 13 different sects of Islam. The Muslims were by far the most populous group, having three times as many members as everyone else. While only about 30 guys consistently attended the Christian chapel services, more than 350 inmates claimed to be Muslims. Most of the Muslims joined because Islam's militant and macho image afforded them protection, not because they sincerely believed its religious teachings. Consequently, the Muslim population was plagued with the same immoral behavior that infested the rest of the prison. That hypocrisy led those who were devout to break away and form their own small sects.

Because the foundations of Islam in America had been so anti-Christian, with Elijah Muhammad and Malcolm X setting the tone with their biting rhetoric against the church, there was a built-in tension between the Muslims and the Christians. Most of the Muslims, despite having been raised in the church, felt they had to adopt a hatred for Christianity upon converting to Islam. That posed quite a problem for those who tried Islam and found it wanting. Over the years, several Muslims came to our chapel services and sat quietly in the back. After weeks of attendance, they usually would approach Milton or myself and ask us about Christ. Many of them privately made commitments to Christ but continued to go through the outward motions of Islam because they feared being attacked by the Muslims. The unwritten rule of penitentiary Islam was to kill those who left the faith, especially if their destination was Christianity. I can recall at least three former Muslims putting up such a façade before being transferred to other prisons and openly taking part in Christian services.

Large contingents of Lewisburg's Muslims were running one of the biggest drug operations in the prison. Milton and I spoke out against it and ended up with a contract on our heads. We didn't single out the Muslims; we spoke out against all drug trafficking and abuse, but because we were practically the only voice of morality in the penitentiary, the Muslims decided that we needed to be silenced. Having seen them deal with enemies in the past, we knew to take them seriously. But we also knew that we couldn't stop preaching the truth. We prayed intently about the contract and then left it in God's hands, saying, "If they kill us, they kill us." The contract was a hot topic of conversation for about a week and then suddenly, the talk stopped. Nothing else was said or done about it. It was as if it had never been an issue. Milton and I still don't know what happened, whether some of our old partners intervened or what; we just credit God.

In many ways, Christians and Muslims were perceived as being on the opposite ends of the religious spectrum. While Muslims were seen as hard and manly, Christians, for the most part, were viewed as soft and weak. Basically it was the same perception that existed on the streets. Also, while joining the Muslims provided one with protection, becoming a Christian made one vulnerable. The perception was that we were easy targets for attack, probably because of Jesus' admonition to "turn the other cheek." I was

147

committed to adhering to that scripture, but I also recognized that I was in a position where I might have to act to protect my life. You could not be pushed around in prison and have a strong voice. So, as I said earlier, I put my trust in God and committed to throwing blows only as a last resort.

My faith in God's protection did not go without reward, as He made sure that I never had to ball a fist during my entire time at Lewisburg. He used numerous means to cover me, one being my former reputation. Most of the guys I came into contact with knew about my life of crime and were unsure of whether I would resort back to my old ways in a conflict. I also kept myself physically fit by lifting weights – at one point, I could bench press 290 pounds – and by running 45 minutes a day. So guys knew I was capable of protecting myself in a scrum. As a result, no one tested me.

God also used other inmates to guard me. Because of my previous prison experience, I knew that guys who didn't drink, smoke, do drugs or mess with homosexuals were usually left alone by other convicts. It was a respect thing, where if the inmates knew a guy was sincerely trying to turn his life around, they would support him. But if they saw that he was a hypocrite, they would attack him. In my case, guys, particularly those I had hung with before my conversion, knew I was serious and because of it, did not let anyone bother me.

The third way God protected me was through the miraculous. One day I was in the chow hall wearing a scarf on my head that one of my homeboys from North Carolina had gotten from outside of the prison. Anything from outside the prison walls had inflated value, which I guess is what led a brother to try and take the scarf from me. Walking aggressively toward me and looking me in the eye, this guy said, "That's my scarf." I told him that it wasn't, and he grew angrier, reiterating that it was. Finally, I said, "It's not your scarf, but if you want it, I'll give it to you." Not pleased with my answer, he looked at me with a vicious scowl and said, "Be here when I get back," and walked away. I knew he was going to get his shank so I began mulling over my options: I could tell someone to give me a shank and get it on with the brother; but that would have adversely affected my Christian witness. I could go back to my cellblock and avoid the confrontation; but then I would have had to hide from him for the rest of my imprisonment, which also would have damaged my witness. Or I could trust God.

That morning, a friend named Gerald Jenkins and I had read a devotional based on 1 Chronicles 16:22 - "Touch not my anointed. Do my prophet no harm." Upon reading that scripture, Gerald began saying how the Bible was alive and applicable to our every situation. So with his words in my mind, I said to God, "Well, I'm going to see if your Word is true because I'm not about to spend the rest of my life running from this guy." So I waited.

Sure enough, the guy returned in a fury and stormed toward me. He reached inside of his shirt to get his shank and then, his anger abating in an instant, said, "Oh, I'm sorry man. My scarf is black and yours is blue." He was less than 18 inches away from me and could have easily killed me right then and there. But I just stood there, motionless, and God protected me. Two days later, some brothers I didn't even know started beating on that brother every day for about a week and a half. I don't know if they heard that he had loud-talked "Rev" or what, but they whipped him something awful. He finally had to check into the protective custody unit, which was the exact spot the devil had tried to get me to run to. As the Bible says in James 4:7, I resisted the devil and he fled from me.

Just by exhibiting steadfast faith in Christ, Milton and I went a long way in changing the prevailing sentiment that Christians were weak. One reason Christians were perceived in that way was because in many instances, they were. Before I was born-again, most of the Christians I met in prison were too timid about their faith to be taken seriously. One thing about the penitentiary is that you have to be tough. If you're not tough, brothers will see right through you and give you no respect. Once I became a Christian, I couldn't understand why so many of the brothers were soft. The Bible told me that neither Jesus nor His apostles - nor the Old Testament prophets for that matter - were soft, so it didn't make sense for so many so-called disciples of Christ to walk around like wimps. Since Milton and I hadn't been soft before salvation, there was no way we were going to be after meeting Christ. In fact, our conviction was that He made us stronger, not in a physical way, but in terms of our character.

While we were mostly at odds with the Muslims, we did have a few positive encounters. Some of the more sincere ones truly respected Milton and I for taking a adamant and vocal stance against the rampant depravity that went on in the prison. One day a Muslim, having heard me speak out against almost every type of sin for a year or two, asked me what I thought about the prejudiced White guards who had been mistreating the Black inmates. When I replied, "I'm a Christian," he shook his head in disgust, saying, "Man, that doesn't have anything to do with it. You better quit being

149

so naïve and wake up." Though it took a while for his comments to sink in, I eventually started to pay more attention to the actions of the guards and determined without a doubt that they were racist. Then I started asking myself why there were so many of "us" in prison. Every jail or prison I had ever been in was at least 50 percent Black. That didn't make sense to me, being that we accounted for only 12 percent of the nation's population. The argument that we were committing more crime didn't wash with me because I had enough connections and hustling experience to know that Whites were committing just as much, if not more, crime than Blacks.

A few months later, another Muslim brother handed me a book and said, "Look, I know you're not going to convert to Islam, but just read this material so you can know." I looked down and saw that it was a book on the prevalence of Black people in the Bible. Though one of my goals since conversion had been to bring Black people to the Bible, I had never thought about searching for us in the pages of scripture. Common sense told me that Jesus, the apostles and the rest of the Biblical personalities, except perhaps the Romans, did not look like the blond-haired, blue-eyed portraits I had always seen. Almost the entire Bible was set in Africa and the Middle East, so I knew the characters were not European. But because of the pictures I had seen throughout my life, I definitely envisioned White people when I read God's word. Those images were so subconsciously imbedded that I didn't even think about it until that Muslim gave me that book.

Intrigued, Milton and I diligently researched the information, using all the resources available to us. There was no prison library or resource center, but family members and friends could mail books to you. When we found that many, and perhaps most, of the people in the Bible were Black, I was relieved; not because it made me feel proud or superior but because it confirmed the things I had been feeling in my heart and oftentimes putting down on paper. In my personal writings, I would propose Biblical solutions for the problems facing the African-American community, and this gave me a historical basis from which to work.

As had been the case years earlier when that brother exposed me for having a slave mentality, my eyes had been opened. This time, however, I would react positively by studying and applying Biblical and historical truths to White America's racism and Black America's plight. I would not respond with anger toward Whites. I was the inmate-leader of a racially integrated group of Christians and could honestly say that I didn't love the

Black brothers any more than the White ones. In fact, besides Milton, most of my closest Christian friends in prison were White. That didn't change my desire to help Blacks, but because I was a Christian, I never felt that meeting the needs of my own meant neglecting the needs of others. Even before I was saved, I don't think I really ever hated Whites. I just resented the fact that they seemed to be so mean and selfish and always got away with pushing Blacks around. So when I became I Christian, I didn't need to be cleansed of great prejudice. I just needed to be freed from the envy, anger and bitterness that I felt towards White people. The one thing I did not want to do was take on the ways of the oppressor.

At Lewisburg, my cell was always located next to that of Gerald Jenkins, a White Christian brother who was instrumental in my maturation in the Lord. Whenever I was moved to another cell, Gerald was also moved and vise versa. Perhaps this was the authorities' way of keeping a watch on us since we both had violent pasts. Another close friend of mine was a White Christian brother named Eros Timms. Eros, who was doing a life sentence for murder, was withdrawn and moody, but we always had a great time together in Christ. He was actually the first White man I could truly call a friend, and he became one of the closest friends I've ever had. I was 31 years old when we met. Eros joined Milton and I as early-morning prayer warriors and became my prayer partner. He was a very affectionate person – not gay, just affectionate - who was small and slim in stature, which made him a target for some of the perverts. One of his greatest hobbies was planting flowers, and he would always plant flowers around the mechanical services buildings where he worked. He would also bring live flowers into the chapel to make it look nice. I was crushed when Eros became a casualty of the most malicious cycle of organized murder I have ever seen.

It was 1984 and open season on White inmates as at least 11 White men were murdered in Lewisburg within a year's time. The killing spree began when the Aryan (a White supremacist group) Nation killed some Black guys at the Federal prison in Marion, Illinois. The Aryans were big in the Federal system and naturally, often at odds with the Blacks. Word of the Aryans' crime spread throughout the prisons as if it had been broadcast on television in every inmate's room. Suddenly, brothers, most of them with a history of murder, were being transferred to Lewisburg from all over the country. In a very calculating, systematic fashion, the Blacks began murdering one White inmate a month. I would be walking down the hall, and guys would come up to me saying, "Pray for me, Reverend Olds." I would casually say all right, planning to mention them in my prayers later that night, and they would grab me frantically and say, "No. Pray for me right now!" White guys needed eyes in the back of their heads that year. It was so dangerous that they were afraid to go into the TV room by themselves. Prisoners were so uneasy that someone could drop a tray in the cafeteria and 500 men would go silent. Our Christian group prayed fervently during those days, particularly for our White brothers.

Eros was targeted when he innocently found a knife owned by some Black guys. Without thinking about it, he turned it in to the guards, and the brothers began calling him a snitch because of it. For the next couple of weeks, they hounded him, telling him they were going to show him what happened to snitches. One morning when we were praying, he told me he had dreamed of being killed the night before. The administration began making plans to transfer him to another prison, but despite being afraid, he wanted to stay in Lewisburg, mainly because of the strong Christian fellowship we had. Also, he had just planted new flowers around the maintenance shop. One day, word got out that he was about to be transferred, and the brothers killed him that night.

I never thought I would cry over the death of a White man, but I felt the tears forming in my eyes when I heard the news of Eros' fate. But a Black inmate named Henry T quickly reminded me of where I was. He saw me standing alone solemnly after Eros' death, and said matter-of-factly, "You better not be seen crying and shedding tears for no White man. I know you guys were close, but Rev, you better always remember where you are." Those words made me pull it together real fast. Henry T was not a Christian, just a brother who knew what it took to survive in prison. That experience turned into a great and valuable lesson, one I often draw resolve from when counseling people today. It taught me that you can feel pain, but at the same time retain the strength to function effectively. Also, the entire inmate population had always viewed me as a strong leader, and Henry T was a reflection of African-American men desiring solid leadership. At that moment, I realized that as a leader, I could display concern, understanding and sensitivity but never weakness.

Interacting with White Christians in prison taught me how to relate to them as equals. In America, and throughout much of the world for that matter, Blacks are constantly forced to react to Whites as superiors in subtle and not so subtle ways. We must talk as they want us to talk or dress as they want us to dress to get a job or be admitted to a university. Most of what we are taught from kindergarten through college is from a Eurocentric perspective, and the list of societal biases goes on and on. In prison, however, that was not the case. The Whites I was close to were not my employers or teachers. In fact, I was teaching them. Since we all were in prison, economic status was not a factor, and unlike mainstream American society, our common penitentiary culture did not promote the idea that their skin color made them better than me. As a result, we viewed one another simply as brothers.

That acculturation process continues to manifest itself in my dealings with Whites today. Though most of my fellowship is with Black Christians, I would venture to say that I interact with more White ministers than 80 percent of America's Black preachers. And our correspondence is in no way paternalistic. We exchange resources based on the principle of sharing found in the Biblical Book of Acts. I do not want their help if it is rooted in pity or sympathy. If they help me, they help me as a brother, not a father.

Chapter *VIII*

REVEREND OLDS

A s our Christian meetings gained strength and stability, Milton and I began contemplating a name for the group. After much prayer, fasting, scripture study and deliberation, we settled on "The Solid Rock Christian Foundation." The name was prophetic in that I would go on to work in both the ministry and the broader non-profit community, and Milton would go on to name the first church he pastored The Solid Rock Church of God. Later, after four years at Solid Rock, Milton would take over the pastorate of the Plainsfield Church of God in Plainsfield, Pennsylvania, becoming the first African-American pastor in the Church of God denomination to lead an all White congregation.

Though nothing in our operation changed, having a name gave our group more distinction, the perception being that we had gone from a loosely structured band of believers to a brotherhood. As the leaders of the group, Milton and I saw our stature soar in the eyes of the convicts, especially once I became the unofficial Christian chaplain to the inmates. I was elevated to that position when Chaplain Bryn Carlson, whom I had worked for as an administrative assistant, was named chaplain of the entire Southeast region and moved to Atlanta.

Despite the religious diversity that exists amongst prison populations, most facilities have only two chaplains. For years, those positions automatically went to a Protestant and a Catholic, so the inmates that were Islamic,

Jewish or of some other religious faith conducted their services and determined their direction on their own. That autonomy is one reason the Muslims became so popular, since few inmates wanted to submit to a leader who was employed by the bureau of prisons.

But after Chaplain Carlson left, the prison installed its first Islamic Imam, Matthew Bilal Hammidulah. Interestingly, Chaplain Hammidulah had been a classmate of mine at North Carolina A&T. He was known as Matthew Simpson back then. Though he was a sincere Muslim, Chaplain Hammidulah's presence helped to spark a proliferation of Muslim sects in Lewisburg, as brothers, refusing to submit to the prison's Imam, broke off and started their own groups. There were so many little pseudo-mosques around that they reminded me of the storefront churches in inner-city Black neighborhoods. The Catholic chaplain remained on board, so we Protestant inmates were able to enjoy what the Muslims had always benefited from: the ability to govern ourselves.

Now, instead of preaching a few times a year, I was delivering sermons once a month. I also was in charge of bringing in guests for special weekend services. Naturally, we had to have our requests ratified by the Catholic Chaplain, but since he was unfamiliar with most Black Protestant congregations, he basically accepted our recommendations automatically. When the inmates witnessed the type of authority we had, they began treating us with more respect, even seeking us out for prayer and counsel. For instance, numerous convicts who had contemplated suicide came to us for words of encouragement and insight into the meaning of life.

We even counseled free folks, usually women who came to the prison to visit their husbands or boyfriends. Since as convicts we could not go to the visiting room at our own discretion, this type of counseling took place while we were meeting with visitors ourselves. It got to the point where guys were coordinating their visitation schedules with those of myself and Milton in order to receive our counsel. Since many couples were without any church affiliation on the outside, they would ask our advice on keeping their families together under such trying circumstances. Our counsel was not limited to the three dozen or so members of Solid Rock. Because we tried to pattern ourselves after Jesus' example of unconditional love, we advised Christian and non-Christian inmates alike. Our advice was always Biblical and intended to lead a person to faith in Christ, but we never turned away non-believers.

156

Shortly after Solid Rock began functioning as an independent organization, a brother named Willie from Mississippi told me about a radio broadcast he listened to on WBAL out of Baltimore, Maryland. Oddly, you could only pick it up on the east side of the prison. Trying to take in as much "Word" as possible, I tuned in whenever I could get a decent reception. I had never really paid attention to Christian radio before prison, and my only reference point was Reverend Ike, who came on WWRL, one of New York City's Black-oriented radio stations in the 1960s and 1970s. After getting home late on Sunday nights, usually in an intoxicated state, I would hear him on the radio and wonder how people could be foolish enough to send money to a man promising healing and deliverance from a cloth. While I still had my questions about that sort of thing, I was enthusiastic about catching the messages of legitimate Christian preachers over the airwaves.

Before I became aware of WBAL, I listened to a station out of Wheeling, West Virginia that offered a melange of African-American preaching, from the sound to the absurd. Milton and I had to carefully decipher the messages we heard because some of the doctrines were way out in left field. Even so, I was thankful for the opportunity to listen to sermons by preachers from all over the country. My Christian foundation was strengthened through the teachings of men like Dr. Walter S. Thomas, Dr. Clay Evans and Dr. Jeremiah A. Wright, Jr. After my release, I had the pleasure of meeting and dialoguing with Dr. Wright, and was blessed to have him write the foreward to a manual for a Christian Rites-of-Passage program I eventually developed called "Redirection of Young Minds (Christo-Centric Passage)."

While I was fond of all of these men, it was Dr. Harold A. Carter of New Shiloh Baptist Church in Baltimore who most impacted my life. I thought Dr. Carter was phenomenal. That man preached the gospel like I had never heard it preached before. The main point of his message was always the nuts and bolts of salvation, but the way he applied the gospel to daily life made you want to get saved over and over again. I cannot understand how anyone could reject salvation after hearing him preach. I began listening to Dr. Carter as often as possible and eventually wrote him a letter to let him know how much I appreciated his radio broadcast. When he wrote back saying he would like to visit our fellowship, I was beside myself.

We pulled everything together as quickly as possible, and a few weeks later, Dr. Carter and some of his church members visited Lewisburg one

Saturday morning. A number of non-Christian inmates familiar with his broadcast came to that service and after hearing his message, stepped forward to accept Christ. I have heard Dr. Carter preach dozens of times since that first meeting and never have I seen him leave the pulpit without a new convert at the altar. Of all the ministers I know - Black, White, Hispanic, male, female, Baptist, Pentecostal, Charismatic, whooping and hollering, quiet and reserved, seminary-trained, and streetwise - he is the only one I can say that about. After that first visit, our relationship took off, and the evangelists from New Shiloh became regular guests of our group.

Several months later, a hardy looking man who stood about 5-feet-10 inches tall and weighed more than 200 pounds accompanied our visitors from New Shiloh. As the procession of guests made its way toward the chapel, inmates of every ilk began staring, pointing and whispering about this man's presence. Many of our members recognized him as well and one nudged me in the side and said, "That's Howard Lyles, warden of the Maryland State Penitentiary." My typical reaction would have been to think he had been sent to spy on us, but it was clear almost immediately that this man had come to worship, not to investigate. He sang hymns with passion, was attentive to the preached word and quite obviously, was a Christian himself. He even tried to downplay the fact that he was a warden and introduced himself as Deacon Howard Lyles. Once I put together the scenario in my mind, I was radically impressed. I thought it was awesome that a man who spent five days a week at a penitentiary would give up his Saturday to drive five hours to worship with inmates at another prison. After getting to know him, I realized that Warden Lyles had not even thought about it in those terms. He just wanted to praise the Lord.

Warden Lyles had the same fire for Christ that I did. He had become a Christian on April 10th, 1975 - he even remembers the date! - and as a result, had experienced a fundamental change in his approach toward dealing with people, particularly inmates. The fact that he was 43 years old when he gave his life to Christ was remarkable in itself. At that age, most people, even if they feel the need to change, are so set in their ways that they refuse.

Before he became a warden, Howard was an extremely strict, totally by-the-book corrections officer with a reputation for being anything but Christ-like. He was converted after hearing one of Dr. Carter's sermons and he subsequently joined New Shiloh's Bible-training class. The study lessons made him realize that much of the harshness, if not downright brutality, he displayed toward inmates was unnecessary. He once told me that his former actions had been based in conceit and a burning desire to make the inmates feel as base as possible. He wanted them to hate themselves, not just what they had done. Though his attitude and actions had changed, the convicts at Lewisburg knew only of his former ways, so they were shocked when they saw him singing, clapping and raising his hands toward the heavens with us. Because he was known as a no-nonsense type of guy, his presence gave our group even more credibility among the convicts. And it made a lot of skeptics curious about a Jesus who could turn such a hardened overseer into a humble, though still rigid, friend of inmates.

While I obviously knew from personal experience that Christ could completely change a man's heart, even I was surprised at how unassuming Warden Lyles acted around us. He truly went out of his way to make us feel like equals, even though that was all but impossible under the circumstances. I saw one of the greatest examples of the bond Howard built with Christian inmates in a Baltimore-area newspaper. A brother from Maryland who subscribed to his hometown paper approached me one day with a look of disbelief on his face. The paper in his hand had a picture of Warden Lyles singing a solo at a baptismal service for some inmates at the Maryland House of Corrections, where Howard had formerly served as warden. That brother was amazed that a warden would show such concern for convicts.

As the leader of our fellowship, I got to know Dr. Carter and Warden Lyles well, Dr. Carter becoming my father in the ministry and Warden Lyles a close friend. My relationships with them developed quickly and within weeks of our introductions we were corresponding regularly through the mail. I was even granted the privilege of calling Warden Lyles at his office in the state penitentiary. When other inmates found out that I had the ear of Warden Lyles, they suggested I ask him for favors, but I never entertained the thought of abusing his friendship. The letters I wrote to Warden Lyles were always spiritually based. I never griped or complained about my conditions and never carried on about mundane issues like sports. I wrote about my growth in the Lord, my vision for our Solid Rock fellowship and my witnessing to other inmates. I called him about three or four times a year, usually before New Shiloh was scheduled to come visit us.

Howard and I became such good friends that he invited me to stay at his home with him and his family within months of my release in 1989. I was in Washington D.C., visiting my brother Aaron and I decided to give him a call. My brother, not understanding the nature of our relationship, thought I was crazy. He said a warden wouldn't want anything to do with me. I didn't have Howard's home phone number or address so after looking it up in the phone book, I called, saying, "Is this the Howard Lyles who is a warden at the Maryland State Penitentiary?" When he answered yes, I said, "This is Mark Olds from Lewisburg." Howard was so glad to hear from me that, as soon as he found out I was in the area, he asked me to come over and meet his wife, Shirley. I ended up staying with them the entire weekend. Knowing I didn't have any money, Howard gave me $200 before I left. Years later, he joked, "That's when I knew I had been converted: when I brought an ex-con into my house to sleep." Now, whenever I'm in Baltimore, I stay at the Lyles' home.

I realized that Howard was an even greater friend when he showed up unannounced at my mother's funeral in 1993. He and four other deacons from New Shiloh drove nearly 7 hours to attend the morning service at my childhood church in Maury, North Carolina. When I saw Howard, I was both comforted and stunned. I could not believe he had traveled such a great distance to pay respects to a woman he had never met. In turn, three years later, Milton and I went to the funeral of Howard's mother. He actually had us say a few words to those in attendance. I had never met his mother, but the bond between us had grown so strong that we thought it both appropriate and natural to be there for one another in a time of such grieving. That is how close we have become: that we are involved in each other's lives not only in times of triumph, but also in times of sorrow.

I will admit that in those early years I had an ulterior motive in corresponding with Howard, but it had nothing to do with his being a warden; it was because he was free. I made it a point to communicate as much as possible with people outside the prison walls. Besides Dr. Carter and Warden Lyles, I kept up with most of the local pastors and Christians who ministered to our fellowship. Such correspondence was critical to my continued development, not only as a Christian but as a human being. To speak only with convicts would have put me in a mental box that would have been difficult to unlock upon release, so even though I was incarcerated, I tried my best to think as a free person. I refused to let myself think, talk or act like an inmate. Almost all my interaction with convicts besides Milton and a few other Christians was either on an advisory level or of some other positive nature. Otherwise, I aimed to distance myself from the prison culture as much as I could.

160

My decision was rooted in my concern for how I would make a successful reentry into society. Though my sentence was lengthy, I believed firmly that God would eventually restore my freedom, and with verbal language being my foremost tool of communication, I took pains to make sure I spoke in a way that would enable me to transition comfortably once He did.

That meant giving up the dialect of the convict, which is dominated by curse words and slang. Many inmates curse every second or third word and, out of defiance, make slang the standard form of speech. I was so intent on breaking free from that mold that I even refused to partake in many seemingly innocuous prison customs. For instance, when inmates would watch a basketball game on television, they would yell "Trash Out!" whenever a player had his shot blocked. The term stemmed from its usage by the prison police, who would holler "Trash Out" when it was time for the orderlies to take the trash out of the cellblock. Thinking there was no way I could sit in someone's living room and yell "Trash Out!" during a basketball game, I refused to use the phrase.

While that may seem like an extreme, I realized that I could not get cozy in the prison subculture and at the same time prepare myself for life on the outside. I knew the reason that many former inmates hooked up with ex-convicts after being released was because they were looking for somebody they felt comfortable with. They were looking for someone who could relate to the subculture they had become accustomed to. Those convicts who immerse themselves in the prison subculture cannot communicate beyond a superficial level with anyone who has not spent time in a penitentiary. As a result, they bond with felons or other ex-cons, a move that often leads them back into a life of crime.

I also made a conscious effort to slow down my speech. I used to speak extremely fast and often failed to complete thoughts. But now that I had something legitimate to say, I concentrated on speaking clearly and making points. Instead of answering questions with a five-word sentence, I would give a person a paragraph or two. I would be lying if I said I did not enjoy and take pride in my developing eloquence, but I made sure not to become excessive, for I did not want to fulfill the stereotype of the verbose prison intellectual.

In addition to Dr. Carter, Warden Lyles and other Christians, I spoke frequently with my brothers and my longtime friend from North Carolina,

Jasper Ormond. By this time, Jasper had earned a Master's Degree in Psychology from Fisk University and a Ph.D. from Portland State. The degree programs he went through were very Afrocentric and his dedication to Black people was the driving force of his life. He wasn't a Christian, but because of his intelligence and seriousness, our dialogue was always positive and uplifting. Our discussions helped to formulate my views on justice and liberation.

During my incarceration at Lewisburg, Jasper worked as the chief psychologist for the Washington D.C. Department of Corrections, and though I obviously was not nearly as accomplished as he was, he continued to speak to me as an equal, just as he had done when we were young boys. He even sent me money periodically without being asked. Jasper never viewed me as a criminal, before or after my conversion. In fact, my commitment to Christ did little to affect the way he thought of me. He didn't take my faith seriously and believed I was just going through "a religious phase" because of my incarceration. But he did think I was sincere in turning away from crime, a period of my life he also considered to be a phase.

In observing the media's treatment of Black America and how that treatment affected our people's behavior, Jasper concluded that the glorification of the "Superfly" image on television and the radio led me and countless other Black men to embrace hustling as normal conduct for Black folks and education, family and racial pride as abnormal. He would share this theory with the inmates while working at the Department of Corrections. He noted that the predominant images of Blacks in the 1960s - the morality of Martin Luther King Jr. and the Civil Rights Movement, the pride and intelligence of Malcolm X, and the militancy and political savvy of the Black Panthers - were threatening to White America. As a result, the powers that be consciously ushered in an era of Black foolishness, ignorance and buffoonery during the 1970s. His view is that the same trend took place in the 1980s and 1990s, this time through rap music, perhaps the most influential art form in the lives of African-American youth.

In the late 1980s and early 1990s, many of the most popular rappers made songs steeped in politics, African history and racial unity and pride. Public Enemy spoke out against drug abuse, negative images of Blacks in the media, and America's racist criminal justice system in their hit albums "Fear of a Black Planet" and "It Takes A Nation of Millions To Hold Us Back." KRS-One cut a record about Blacks in the Bible called "Why Is

That?" and many of his songs urged Black youth to learn their history. He also started a movement with nearly a dozen other rappers called "Stop the Violence." And popular groups and individuals such as Stetsasonic, X-Clan, The Jungle Brothers, Brand Nubian, Eric B. and Rakim, and Queen Latifah followed suit with Afrocentric lyrics in their music. That racially-charged rap music stimulated a massive interest in Malcolm X and Afrocentricity on the part of young African-Americans, and created an atmosphere that demanded the making of movies such as Malcolm X by Spike Lee and Panther, a film about Huey Newton and the Black Panthers, by Mario Van Peebles. But as was the case in the 1970s, this redemptive message was soon replaced by the largely negative gangsta rap that emerged and dominated the decade of the 1990s, the only difference being that instead of emulating "hustlers" like SuperFly, young Black men were led to model gangsta rappers who boasted of pimping women, murdering one another and abusing drugs.

Thought provoking conversations about subjects such as that enabled me to think like a free citizen rather than an inmate. Also, at a time when my interest in social and political issues was burgeoning, I was able to share my views with folks from nearly ever rung of society – Black and White, incarcerated and free, Christian and non-Christian, rich and poor, law abiding and criminal. Most of those I spoke with commented that my opinions were astute and on time, and their positive feedback led me to put my ideas down on paper.

I first began addressing contemporary issues in print through the recreation department, which published a booklet every holiday season. Gene Cross, the supervisor of that department, was a devout Christian whom I had often prayed with, so he let me write editorials for the booklet. My columns were such a hit with the inmates that some of them sent them home to their family members. That reception led me to branch out on a broader scale, and I decided to send a column to The Carolinian, a Black newspaper I subscribed to out of Raleigh, North Carolina. When the paper printed my editorial, I was thrilled. It saw it not only as tangible evidence of my ability to fit back into society but as proof that I could make a contribution and become an advocate for change.

Now galvanized, I got a listing of all the Black newspapers in America and began submitting editorials. I also wrote to the editors, asking them what they looked for in their editorial pieces. I explained to them that I was an inmate and was glad to see that my condition did not negatively impact their views on my articles. Often, after printing one of my columns, they would send me a copy of the paper.

From 1983 to the time of my parole in 1989, I had pieces published in about 15 Black newspapers nationwide, including The Goldsboro Times in North Carolina and The Call and Post in Cleveland, Ohio. Though my columns were laced with concerns of morality and justice, I did not write Christian articles. I simply applied Biblical values to the problems facing the nation. For example, I judged America's treatment of the poor against the Biblical standard and found it wanting. I addressed racism, poverty, welfare, education, politics, the criminal justice system, drug and alcohol abuse, broken homes, environmentalism, South African apartheid and other hot-button issues from a Biblical perspective, all without alluding to specific scriptural verses or the Christian faith. Of the approximately 60 articles I sent out, I would estimate that 85 percent of them were published.

I saw my ability to write cogent articles for newspapers as verification that I could hurdle the obstacles that incarceration placed before me. So my next step was to validate my calling through ordination. Most prisoners, even the most spiritually devout, would never think to receive their ordination while behind bars, and even if they did, they would be rebuffed quickly since many people, Christians included, do not put much stock in prison conversions. To my knowledge, no inmate in the history of the United States had ever been ordained as a religious minister while serving a sentence in a Federal prison. But by this time, my faith was large. I did not put anything past my Lord. Though I could not claim like King David that God had kept me out of the jaws of hungry lions, I could state that He had kept me from the paws of violent inmates. So though I realized the odds were against me, I began praying for my ordination. I truly believed that my inclination to be ordained was from God rather than any egotistical, self-driven desire of my own and soon I received evidence to support my case.

I shared my desire to be ordained with Warden Lyles, and he was nearly as excited about the idea as I was. He even volunteered to speak to Lewisburg's warden on my behalf. He knew the warden well because his brother, Richard, who was the chief executive officer in charge of hiring minority wardens for the U.S. Bureau of Prisons, had hired him. In what seemed like an instant, Howard contacted the warden, told him about our unique relationship and also vouched for my Christian manner and lifestyle.

While the warden was aware of my commitment to Christ, Howard's endorsement was priceless, and soon thereafter, I received the incredible news that in three months I would become the first person in American history to be ordained as a minister while incarcerated in the Federal prison system. The date set was December 1, 1984.

I cannot explain how ecstatic I was. Though I had long ago accepted God's forgiveness for my previous crimes, being ordained would confirm that man had forgiven me as well. It was proof that my past could not hinder my future, that in spite of all the detestable things I had done, I could indeed be given a clean slate. Besides having my articles published, it was the first legitimate accomplishment of my adult life; and what an accomplishment - the first person ever!

Though I had no idea if or when I might be released, I planned to return to North Carolina if it ever happened. Therefore, I figured I would find a minister from North Carolina to moderate the service. I valued ordination, but I did not envision an arduous preparation process or a large ceremony. I thought someone would ordain me by laying his hands on my head and praying over me. The picture in my mind was that of Samuel pouring oil on David's head. But God and Dr. Carter had other plans.

After I informed Dr. Carter over the telephone that I wanted to be ordained, he took me completely by surprise by saying he would like to lead me through the process as well as perform the ceremony. I was floating now, knowing that one of the nation's most accomplished ministers would put his stamp on my Christian experience. Even so, I could not comprehend the magnitude of the blessing God had in store for me.

While I had imagined the laying on of hands, some anointing oil and a prayer, Dr. Carter planned to take me through a real ordination process. His vision was much more prophetic than mine and he was thinking ahead to the questions people would have about me. He knew that my background, not to mention my state of incarceration, would lead people to question the legitimacy of my ordination, so he sought to remove all doubt by making my experience as near as possible to that of the ministers in his church. Instead of the small, "down-home" service I had in mind, he told me he was going to put me before the Baptist Minister's Council of Baltimore and Vicinity for an intense oral examination. In preparation for this, he sent books for me to study and told me what types of questions the ministers were likely to ask. It was like I was taking a correspondence course.

At the time, it did not occur to me how much Warden Lyles and Dr. Carter were risking by supporting me. After all, literally thousands of inmates have confessed to be born-again Christians only to return to lives of crime once they were released. Even many of those who appeared to be sincere while in prison have turned out to be, at worst, hypocrites and, at best, weak when faced with the world's temptations. It was not like these two men were naïve. They had been involved in prison ministry for years and were well aware of the fragile faith of many convicts. For them to recommend the unprecedented ordination of an inmate they had worshipped with only a few times, one who had served only five years of a 30-year sentence, was practically inconceivable. If I so much as frowned at a guard or cursed at an inmate it would reflect poorly on them and lead to questions about their discernment. Fortunately, they felt that I was up to the task, and by the grace of God, I was.

Things continued to progress smoothly until the night before the ceremony. We were having a Bible study led by a local Mennonite lay minister named Ken Martin when a Black inmate trudged through the corridor inside of the chapel. He raised one hand toward a window and those of us who were facing the window thought he was waving. He continued down the corridor toward the main sanctuary where an Islamic service was in progress and less than two minutes later, we saw two other inmates helping the brother walk out of the chapel. They were moving with urgency and we could see that he had been stabbed because blood was blanketing his clothes. The Mennonite volunteers were visibly shaken and officers immediately began pouring into the chapel area. Naturally, we were forced to leave and the chapel was locked down. This was during the period of Black-on-White murders that I mentioned earlier, so the attack was just one of the many that had recently taken place.

Initially, we thought it was a retaliation hit by some White inmates, but we were mistaken. It was a Black-on-Black crime connected to the drug trade. Since similar incidents had been occurring for nearly a year, I began to wonder if the prison would permit the ordination, especially after a Hispanic inmate was stabbed near the chapel the next morning. With two stabbings having transpired within hours, it seemed quite possible that, if allowed, the ceremony itself would be interrupted by a brutal assault.

To my surprise, the authorities did not say a word against having the service. They said everything would go as planned and summoned some orderlies to clean up the chapel. They actually had to scrub blood off the chapel doors. By the time the ministers and other visitors arrived for the ceremony, the place was spotless. It looked as peaceful as could be, though just hours earlier, hell had had its way.

The diabolic series of events only strengthened my spirit, as I was determined not to let anything keep me from reaching my goal. The ceremony turned out to be beautiful. There were between 70 and 80 people present, which by itself seemed to add more credibility to the service. Dr. Carter was joined by about nine preachers from the Baptist Minister's Council and about 30 Christians who regularly visited us at Lewisburg also attended. Nearly 40 inmates, eager to see one of their own receive a dose of positive recognition from the outside world, came as well.

Naturally, I was nervous and once the presbytery, led by Dr. Carter, began questioning me on Christian theology, I grew more tense. The questioning was ardent and at times took on the feel of an interrogation. Part of me felt like some of the ministers were attacking me, trying to stump me on some Biblical concept to prove my unworthiness. But I kept my composure and represented myself well. I had spent countless hours researching the information Dr. Carter had given me, so my knowledge was substantial. While I think my aptitude surprised some of the ministers, I could see that Dr. Carter was proud of me. When he presented me with my certificate, along with a Bible that was signed by every minister in attendance, he had the look of a father who had just watched his son follow in his footsteps. The inmates were also beaming, and I had each one of them sign the Bible too. I still have that Bible, and I cherish the signatures of the inmates as much as those of the ministers. I am truly appreciative to my former prison mates for supporting me and helping me along in my quest. Without the hours of group prayer, study and discussion, I would not have advanced as quickly in my Christian walk, and without their willingness to submit to my leadership, there would have been no Solid Rock Foundation. In a very real sense, my accomplishment was not only a testament to my spiritual maturity but to theirs as well.

Dr. Carter, who had already gone far above and beyond the call of duty on my behalf, had one final surprise for me: a church. After ordaining me, he explained that he had not merely licensed me to preach but also to pastor. So with everyone looking on in amazement, he asked all the members of Solid Rock to stand, set us apart as a church and had me appoint deacons

167

right there on the spot. Now, in addition to being the first ordained inmate, I was pastoring the nation's first all-inmate church.

Dr. Carter allowed me to make history on two counts, which is why I value him so much and always refer to him as my father in the ministry. A man of his stature had nothing to gain from ordaining, or even befriending, a convict. Yet, in an entirely selfless act, he put his reputation on the line for me. There is no greater gift he could have given me.

The immense responsibility I had taken on did not fully hit me until everyone had gone and Milton and I were left alone in the chapel. We had just finished praying and all was quiet when Milton looked me in the eye and said, "You can't turn back now." While the thought of leaving Christ had not entered my mind in years, I had also never thought about my future in the way Milton had put it. He was saying that my ordination meant I had to be a Christian for the rest of my life. It was a new level of commitment, like going from engagement to marriage. A step of great magnitude, it was one I took as a challenge and not a threat.

Since leaving prison, I have been ordained by three churches or denominations, but out of respect for Dr. Carter, none of them have put me through a major ordination process. I received these ordinations not to replace my first one, but because most denominational bodies require ministers who are active in their churches to have distinct credentials. Shortly after being paroled, I was ordained by the Freewill Baptist Conference, which oversees the church I grew up in in Maury, North Carolina. Some of the ministers wanted me to go through the long, drawn out process all over again. But upon seeing my ordination papers, one of the bishops recognized Harold Carter's name and said, "If he's good enough for Harold Carter to ordain, I don't see any reason to examine him again." That settled it. I have also been ordained by The Praise, Prayer and Worship Revival Center, which is an independent church in North Carolina, and The Full Gospel Evangelistic Center in Cleveland, Ohio. In addition, I have an annual license from the Church of God.

After Dr. Carter transformed the Solid Rock Christian Foundation into the Solid Rock Baptist Church, my already strong influence among Christian and non-Christian inmates increased. Even the prison staff began to show me more respect. Before, many guards and administrators had treated me nicely because of my conduct, but I now sensed a small bit of admiration on their part. Of course, there were also numerous staff members who, thinking I had been given too much standing, resented my ordination. Both attitudes served to raise my esteem in the eyes of the inmates. While it was good to be held in regard among the authorities, anyone who was too close to the staff would be viewed with contempt by the prisoners. But the indignation that some staff members felt toward me created the feeling that I had earned my position, rather than been handpicked for recognition because I was non-threatening. The inmates felt that the staff had given me its respect grudgingly and naturally, they liked that.

Now that I was ordained, I became even more entrenched as the prison's unofficial Protestant chaplain. There was no official recognition, no papers drawn up or signed, but I served as the chaplain in every capacity. My office, which I had been in since becoming the chaplain's administrative assistant, took on more of a symbolic meaning. I did everything from schedule services for the various religious groups, to conduct memorial services for inmates who had died, to mediate differences between the prison population and the authorities.

One example of my authority recognized within the prison took place when I was paged over the public address system, supposedly to go to the hospital. I was in the recreation area lifting weights and reacted casually when I heard the page. When I exited through the gate, I was first taken to the infirmary. Then, I was escorted through a long and winding hallway and down dozens of steps into a small room, where I met face to face with Willie Johnson, Assistant Warden of Programs.

Justifiably, the inmates had been complaining about the food - the green eggs, the stale bread, the rotten fruit - and the buzz throughout the prison was that there was going to be a work stoppage. The atmosphere in the prison was tense and the angry mood could have easily set off a full-scale riot. So as soon as I sat down, Mr. Johnson asked me point-blank what could be done to avert the coming commotion. I responded candidly that they needed to do something about the food, that while I didn't condone a riot, I understood and agreed with the prisoners' protest. I further stated that some degree of restraint had to be exercised by the correctional staff and that more respect for the inmates had to be displayed. The guards were treacherous to the convicts, and I told him it would not be long before the combination of bad food and bad blood led to a tumult. Finally, I let him know that I was not ignorant to the negligence of the guards. I had noticed that the officers were never at their security points when a race-based killing took place, and that whenever someone was stabbed, the guards would always show up just moments too late. That could not be by coincidence.

Mr. Johnson took what I said to heart and after that, the guards behaved a little better. The meeting was kept a secret and soon thereafter, the inmates who worked in the prison industry went on strike. The prison began shipping the insubordinate workers to different prisons and bringing other inmates to Lewisburg. Their plan worked, and the strike ended after a week. The prison did improve the food, albeit only slightly. At any rate, God was glorified in this process because the serial killings soon ceased. Whatever faction had been responsible for the savage racial murders must have been caught up in the aggressive reshuffling of inmates and removed from Lewisburg.

At that time, I was at the height of my ascendancy, but soon circumstances conspired to knock me off my pedestal. My downfall began when some Christian convicts grew envious of the authority I had over the Protestant fellowship. The same spirit that led numerous Muslims to start their own sects infected Solid Rock and several brothers began to oppose my leadership. They argued that they were not Baptist so Solid Rock's affiliation kept them from practicing their denominational beliefs. They also said my position gave me an unfair advantage within the prison population because I had a platform from which to speak that other inmates did not. There were no gripes over my authority from the majority prison population. This was solely the work of Christians. None of the men who had witnessed my ordination protested, but later some of them joined the dissenters. Eventually, some inmates complained to their caseworkers about this "inmate-chaplain" and, in turn, their caseworkers wrote letters to the warden, demanding that I be removed from office.

That is one reason why when Chaplain Hammidulah, the Islamic Imam, resigned a few months later, a Black Protestant chaplain was hired as his replacement. It was clear right away that the new chaplain, whom the inmates quickly named "Too Thin Slim," was more concerned with putting me in my place than with preaching the gospel. He was intent on reestablishing the authority of the civilian official over that of any inmate, perhaps at the urging of the administration, and as a result sought total control over the Protestant fellowship. For months, he slowly chipped away at my authority until his aggravation with me came to a head.

I was still working as the chaplain's administrative assistant, and since I had now been in Lewisburg for six years, I had accumulated favors from various inmates and guards. So I asked a couple of those inmates to build some shelves for me and to rearrange my office. Well, the new chaplain had been trying for weeks to get his office refurbished, so he got upset when he saw them fixing my place. The next thing I knew, I had been transferred from the chapel to the mechanical services department. In May of 1986, a mere 18 months after I had been ordained, my official affiliation with the chapel came to an end, all but assuring the demise of the Solid Rock Baptist Church.

At first, about seven or eight of us continued to meet in the yard for Bible study and prayer, but the correctional officers always came along and broke it up. So rather than go through that hassle, we decided to disband totally. Unfortunately, because of envy and protocol, what had been a vibrant, rewarding and historical alliance was reduced to nothing.

Obviously, I was disappointed, but my spirit was not broken. My work had not been limited to the church so I could not be defeated so easily. In addition to my editorial writing in Black newspapers, I had composed dozens of manuscripts, study guides and booklets on various topics relating to Christianity, African-Americans, and America as a whole. Some of these had been used in Bible studies, but I did not intend to unveil most of them until I was released. That changed, however, when Elder Shumpert Watts, a New York City pastor whose church often visited Lewisburg, suggested I put my thoughts together in book form.

A native of Mississippi, Elder Watts was a proponent of getting pertinent, liberating information into the hands of Black people. Inspired by his idea, I began writing at once and later that year, *Words of Liberation From Prison* by Mark C. Olds was published. Elder Watts believed so strongly in my ministry that he provided the financial support for the project. More of a pamphlet than a book, *Words of Liberation From Prison* was a small work of 32 pages that addressed contemporary American issues. Though incarcerated, the love of Christ had made me feel more spiritually, mentally and emotionally free than many of the citizens who lived outside of prison walls. Having been imprisoned in my mind long before my arrival at the penitentiary, I knew it was possible to be more liberated in prison than out of it. So even though I was locked up, I felt I had something to offer those who were physically free, but emotionally and spiritually bound. Hence, the eye-catching title.

Although the topic of the book was similar to what I had written about in my editorials, the tone was much different. Unencumbered by a secular media outlet, I wrote in an almost entirely spiritual manner. Dozens of Biblical verses and words of praise to God were interspersed throughout the book. While I still agree with the content and message of Words of Liberation, I now realize that many people may not have been able to follow it because of its intensely spiritual nature.

To a certain degree, I was stepping out into uncharted waters with my unique version of liberation theology. Of course, theologians (particularly ones of color), had espoused liberation theology for at least two decades but not many had made a direct correlation between social and spiritual liberation. In other words, most theologians who advocated a social gospel of liberation did not emphasize or even recognize the necessity of personal salvation or the born-again experience. Conversely, most evangelicals who preached "you must be born-again" did not make a connection between personal salvation and social transformation. They would preach about how individuals need to be saved, but neglect issues such as apartheid, racism and inadequate housing.

In my understanding of God's justice, which was inspired mainly by the Old Testament, when people were liberated spiritually, God always responded by liberating them socially, economically and politically. For instance, after Moses experienced a spiritual awakening when learning about God from the Ethiopian priest Jethro, God sent Moses to Egypt to bring political deliverance to the Israelites. This relationship between spiritual and social freedom also is seen in the Israelites experiences in Babylon and Persia.

Furthermore, when one is born-again he is essentially set free from sin. The chains of sin are broken off of him, and he no longer has to obey his sinful desires. This clearly was the case with me, as my being born-again delivered me from the bondage of gambling, drug dealing, sexual immorality, greed and a myriad of other vices. That being the case, it seemed clear to me that the way to get people to behave properly was to get them to be born-again. Evangelicals stress this viewpoint in terms of sexual immorality and substance abuse but rarely do they apply it to racism, criminal justice, economic inequality, inadequate public schooling and similar social issues.

In addition to my personal Bible study, I developed this type of thinking by reading numerous extra-Biblical and Black history books. For instance, I read all of Dr. Martin Luther King's works. Listening to ministers such as

Dr. Carter, Dr. Jeremiah Wright and Reverend John Bryant on Christian radio shaped my beliefs as well. Those men impressed me greatly because they mixed the spiritual and social aspects of the gospel better than anyone else I had heard. Another person who influenced me in this area was a White Christian brother named David Hayden.

I met David one Saturday afternoon in 1985 during visiting hours. He had brought a woman named, Alice Ferguson, to see her husband, Joe, a White brother who was one of the original members of Solid Rock. While Joe and Alice talked privately, David and I struck up a conversation and soon found that we had similar interests. At the time, David was a seminary student who had left a successful job at a pharmaceutical company to go into the ministry. He had been a member of the Assemblies of God, a Pentecostal denomination, but left it for a Mennonite church because he thought the Mennonites did more to meet the practical, everyday needs of individuals. Deeply concerned about the plight of the homeless, he started a movement in Roanoke, Virginia called Justice House. With so much in common, we quickly became great friends who would dialogue all day about ways to apply the gospel to America's social ills. Since he was a seminary student, he read a glut of books and introduced me to a whole new world of texts. He directed me to numerous books that dealt with social oppression from a Christian perspective, including those by James Cone, the eminent Union Theological Seminary professor who is regarded as the father of Black Liberation Theology.

Since I was learning so much from my reading and praying, I had no time to be bitter about what happened to Solid Rock. In fact, I began to see it as God's will because as the lessons from that experience passed, new lessons were unfolding. For long stretches of time, all I did was read and discuss and soon God exposed me to a side of Christianity I had not seen before.

Among Christians in the prison which I later found this to be true on the outside as well, there was always an ongoing debate about speaking in tongues and the other gifts of the Spirit. Though I had been saved for nearly eight years, was an ordained minister of the gospel, and was viewed throughout the prison as a knowledgeable Christian, I did not know what speaking in tongues was and had never been exposed to any supernatural gifts, such as healing. Asking Christians, whether preachers or inmates, about these things did not help. Some told me the gifts were not for today, that they were limited strictly to the apostles. Then they gave me books to read that supposedly used the Bible to prove that point. Others told me that speaking in tongues was the evidence that a person had been baptized in the Holy Spirit and that this experience would open them up to the possibility of expressing the other gifts. Of course, they also provided books to back up their claim. This only served to confuse me even more.

While I had questions concerning all of these things, it was not until a charismatic minister visited the prison that the gifts of the Spirit question began to consume my mind. What we thought was going to be a normal service became a supernatural experience when this brother began prophesying over inmates, naming their ailments and exposing those whose hearts were hurting because they had not received any mail. Grown men began crying when he described past experiences that had caused them pain.

We were dumbfounded. We did not know whether this brother was a magician or what. We had never seen anything like it before. We could not deny what he was saying because all of it was true, so those of us with a desire to know more about the Lord had to begin looking at things from a different perspective. After that, I began studying diligently what the Bible said about the gifts of the Spirit: speaking in tongues, prophecy, word of wisdom, words of knowledge, healings and miracles. Though I had still never heard anyone speak in tongues, I determined that the gift was indeed for today because the Bible never said it was limited to the first century. Shortly thereafter, I received proof.

I called a female pastor from Atlanta named Yvonne Cuffee, who led two congregations known as Powerful Truth Sanctuary in Atlanta and Macon, Georgia. A friend of mine from Columbus, Georgia had given me her name a number of years ago while I was awaiting trial for bank robbery in Georgia. Though we had never seen each other, we spoke often by telephone. On this particular day, I had not called her to talk about speaking in tongues, but the subject came up when she asked me if I had been baptized in the Holy Ghost. When I said yes, she asked if I had spoken in tongues. I responded no and she said that I needed to speak in tongues to truly be baptized in the Holy Spirit. Then she began praying for me over the phone, asking God to baptize me in the Holy Spirit. When she was done praying, she told me to go back upstairs to my cell and speak in tongues. She was very frank about it, leaving no room for doubt.

Though puzzled, I did exactly as directed: I hung up the phone, returned to my room, lay on my bed and spoke in tongues. There was no build up, no

174

30 minutes of prayer, no saying "Jesus, Jesus, Jesus" as fast as I could, just an immediate response to her prayer. I had never heard speaking in tongues before, so I didn't know what it sounded like, but I knew that the language coming out of my mouth was "tongues" and that it was from God. Excited, I ran downstairs as fast as I could and called Pastor Cuffee. As soon as she answered, I said, "I spoke in tongues! I spoke in tongues!" Not sharing in my astonishment, she replied, "Look, I have to go. I knew you were going to speak in tongues. That's why I told you to go upstairs and do it." Then she hung up. It was amazing.

This opened me up to a whole new realm of my faith. I began watching Christian Television, tuning in to the "700 Club" with Pat Robertson, the "Praise The Lord Club" with Jim Bakker, and Jimmy Swaggert's show. Milton and I experienced greater freedom in our music ministry. Since he was a musician and I could write lyrics, we began writing praise and worship songs. We had done this in the past, but now the rhythm and tempo of our songs was more upbeat and contemporary.

One thing bothered me, however, about the Charismatic Christian movement. While the emphasis they placed on Jesus Christ's ministry of deliverance appealed to me, I found most members of this group to be utterly conservative in their political views. This clashed with my justice-oriented political and prophetic bent, so I figured that God had a unique ministry in mind for me.

It was an enlightening time and I felt like I was ready to explode. I had all of this fire in my belly and knowledge in my head - Blacks in the Bible, Black history, the social gospel, the gifts of the Spirit - but was unable to share any of it in front of a group. I loved preaching, so having all of this information without being able to teach it in public was driving me crazy. The way I saw it, there was only one thing left to do - get out of Lewisburg.

Of course, escape was no longer an option so in pursuit of legitimate release, I began writing letters to the Commissioner of the North Carolina Department of Corrections. My goals were to get the escape warrant and the six- to eight-year sentence I owed the state of North Carolina dropped. That way, with a single 30-year sentence, I could go before the Parole Board after serving 10 years and potentially be a free man shortly after my 40th birthday. That would give me plenty of time to fulfill the proclamation I boldly made to the inmates shortly after receiving salvation: that God had called me to evangelize within America.

Naturally, I tried to impress the Commissioner and show him that I had indeed been rehabilitated. While I knew my conversion to Christ was real and responsible for all I had become, simply stating that I was now a born-again Christian would have done very little to move the man. With that in mind, I wrote down everything that I had achieved while in Lewisburg. With such a distinct resume, I smiled as I dropped that first letter in the mail. I say first because there were many more. As the weeks and months went by without any positive response, I cranked out letter after letter, making each one a little more glowing than the first. Finally, I called Warden Lyles and asked him to pray about my attempts to gain freedom. I told him about all the letters I had written, and he responded with the best explanation I could have hoped for: I had written the letters to the wrong person. He told me that I needed to write to the North Carolina Parole Commission. Less than an hour later, another letter was in the mail.

Soon, I was informed that the North Carolina Parole Commission had paroled me to the Federal authorities, in effect, dropping my six-to eight-year sentence. Next, the state's attorney for the Wake County Jail in Raleigh, North Carolina wrote, saying I would not be prosecuted for the escape charge. They said I had served enough time. I said "Praise the Lord!"

A year later, in an amazing development, I was paroled without going before a parole board. I was walking down the hall in Lewisburg when I bumped into my case manager, Mr. Wagner. He said he had been looking for me and that I had been paroled. Totally shocked, I said to him, "Man, don't play with me. I'm going to call my momma, and she's too old for me to be playing with." He laughed and assured me that it was legitimate.

The God who had turned me from a peddler of dope to a preacher of righteousness, who had kept me safe in one of the most dangerous places in America, who had made me a living, breathing miracle, released me from prison in the most marvelous manner. In truth, it was the only way for me to go. After all, with all of the extraordinary things He had allowed me to do in Lewisburg, I had to leave in a way that was unorthodox and distinctive.

Chapter *IX*

OUT AND ABOUT

Throughout my incarceration experience at Lewisburg, I watched several devout Christians leave prison with grand plans of serving the Lord, only to return to a life of crime and eventually, the penitentiary. Each time a brother who loved the Lord came back in defeat, I asked him what went wrong, not in a condemning manner, but out of legitimate concern and curiosity. I must have asked about 15 convicts that question, and almost to a man, they told me that the two leading factors in their downfall were that first, they did not have a plan, and second, they expected more aid than was practical from church folks and family members. So in order to survive, they reverted to their old comfortable life on the streets. These were guys who were sincerely committed to God, and had been Christian warriors in prison.

Long before I was paroled, I put together a plan for whenever I was released. I divided my plan into three years, and during the first year, I intended to return to North Carolina and validate myself as a minister. I wanted people to scrutinize my walk with the Lord and see that I had indeed been converted and changed. I hoped that during that time I would also be able to use the pastoral contacts I had established to get myself rooted in an itinerant ministry. My aim in my second year would be to establish a political base, and in my third, I wanted to start an alternative political party, one whose major focus was on improving the quality of life for poor people of all races.

The most significant part of my first-year plan was to return to Maury to live with my mother. Though that would certainly ease my economic burden, money had nothing to do with it. I had been away from my mother for 10 years, and my father had died during that period, so I just wanted to spend some time with my mama. Like most mothers, mine was my strongest supporter while I was at Lewisburg. But her connection to me went beyond the already deep personal bond that is natural for a mother and her child. Because of my salvation, we had bonded on a spiritual level, and that was something my mother had never had with any of the men in our family. The fact that I was her youngest child and had strayed further than probably anyone in the history of our family made it that much sweeter when I became her first son to accept Christ. The joy she experienced over my salvation overrode the pain she felt over my confinement. Of course, it was still her constant prayer that I would one day be released and when I was, we grew closer than ever.

One of my mother's greatest pleasures was to hear me preach. As I began to make my way around the churches of rural North Carolina, preaching every chance I got, I brought my mother along as often as possible. I always introduced her to the congregation and I could see in her face how much it meant to her to have a son who was a minister. What I found rewarding was answering my mother's questions about the faith. She would sometimes ask me to interpret a specific scripture for her or she would tell me she had heard a certain doctrine on the radio, on the television or from a friend and she wanted to know my opinion. Knowing that my mother viewed me as a spiritual authority made me beam with pride. It felt so good to give her the type of relationship she had long desired. She loved that one of her sons finally understood this Jesus she had talked about for all these years.

Our special, lengthy and frequent conversations did not end when I moved away to Cleveland in 1991. I visited a lot and called every Sunday morning at 7:30. We spoke during the week as well, but Sunday morning was our designated time together. We would talk for about 30 minutes, almost always about Christ. In 1993, my mother died of natural causes at the age of 81. For the next several months, I found myself reaching for the phone every Sunday morning.

My mother was the main reason I believed so strongly that I would eventually be paroled. In 1980, just a few months after I had given my life to Christ, she said she had seen a vision of me dressed in all white and speaking before a massive throng of people. My faith in my mother's relationship

178

with God was unwavering, so when she told me of her vision, I did not doubt it for a second. I believed that if God had shown her something, it would come to pass and recognized that my part in fulfilling the vision was to get as close to God as possible. I have spoken in front of thousands of people before but I have never felt as if I was completing her vision. Someday I will. I don't know how or when, but I will. The first part, however, was fulfilled on August 1, 1989 when I left Lewisburg as a free man.

Before returning home to my mother, though, I had to spend 64 days in a halfway house in Fayetteville, North Carolina. My unit manager at Lewisburg, Robert Wagner, was a fair and decent man who had been impressed by my transformation. So he was almost as excited about my release as I was; so excited, in fact, that he forgot to give me the address of the halfway house. He just gave me $100 and a bus ticket to Fayetteville and told me I had to report by midnight. Almost scatterbrained because of my enthusiasm, I didn't even think to ask for the address.

After the prison van dropped me off at the bus station, I left Lewisburg at 8 a.m. It was a 14-hour ride to Fayetteville, but it seemed more like 14 days. It was too much time to think. I spent the entire trip bouncing from one thought to another. My mind was jumbled. Sometimes, I reflected on how 9 years and 10 months earlier, I had taken the bus the opposite way: from Fayetteville to Lewisburg. And now I was returning to the place where I had been sentenced to spend the rest of my life in prison. Other times, I thought about the uncertainty that lay before me, of how I was returning home for the first time since my father and my sister had died. I also would get anxious about what I was going to do and what new obstacles awaited me. Then, I would override those anxieties with thoughts of all the great things God was going to do, thoughts of carrying out my plan and fulfilling my dream. Suddenly that pleasant time would be ambushed by the realization that I had nothing to work with besides my $100 and the clothes on my back. All of those mixed emotions made the ride an excruciating one. I was so uptight that I didn't sleep a wink or say a word. I just thought and prayed.

Finally, we arrived in Fayetteville around 10:30 p.m. But just when I thought the worst part of my day was over, I realized that I didn't know where I was going. Hoping there was only one post-penal residence in town, I hopped into a cab driven by a Hispanic man and told him to take me to the halfway house. When he responded, "Which one?" I knew I was in trouble. And when he asked, "What street is it on?" I thought I was going back to prison. It was already closing in on 11 o'clock, and if I didn't check in by midnight, I would be charged with escape. I told him I had an hour to get there, so he said, "Don't worry. We'll find it." That calmed my nerves because I figured that, as a cabbie, he knew every place in town. But we stopped at about four places that once served as halfway houses and each one had been closed down.

As our fruitless journey continued and time flew by, I sat in the back, partly in prayer and partly in panic. Neither of us had a clue as to where that halfway house was. As I was planning to call the U.S. Marshals to let them know that I was lost and not attempting to escape, the cab driver pulled into the Lemon Tree Inn, hoping they would be able to point us in the right direction. And by the grace of God, one wing of the motel served as the Federal halfway house we were looking for. It was 11:55 when I checked in. When I went to pay the driver the $40 that was on the meter, he pushed my hand away and said, "Nah, I've got a brother who gets into trouble sometimes. And besides, you're going to need all the money you have to get started again." I chalked the man up as an angel.

After being processed that night, I woke up bright and early the next morning and sought out a church. In prison, my favorite verse of the Bible had been Psalm 142:7 - "Bring my soul out of prison and I will praise thy name" - so I wanted to find a church and let everyone in it know that God had miraculously delivered my soul from prison. I began searching in downtown Fayetteville and to my surprise it was all but deserted. It was a Monday, so I expected the area to be booming with business, but practically all of the stores and shops had moved into malls. In the 1970s, when I was running the streets, there were very few malls and the downtown area was always bustling. But a decade had passed and things had changed. I went to a number of churches before finding one that was open. It was a tiny storefront church called Townsend Temple and it was advertising an appreciation ceremony for Apostle Moses Townsend, its pastor.

I entered and found a middle-aged Black man and his female administrative assistant and immediately began sharing my life's story. Speaking at the speed of light, I told them I had been locked up in one of the most heinous prisons in the country, and that God had supernaturally set me free after only 10 years of my 30-year sentence had been served. I quoted Psalm 142:7, saying it had inspired me to find a church so I could give God some praise. I was so elated and speaking so quickly and fervently that I must have sounded like a tape playing on fast speed. Excited as well, they invited me to come back for a church service, and there began a relation-

180

ship with Apostle Townsend that continues to this day. He still has his congregation in Fayetteville, although it has since moved into a church building, and he now oversees a group of churches in various parts of the country.

Under the conditions of my contract with the halfway house, I had three weeks to find a job. If I did not secure employment within that time frame, I would be sent back to the penitentiary to complete my 64 days of transition. After I looked to no avail for two weeks, Apostle Townsend took me to a Kroger supermarket and introduced me to the manager, a young Black man who greeted me with a warm smile and a firm handshake. Moses had told him beforehand that I was a member of his church and in need of employment. The manager, who was a Christian, had given Moses every indication that he would hire me. He told Moses I just needed to go through a few formalities, such as meeting him face-to-face and filling out an application. Anticipating a job, I hastily filled out the application until reaching that nightmarish question that every ex-convict hates to see: "Have you ever been convicted of a felony? If yes, explain." Being a Christian, I was compelled to tell the truth, although I felt a great temptation to lie. So I penciled in "Yes" and then the words "armed bank robbery" next to it. I handed the application back to the manager and his eyes seemed to go straight to that question. His eyebrows jumped when he saw my answer and I could tell by his reaction that I would not get that job.

I started calling some of my Christian friends who had visited the inmates in Lewisburg and asked them to pray that I find employment. One couple I called, Harold and Marion Spellman of Pennsylvania, put in a good word for me with a pastor they knew in Fayetteville. Then, early into my third week at the halfway house, he telephoned me, introducing himself as Pastor Ken and saying he had landed me a job as a mechanic's helper at an auto body shop. He also said he would pick me up on Wednesday night to attend Bible study at his church, the East Russell Street Church of God.

The owner of the garage gave me the job based on the word of Pastor Ken, who had never met me himself but acted solely off of the Spellman's recommendation. On top of that, the owner, who had been told about my past, arranged for someone to pick me up and drop me off each day. I knew I was indebted to the shop's owner, a tall and brawny Black man in his 50s, but he had only one request besides an honest day's work: that once I was established and doing well that I would help someone else. With plans to have a career in ministry, I certainly was agreeable to that.

While I was thankful for the job, I foresaw one major problem: I did not know the first thing about fixing an automobile. But in the midst of my apprehension, I called to mind Philippians 4:13 - "I can do all things through Christ, which strengthens me" - and walked proudly into the shop, intent on learning all that was necessary to become the best mechanic's helper I could.

My first assignment was to remove the battery from a Volvo, a simple chore for most people in my position but the equivalent of performing brain surgery for me. I was stunned and almost light-headed before I even popped the hood because as soon as I opened the door, the car started talking: "The door is open. The door is open." Needless to say, there were no talking cars when I was shipped off to Lewisburg in 1979. I felt like I was on another planet. Once I settled down and regained my wits, I began the surprisingly perplexing task of figuring out how to open the hood. I combed the inside of the car, looking for the latch that would pop the hood. I checked the glove compartment, the dashboard, the steering wheel. Twenty minutes went by before I finally located it and with great relief, pulled. I was already dripping in sweat and I hadn't even attempted to find the battery yet. When I got out of the car and lifted the hood, my anxiety heightened, as I was baffled by a fabulous European design that I admired, but was completely clueless about. The only thing I could identify with confidence was the engine. I couldn't even find the compartment that held the windshield wiper fluid. After an hour had passed and I was still in search of the battery, the mechanic finally ambled over and showed me that the battery was located beneath the back seat. Embarrassed, I forced a smile and said, "They didn't have cars like this in the '70s."

Because I lacked the mechanical aptitude to contribute to the operation of the garage, I decided to put the administrative and organizational skills I had acquired as the chaplain's assistant to use. Creating a position that was part administrative and part custodial, I cleaned the garage and organized the owner's inventory. I turned out to be quite the janitor, keeping the place spotless while always seeming to have a broom in one hand and a rag in the other. After guys would use the tools, I would clean them with solution and shine them so well that you could see your reflection in them. I had the bathroom looking nice and the waiting room smelling fresh. As an administrator, I put together the shop's first inventory system and updated it daily. My system increased the shop's profits substantially because the garage had previously been spending money to buy parts it already had in stock. For instance, a mechanic would often think we were out of something such as oil filters because the garage was so cluttered that he could not find one. So he would send someone to a parts store to buy one, only to discover later that we had three oil filters all along. My simple system of documenting the shop's parts put an end to such unnecessary spending and quickly made me one of the owner's favorite employees. His shop running smoother than ever, he spoke of me as if I was some sort of organizational genius.

After about a week on the job, the one no-frills outfit I left prison with was soiled considerably, even though I wore coveralls in the garage. So my first paycheck went toward paying my tithes to Townsend Temple and updating my wardrobe. The days of wearing suede and lizards were on hold, though. As a minimum-wage earner, the only place I could afford to shop was at a thrift shore, a fact that really bothered me. It was one thing to be out of style in prison, where everyone wore uniforms, but to be so tacky on the outside was almost too much for me to handle. I had always prided myself on being a fashion plate. Even though I was now a Christian, my taste for fine clothing had not changed. So walking down the aisles, picking up outdated, used clothing, greatly tested my resolve. In fact, I believe that day was the first time I had a real conversation with the devil.

On the verge of tears as I walked from rack to rack, I heard the devil say, "Mark, you know you don't have to buy used clothes. You know how to get money so you can dress like you want to." I stayed strong as he peppered my mind with temptations, but it wasn't easy, and by the time I brought my second-hand items to the checkout counter, I was in tears. I don't even remember the reaction of the clerk - or if the clerk was male or female, for that matter - because I was too busy wiping my eyes. When I stepped outside, used clothes in tow, I heard the spirit of the Lord say to me, "You will never have to do that again." That's when I realized that it was a test, one that had served to quell the pride that was still prevalent inside of me. When I realized what had just occurred, the three shirts and three pairs of pants I was holding didn't seem so bad anymore. I actually still have one of the outfits I bought that day hanging in my closet. It's a beige terry clothed, v-necked, pull-over sweater with yellow trimming and a pair of brown pants. Every once in a while I pull it out to remind myself of how far the Lord has brought me.

Now that I have an abundance of nice shirts and suits, that old outfit serves as a testimony of faith and perseverance. I tell my wife that she can throw away any of my other clothes, but never to touch that sweater and pair of slacks. That outfit keeps me humble and gracious in my interactions with those who have little and keeps me aware of the often quoted, and always true statement, "but for the grace of God, there go I."

Shortly after I began working, I made my pulpit debut in Apostle Townsend's storefront church. Of course, this was the moment I had been waiting for since my ordination in Lewisburg. I had spent many nights on the bunk in my cell, staring at the ceiling into the small hours of the morning, envisioning myself behind the sacred desk. Borrowing techniques from some of my favorite ministers, I contemplated my mannerisms, speaking cadence, attire, everything. No detail was too trivial for me to cover. I planned to go from prison hero to pulpit prince within months of passing through the exit gates of Lewisburg. Reality, however, was much different than my dream. Apostle Townsend's modest 25-member church was not the gleaming tabernacle I had pictured myself delivering the word in. Neither was my attire up to the standard I had imagined. Instead of a sharp, double-breasted suit, I was wearing jeans and sneakers. But none of that seemed to matter. I was simply thankful and overjoyed for the opportunity to preach.

As a young preacher, I spoke strictly from a manuscript, reading my compositions word for word. I had written about 15 or 20 sermons while in Lewisburg and those were the messages I preached over my first year or so out of prison. Whatever was printed on the sheet is what the congregation got, without deviation or discernment. Chock-full of information, my messages were lengthy and always lasting at least an hour. Some of my sermons were 30 pages long and I would not stop preaching until I finished the last line. I was schooled enough to make eye contact with the audience and deliver the message well, but I was not comfortable enough to move around the pulpit. Instead, I was frozen behind the lectern, as if my heels had been nailed to the floorboards. I also was not mature enough to tailor or adjust my message to the needs of the people. If they were not attentive to what I was saying, I did not have the sensitivity to alter the sermon so they could understand it. And I certainly was not at ease enough to add humor. My messages were always straightforward and serious, more like lectures than sermons. I spoke with a power and authority that demanded intense listening, but I did not whip anyone into an emotional frenzy because I was so staid myself.

As an ex-convict, I think I was so concerned with proving I was not doltish that I often spoke over people's heads. My written vocabulary is much larger than my speaking one, so in reading from a manuscript, I was using big, $20 words that most members of the congregation had probably never heard before. My command of the English language had people marveling at my messages, especially those that knew I had been in prison. But few of my listeners understood what I was saying. Once, after I had delivered an extensive and eloquent sermon, a preacher approached me with a smile and said, "They don't know what you said, but you sure said it pretty." Many of the people were astonished that someone straight out of the penitentiary could speak so intelligently, display such a deep knowledge of the scriptures, and meld it all together in the context of the current events of the nation or region. My messages were always based on the Old Testament prophets and always dealt with a pertinent social issue. Then, I would draw to a close by showing how personal salvation was the first step toward social renewal. I guess that part stemmed from the influence Dr. Carter had on me.

I purposely incorporated little, if any, of my testimony into my messages. In observing the Christian inmates at Lewisburg who had fallen back into a life of crime upon release, I saw that incessant testifying could be detrimental. Wanting no part of anything that might impede my progress, I went to the extreme. I based my decision on a brother who had been an exceptional Christian in the penitentiary. All of the Christian inmates admired him and when he got out of prison, all of the Christians who had visited Lewisburg wanted him to visit their churches to share his powerful testimony. Happy to oblige them, he moved from church to church, telling people how God had delivered him from a lifestyle of recklessness and violence.

But he was so busy giving his testimony that he never got rooted in the Bible while outside of prison. Every time he went to a church, he was the focal point. He never went and learned at a Bible study or sat underneath a pastor who would teach him how to apply the Word of God to his daily struggles. Consequently, he regressed to the point where he was back on the streets and before long, back in the penitentiary. So I determined that I would never deliver my testimony. Whenever people asked me to speak about my background, I told them that I was a preacher first and foremost. If I incorporated my past into my message, fine, but my chief intention was to preach the Word of God. But I was so adamant in my stance that I never worked my testimony into a sermon. The only way my listeners knew I had been to prison was through the pastor's introduction of me. It was a couple of years before I realized that sharing my testimony was actually a blessing to people.

One Christian, however, who did not need to be told about my past was the Kroger's manager who had refused to hire me because of my record. But he and I were reacquainted at Pastor Ken's East Russell Street Church of God in what proved to be a valuable lesson for the young brother. I was nearing the end of my stay at the halfway house and preaching at Pastor Ken's church for the first time when I noticed a guy sitting in a rear pew, shaking his head and looking at the floor. When he finally raised his head, I noticed that he was crying. The more I preached, he began to sob as his tears fell even more. I did not recognize him and I was thinking, "What's wrong with that guy? I know I ain't preaching that good."

When the service ended, he approached me and grabbed my hand to shake it. Then he hugged me and told me he had promised God that if he received the job at Kroger he would help young Black men. Yet when I came to him for help, he refused to lend a hand. Clearly torn up by the situation, he said seeing me in the pulpit let him know that God meant for him to give me that job. I was touched and when he offered me the job moments later, I almost took it just for his sake. But in the end, I turned it down because I had only a week left at the halfway house and my career as an itinerant minister beckoned.

My enthusiasm for preaching was matched by my enthusiasm for leaving the halfway house. When I exited the motel doors, the sunlight caressing my forehead, I felt totally free for the first time in 10 years. No more chow time. No more lights out. No more reporting every act of my life, no matter how mundane, to another human being. While I still had to meet with my parole officer once a month, my times of being monitored for the better part of the day were finally over.

My old friend, Jack Best, met me outside of the halfway house. At that point, I don't know whether Jack thought I might slip back into my old ways or not. We had kept in touch during my years in Lewisburg, speaking by telephone about once every week, so he was well aware of the progress I had made in my spiritual journey. But he was also aware of how inviting the temptations of the world could be to an ex-convict. If he had any doubts, he never let me know about them, nor did he ever test me with an invitation to join him in an act of crime.

186

In fact, Jack was very supportive of my new lifestyle and new ambitions and would often do things to help keep me on the narrow path. For example, knowing I liked to dress well, he could see that it was a struggle for me to wear the sub-standard clothing that now filled my scanty wardrobe. So, every once in awhile he would give me a shirt, a pair of slacks or a suit that he claimed had been bought for him by someone else. At 6-feet-1, 190 pounds, Jack was slightly bigger than I was and his suit size was a 42 Long. I weighed about 175 pounds and wore a 40 Long, so he would always say, "They bought me the wrong size. See if it fits you." We used to laugh about how excited I would get over some of the suits he gave me. Once, he pulled out this sharp brown suit and said, "Why don't you try this on?" Before he could finish his sentence, I was smiling and saying, "Yeah, it'll fit." He buckled over in laughter because he could tell by my response that I was taking that suit whether it fit or not.

The change in wardrobe was only one of several things I had to adjust to as a free man. Moving from the wholly regimented lifestyle of prison to the semi-regimented lifestyle of the halfway house to the complete autonomy of freedom takes some getting used to. Even the most basic decisions and chores take on the magnitude of life-or-death situations when transitioning from incarceration to freedom. How long that transition period lasts depends on the individual, but no ex-convict is immune to the discomfort of adjusting to life on the outside. Whether it takes weeks, months, years or forever, everyone who has spent more than five years in prison experiences an awkward, frightening phase after being released. I am proof of that.

I was an inmate who did not embrace the prison culture or its regressive mentality. I did everything I could to think like the free folks on the outside. I read about current events in newspapers and magazines, spoke in person or by telephone with upstanding members of society, and made thorough plans for life outside of the iron bars. And yet, leaving prison after an entire decade, particularly the 1980s in which nearly every aspect of society became computerized, was like awaking from a 10-year hibernation. Errands as simple as grocery shopping challenged and scared me.

For example, when I was locked up in 1979, supermarkets had hanging scales on which customers could weigh and price their produce. You simply picked up the fruit, put it on the scale and found out how much it cost. But on my first shopping excursion of 1989, I realized that hanging scales were a thing of the past. Now, you took your fruit to the counter to see how much it cost. Well, I wanted to buy some grapes and since I had only a small amount of money in my pocket, I didn't want to take too many up to the counter and then be embarrassed by not having enough money to pay for them. While the average citizen would have split a batch in half, I wasn't sure whether that was allowable, and my indecisiveness left me paralyzed. Unsure of what to do, I stood there in trepidation, absolutely certain that every person in the store was staring at me and laughing. There I was, a grown man standing in a grocery store and sweating because I lacked the nerve to break off some grapes. I thought if I started breaking off the grapes, everyone would think I was trying to steal them. Finally, I gave up, dropped the bag of grapes and ran out of the store with nothing. While buying grapes sounds like a trivial matter, it was exasperating for me. And I was about as prepared for freedom as an inmate can be.

Sometimes, ex-cons try too hard to fit into society and end up looking foolish. Months before I left Lewisburg, a convict told me that everything at McDonald's was computerized, so customers no longer had to pick up their trays when they finished eating. So I went to McDonald's one day and left my tray on the table when I was done, and people looked at me like I was a barbarian. They thought I was crazy, but I thought I was being normal.

One of my Christian inmate friends, Gerald Jenkins, once told me that he went to a fancy restaurant shortly after being released and panicked when the waitress handed him a five-page menu. It had been years since he had made a decision about what to eat and suddenly, he was being asked to choose the New York strip or the filet mignon, the blackened salmon or the swordfish. Being questioned about how he wanted his meat cooked, medium rare or well done, felt like an interrogation to him. So, completely flustered, he ended up sprinting out of the restaurant before the waitress returned with his complimentary glass of water.

Some brothers, of course, have trouble avoiding the various temptations of society, whether it's women, crime, drugs or alcohol. But because of my devotion to Christ I never struggled with those things. Many former alcoholics or drug addicts can't be around their old vices for any significant period of time without being overcome, but I never had that problem. Though I had used cocaine on numerous occasions, I often walked undeterred into North Carolina crack houses in search of a cousin who had become an addict. Not once was I seriously tempted to indulge, and eventually, I found my cousin and got him off the drug and involved in a church.

Discipline has always been a strong suit of mine, even when I was a criminal. I have never had trouble putting aside things that might hinder me from reaching my goal. Before I became a Christian, my objective was to make as much money as possible, so at one point I gave up smoking, heavy drinking and drug abuse because I thought they might prevent me from becoming rich. When I was born again, I applied that same sense of self-control to my walk with Christ, giving up whatever I thought might hamper my relationship with God and the scriptures. That mentality is what led me to become a vegan.

In January of 1981, while studying the Book of Daniel, I was moved by Daniel's decision to give up meat for a 21-day fast. Since I admired Daniel's spiritual and political outlook, I decided to give up meat myself. But instead of abstaining for three weeks, I gave it up forever. In my study of the scriptures, I had noticed how fasting seemed to produce power in an individual's life and I knew that if I ever got out of prison, I would not be able to consistently go on 7- and 10-day fasts. So, I decided to give up something that would enable me to be on a perpetual fast, and for me, that was meat. To those who knew me as "M.C." or "The Bronx Star," the idea of me becoming a vegetarian must have sounded as radical as the idea of me becoming a preacher. During my years on the street, I had lived off of a cholesterol diet, starting almost every day with a plate of steak and eggs. Then, I would scramble two raw eggs in orange juice and swig it down like a shot of whiskey. Someone had told me that concoction was an aphrodisiac, so I drank it religiously for years.

In addition to giving up meat, I vowed to abstain from fish as well. The vegans (vegetarians who do not eat animal products) in the pen used to have a saying - "Nothing with a face on it (will we eat)." Since making my decision 19 years ago, I have not had one bite of meat or fish. When I first began my fast, I was probably hurting myself because I did not know how to properly balance a meal without meat. But as other vegetarians observed me, they began giving me health pamphlets and books that taught me how to eat correctly. That's when I realized that I was not only strengthening myself spiritually, but physically as well. While my original intention remains the same, I now understand how people destroy themselves by the foods they eat. When I recognized that, living without meat became easy, so easy that I eventually decided to give up desserts too.

When I left prison, I added dairy products to my list of forbidden foods. Now I live off a diet of fruit, rice, raw vegetables, soy, and beans and nuts for protein. I substitute soy beverage for milk when I eat dry cereal. You would think it would be easier to be a vegan or a vegetarian in prison, but because of the limited choices that one has and because the fruit and vegetables are so bad, it actually requires more discipline to stop eating meat behind bars. In society, where you can obtain numerous substitutes for meat, I find it simple.

I was so disciplined when I left prison, and so focused on my goal of establishing myself in the ministry, that the opposite sex was not a distraction either. While in North Carolina, I dated one woman seriously and probably would have married her if she had been willing to move to Cleveland with me in 1991. Besides that, this former womanizer was dateless.

Being out of the halfway house enabled me to take advantage of the graciousness of some of my preacher friends. Naturally, I had not been able to leave the state to preach while living in the halfway house but upon being released, I traveled to Washington, D.C., Baltimore, New York, Pennsylvania and Ohio, delivering the Word of God. My first experience in preaching before a large congregation came at the Full Gospel Evangelistic Center in Cleveland, where Michael Exum, who had become a good friend of mine while visiting our Christian group in Lewisburg, was the pastor. There were about 500 people there and I would be lying if I said I wasn't a bit nervous. But I stuck to my manuscript and all went well.

Soon thereafter, I made an appearance at Dr. Carter's church, New Shiloh in Baltimore. My visit had been unannounced, so I did not preach, but Dr. Carter introduced me to his membership, allowed me to sit with him in the pulpit, and had me say a few words to the few thousand people in the pews. It was unsettling to stand before that many people, but there existed within the congregation a sense of familiarity with me. Because Dr. Carter had often spoken of his visits to Lewisburg and, in particular, of my extraordinary ordination, the folks at New Shiloh embraced me as a son. So months later, when I finally got the chance to preach there, I was comfortable and ready.

Tapping into the network of ministers I had met during my incarceration, I began to build up quite a schedule outside of eastern North Carolina. But while my ministry was thriving outside of the area, I was being all but shunned on my home turf. None of the local ministers welcomed me into their pulpits. I preached in Maury at the church of my youth one time and at a church where a cousin of mine served as a deacon twice but besides that,

I was being muzzled. I believe that many of the young pastors were intimidated by my intellectual messages and that many of the older pastors were threatened because they perceived me as being rebellious. In hindsight, I can understand why the older pastors may have felt that way. In preaching a strong message of change and transformation from the old way of doing things, I did not realize that I was highlighting the shortcomings of the local Black Christian leadership.

Those who enjoyed my message kept telling me that I needed to find my niche, that my views were unique and would not be accepted by everyone. At the time, I could not comprehend what they meant. The way I saw it, I was merely preaching the gospel. But later I understood why I came off as a radical who did not fit neatly into any of the Christian camps.

I was not a prosperity preacher, although I taught that God would provide all of his children's needs. I was not a deliverance preacher who casted out demons and devils, although I knew that some people needed deliverance. I was not a typical salvation preacher, although I never preached without emphasizing that one must be born again. I was not a sociologist in the pulpit, although I always incorporated social issues into my messages. And I was not a prophet in the Charismatic or Pentecostal tradition of supernaturally telling people about their business after every sermon. Rather, I saw myself being in the mold of the Old Testament prophets such as Isaiah and Jeremiah, challenging individuals and society on issues of justice. My mixture of evangelical Christianity, charismatic Christianity and social reform was too much for rural North Carolina and hence, I was perceived and treated as an outsider.

It was not long before I concluded that the only way to establish a local platform was to have my own church. After 10 years of intense and unconventional study, there was no question that I had the Biblical knowledge to lead my own flock. And my skills of oratory and discernment had improved to the point where I was no longer preaching over the heads of those in my audience. Initially, I sought to take over a church that was already in existence, but after being rejected for the few openings I applied for, I decided to open my own house of worship. Apostle Townsend told me that starting a church would be a mistake, that my message was too progressive to be received in eastern North Carolina, but I was convinced that I was doing the right thing. So with sky-high hopes, I opened the doors to the "Vision of Deliverance Justice Center" in May of 1990.

191

On paper, I had everything I thought I needed to be successful. Through the funding of some cousins and old friends, I was able to rent an historic building that used to be known as "Harper's Chapel Church." Like many old Black churches in the South, it had served as a one-room schoolhouse in Greene County years before integration. I thought that historical combination of the spiritual, social and educational made it the ideal setting for my church.

Things started with a bang as we drew nightly crowds of 60 to 70 people during our grand opening revival week. I had some guest preachers come to speak, including Frank Summerfield of the Word of God Fellowship in Raleigh, whose services now appear on Black Entertainment Television, and Donald Fozard, the pastor and founder of Mount Zion Christian Academy in Durham, which over the past few years has developed one of the most powerful high school basketball programs in the nation. Tracy McGrady, the rising star whom the Toronto Raptors drafted out of high school, graduated from Mount Zion in 1997. But most of those who turned out had come just to hear my guests. When the preachers returned to their congregations, I was left with a steady group of only about 8 to 10 adult members.

Part of my problem was the name of the church, which by itself was disturbing to folks in the rural South. The "Vision of Deliverance Justice Center" suggested to some that I had started a radical deliverance church and to others that I was a liberal who had designs on starting another peace movement with flower children. And because my blueprint for some of the social outreach endeavors was based on the Black Panthers' "Feed the Children" breakfast program, some people thought I was a militant. So folks didn't know what to make of me, and as a result, my church did not grow. But I kept myself busy and, rather quickly, my voice came to be heard.

One of the few allies I had in the area was an African-American entrepreneur named Jim Rouse. He owned a Black newspaper and radio station in Greenville and liked me so much that he gave me free access to both outlets. He was tired of the shuffling and compromising of the established Black leadership and saw me as a much-needed voice of enlightenment. He allowed me to write editorials in his newspaper and gave me a free one-hour broadcast every Saturday morning on his radio station. And Jim did not attempt to censor me. In fact, he often thought the more radical my commentary, the better. He also produced a monthly television show called "The Minority Voice," which I appeared on.

Because I was trying to eradicate what I viewed as a backwards mentality on the part of the local Black population, I geared most of my work toward the youth, thinking I could reach them before they were indoctrinated into the old way of thinking. So, my first target for social reform was the educational system, which had maintained the doctrine and practice of White supremacy despite several years of integration. There was not even a hint of African-American history in the curriculum and the books they used featured exclusively White characters. Having been poorly educated because of similar circumstances nearly 30 years earlier, I was not about to stand by idly and watch it happen to another generation of Black children. But the problem went much deeper than the books. The schools were dividing the children into classes along racial lines. They were tracking the Black kids, putting them into lower-level classes while the White kids were being pushed into advanced classes. It was practically like having two schools within one building.

In an effort to bring attention to these injustices and shame to their practitioners, I called a march in Snow Hill against the Greene County Board of Education. Our theme was "No Change This Summer, No School This Fall." We threatened to hold all of the Black children out of school if the curriculum was not updated to include us. It turned out to be a powerful demonstration, though we did not reach our desired objective. My friend David Hayden, the socially-conscious White minister who had been such a blessing to me while I was in Lewisburg, showed up, as did members of the Nation of Islam and the Gay Liberation Army, to my surprise I had no idea that such a diverse assortment of people would come out, but once they arrived, they were too boisterous and committed to be turned back. So, myself and about 100 other protesters, most of them coming from outside of the region, marched up Highway 13, from St. Peter's Freewill Baptist Church to the offices of the Board of Education. While the Black children returned to the same racist schools that fall, the rally afforded me some television coverage in what would be the first of many appearances over the next six months.

Shortly after the march, Jim Rouse put me in the spotlight by calling my first press conference. He told the local television stations that he had a hot scoop, that this Olds guy was about to turn Greene County upside down. What I was about to do was apply for the County Manager's job. I really had no interest in the job, but I wanted to make a statement that it was high time for a county with a Black population of nearly 50 percent to begin appointing some African-Americans to positions of leadership. None of the appointed positions were being given to Blacks and no one was willing to challenge the status quo. I had done research on the surrounding counties and Greene County was about the most backwards of them all. So, with Jim having notified the local reporters, I stormed into the County Commissioner's office with television cameramen from three stations following. I asked for an application for the County Manager's job and the folks in authority just about fainted. So with the cameras rolling, I began my spiel, saying that the last County Manager had been a thief and a drug addict and that I was here to clean things up. The TV stations ate it up and from that point on, I was their favorite Black newsmaker.

Whenever I wanted coverage for an event, I would simply call the reporters and they would show up or write a story. Oftentimes, they would call me and ask what I was doing. There were not a lot of positive things going on in the Black community and the only other Black leader in the area was caught up in a number of vices, so I was like a breath of fresh air to the local media outlets. It got to the point where, from May of 1990 to November of 1990, I was either in the newspaper or on television once a week.

Marching or rallying every three or four weeks, I challenged anything and everything I deemed to be having a negative effect on the Black community, particularly on its youth. For instance, because there was no meaningful recreation for the children after school, I asked the County Commissioner to build a park in Maury for the kids. He scoffed at my request, but I called a local television station, Channel 12 out of New Bern, and they walked with me through the area I wanted converted into a park, filming as we went. When the piece ran on television, the Commissioner was left tongue-tied, trying to explain why he had turned down the creation of a park on land that was not being used for anything. On another occasion, I got two of my cousins to run for local office: Wanda Kay became a candidate for the Board of Education, and Darnell Miller ran for the position of County Commissioner.

My relationship with the press grew so strong that the local NBC affiliate allowed me to host a public affairs special on infant mortality. The program went so well that they offered to give me a monthly, half-an-hour show free of charge if I would work for them as a sales person. But I refused to take the job because it would have forced me to deviate from my three-year plan. Now, I wish that I had taken that job. I could have been

194

syndicated by now. I did not realize that the platform I was so desirous of was there for the taking.

Even though I received a lot of press and was articulate on my sound bites, the local Black aristocracy never accepted me. Most African-Americans with extensive education could not bring themselves to support an ex-convict who had been in prison only five or six months prior. And in my zeal, I was not sensitive enough to people's legitimate concerns about my past. I did not realize that these were people who remembered me for pimping women and bringing drugs into the community. So naturally, they were not about to submit to my leadership. And the Black preachers who had ignored me earlier began speaking out against me. While they rarely referred to me by name, they often used their time in the pulpit to lambaste the thinking behind whatever cause I was fighting for.

While my activism created a stir, it did nothing for my church. And since I did not have an organization behind me, those who supported my ideas had nothing to contribute their money to. I was running so fast and spreading myself so thin that I did not stop to build an organization. I thought the church could serve as the foundation for my movement, but people were baffled and frightened by the Vision of Deliverance Justice Center. Because I did not understand the importance of creating an infrastructure, my activity was without staying power.

Looking back, I think my fervor and hyperactivity was an attempt to overcompensate for the destructiveness, neglect and political absenteeism of my first 40 years of life. Driven by my redeemed spirit, I tried desperately to make up for the time I had wasted. I felt guilty for running the streets, committing crimes and landing myself in prison when I should have been helping to uplift Black people in rural North Carolina. I felt that since I had not been a part of the solution that I had been a part of the problem, which of course I had been. But rather than try to establish relationships with the people and the local leadership, I thought I could gain prominence overnight by making bold proclamations. I thought everyone would automatically view me as this great deliverer for the region if I preached the truth and showed concern for the people. Later, I realized that I was unintentionally showing up the existing leaders.

Obviously, I now understand the mistakes that I made and I'm glad to say that, despite my missteps, my work was not completely in vain. After I moved to Cleveland, many of the changes I pushed for were brought to fruition. The county's manager and all of its officers were replaced. The members of the Board of Education either resigned or were voted out. And the land I asked the County Commissioner to turn into a park was converted into a Little League baseball complex after all.

During the time I was running around making noise in North Carolina, I continued to travel outside of the state to preach. I made two more appearances at the Full Gospel Evangelistic Center in Cleveland and after my third visit, I shared the problems I was having in my home state with Pastor Mike Exum. He and his congregation had been nothing but supportive of me since they began visiting Lewisburg in 1985. In fact, after my Solid Rock Baptist Church was forced to disband, the national organization that Pastor Exum belonged to wrote letters to their local senators and representatives, calling into question why I was being prohibited from practicing my religious freedom. A sister named Linda Billingsly was appointed to correspond with me and record the information that was pertinent to my plight. Then, she sent the letters out to the politicians. That is how I first came into contact with the woman who would become my first wife. Then, when I was released from prison, Pastor Exum sent me money and gave me access to his long distance calling card.

Just as he had always done, Mike came through upon being told of my struggles in North Carolina. After hearing that I was fighting just to stay afloat in the ministry, he offered me a job as his church administrator. In addition to a stable salary, the position came with an office at the church and the promise of being allowed to preach once every couple of months at Full Gospel.

With the way things were going in North Carolina, there was not much to take into consideration. So, after receiving the go ahead from my parole officer, I left for Cleveland in January of 1991.

Chapter *X*

FREEDOM NOW

The Full Gospel Evangelistic Center was one of the liveliest and most exciting churches I have ever been in. In addition to a traditional choir of 40 to 50 people, it had a band, complete with drums, keyboard, bass guitar and horns, making for a sound that was contemporary and exceptional. The driving beat was not unlike that heard on many urban radio stations, but the lyrics, which usually were taken directly from the Book of Psalms, were uplifting and invigorating to the spirit. When the praise and worship was over, Pastor Exum would share insight from the Bible with a congregation that was attentive and, for the most part, quiet. He was a brilliant preacher who spoke straight from the Bible. He did not whoop and holler like many Black ministers, choosing instead to teach the Word of God in a straightforward and composed manner.

Shortly after arriving in Cleveland, I met Linda Billingsly for the first time. Though we had written letters to one another over the past few years of my incarceration, as well as during my time in North Carolina, we had never seen each other because she had always been out of town when I preached at Full Gospel. Our correspondence had been almost entirely spiritual, full of testimonies and Bible verses, and when our relationship continued to develop smoothly in Cleveland, I began thinking in terms of marriage.

As a born-again Christian, I definitely wanted to get married and I viewed Linda as the perfect partner, even though I knew little about her outside of her relationship with Christ. At that time, I could be characterized as "super spiritual," so I did not believe in long and thorough courtships. We had one lunch date and then the next time I took her out, I asked her to marry me. When she said yes and accepted the engagement ring, I kissed her for the first time. I was proud of myself for having been so upright and thought I had done everything by the book. The fact that we had spent just a meager amount of time together only contributed to our belief that our union was "predestined by God." The way we saw it, I was saved and she was saved, so what could go wrong? But five years after getting married in September of 1991, we were divorced.

One of the first career moves I made in Cleveland was to create a non-profit organization called Community Resource Inc. (CRI). Having learned from my mistakes in North Carolina, I decided to build a base before branching out into the development of different programs and activities. Through dialogue with various individuals and research on my own part, I easily incorporated CRI and obtained for it 501-C3 status as a tax-exempt organization. In my proposal, I wrote that the goal of CRI was to service underprivileged youth and to enhance the educational experiences of young people and adults in urban areas.

Jim Rouse, who played a mentor's role in the establishment of CRI, continued to publish my editorials in his newspaper and provided a nice supplement to my salary along with it. One day, as I was flipping through his paper, I came across an article on Paul Hill, a Cleveland-based author, educator and activist who had developed an Africentric Rites-of-Passage program. Seeing that he was the Executive Director of the East End Neighborhood House, a local youth/community service center, I contacted him, and we immediately began an ongoing dialogue on the plight of African-American men. My discussions with Paul and my respect for his insights and programs, inspired the formation of my first and to this day, most fruitful, venture under CRI: Redirection of Young Minds (ROYM).

My intention in starting the Redirection of Young Minds program was to instill an appreciation for African and African-American history and culture in the best and brightest of our young Black men. I wanted them to understand the importance of establishing a covenant with their communities so that upon becoming successful in their chosen fields of endeavor, they would maintain a commitment to the liberation of African-American people. Also fundamental to ROYM was a Christ-centered curriculum that would ground our youth in Jesus Christ so they would not become confused and faithless when encountering other religions in the college classroom.

But from the beginning ROYM was misunderstood. Because of the word "Redirection," people thought that I wanted all of the at-risk youth, that I had some magic wand to wave that would immediately straighten out the young thugs, gangstas and drug dealers. As a result, my first class, which met in 1991, was filled with unruly young men who, like me decades before, seemed bent on learning the hard way.

I began meeting twice a week with 40 young men between the ages of 15 and 19 in the basement of Pastor Anthony Johnson's Mount Pleasant Church of God. These were not churchgoing boys. Only about 15 of them had parents in the church, while the rest were hardened brothers who had been forced to come by their frustrated parents. Most of them, having already been involved in criminal activity for years, reminded me of myself as a teenager. Though appearing obstinate and brazen, they were lost, just trying to live up to their warped idea of manhood in a world that gave them little direction.

The first meeting went well enough and gave me the impression that I would indeed be able to redirect the course of these young men's lives. With my one assistant, a dedicated parent named Carlos Anthony Brown Sr., by my side, I shared my testimony of crime, murder and prison with the students, immediately gaining their respect and, I hate to say it, admiration. They thought I was hard, that I was some kind of O.G. - original gangsta. When I was done sharing my life's story, most of the guy's questions were sensational inquires about my criminal activities or prison experience. Not one of them asked me anything pertaining to Jesus Christ. We met again a few days later and that's when things began going downhill.

I had established a curriculum of Biblical Studies and African studies, which entailed learning about the slave trade and comparing the traditional educational systems of Africa with the contemporary schooling methods of America. The plan was to move through a workbook I had written called "Steps of Preventative Support." But after a few meetings, I was forced to redo the curriculum because most of the students did not have sufficient writing skills. And as far as homework went, they did not even consider doing the lessons I assigned, which led to a lot of improvisational teaching during class.

Part of the problem was that half of the youngsters were men just a few months shy of their 20th birthdays. Thinking they knew it all, they sat in class like beanbags, slouched and lifeless. Discipline was never a problem because after sauntering into the room, they shut themselves down completely. Many of them were involved in the drug game and the various vices that go along with it, so they had more money in their pockets than me. From their vantage point, that gave them little reason to pay attention to anything I said.

That point was driven home one Saturday morning about halfway through the program. I took the 20 to 25 students that remained out to breakfast for what was supposed to be a father-son event. There were far more boys than fathers, though, as many of the kids were without a strong male influence in their home. After we finished eating and the waitress brought the bill, the fathers and myself began putting our money together to pay for the meal. As we thumbed through our wallets, one of the youngsters pulled out a wad of what had to be a couple thousand dollars and said proudly, "Pastor Olds, you having a problem?" Knowing he had not made that money from an after-school job, I took that as a clear indication that my message was falling on deaf ears.

The program ran for 48 weeks, meeting at three different sites: Mount Pleasant; the Schaffer Memorial United Methodist Church; and the Freedom Christian Church. When the final week concluded, only six young men remained. Not coincidentally, those six brothers all had positive male figures in their lives. The rest of the guys had dropped out somewhere along the way. Every so often, I see some of the dropouts around the city, standing on a corner amid a gang of wayward brothers. I think I saw one young man in a penitentiary during one of my ministry trips, but I can't be certain because he turned and walked the other way as soon as he saw my face.

To close out the program on a festive note, we held an event meant to celebrate a holiday of our own making, The African Expatriation Commemorated. The complex name of the holiday stands for "out of Fatherland," which signified our desire to commemorate our African ancestors who had been taken out of their Fatherland during the slave trade. We created a special definition of the holiday that allowed all six of the young men to participate in explaining the meaning of the African Expatriation and the Redirection of Young Minds program.

Another purpose in creating the holiday was to infuse a sense of independence into the youth by having them originate and observe their own cultural celebration without the permission or sanction of White America. Ideally, the holiday would have wrapped up the program with three days of activities, but we had to condense it into one night of performing arts. The show, which was held at the Cuyahoga Community College, featured a number of musical routines and was highlighted by a performance of Porgy and Bess by a group from Youngstown, Ohio.

While the finale went well, I was disappointed and somewhat discouraged by the ineffectiveness of the program. In an effort to improve it, I decided to make some changes. First, I reduced the age range from 15-19 to 14-17 and planned to drop the age limit in each successive year. Then, I made the program co-ed. Those two changes alone made a world of difference, but I went a step further and also altered the curriculum. Though I still taught plenty of African-American history, I moved away from the African perspective and in its place, began focusing on the development of communication skills through print and broadcast journalism. The students, who felt little connection to Africa, did not understand the significance of the history, so it had not impacted them at all.

The emphasis on communication grew out of my desire to help the youngsters become more articulate. My thought was that the only way to change the negative perception that others, and we ourselves, hold about us was to make our young and articulate African-Americans vocal and visible. That would allow us to stop fulfilling the stereotypes that have ensnared us for decades. Over time, I discovered that the more we concentrated on communication skills, the more receptive the kids became to new material, which enabled me to reinsert some of the African history into the curriculum.

The entire second year of the program was held at Pastor Julia Brogdon's Freedom Christian Church and was a tremendous success. The kids produced a half-an-hour radio show that aired on WRDZ, a local Christian radio station. The show required them to interview ministers, activists, musicians and others, and in the process helped them develop skills in broadcasting and writing. The next year, I reduced the ages to 14-16 and began the publication of newsletters and magazines.

Since then, ROYM has progressed to the point where today youngsters must apply to participate. To get into the program, they must sign a contract, write an article, and produce an audiotape on which they interview an adult about his or her career. The program has also been expanded from one year to four years, so children can be involved throughout their high school experience. If the participants complete the terms of the contract, which includes attending regularly, behaving respectably and producing newsletters and a magazine, they can receive up to $1,000 in scholarship money. The first scholarship we established, the Carlos Anthony Brown Memorial Scholarship, was named in honor of Carlos Brown, who died unexpectedly of an aneurysm in 1999. Carlos, the first adult volunteer of ROYM, had worked beside me during that trying first year, when his son, Carlos Jr., became one of the program's first graduates.

Seven years after that inaugural class, four ROYM students, one boy and three girls, graduated from high school and were awarded scholarships to college by the program. That group produced a newsletter called "Today's Youth, Tomorrow's Leadership," and put out two issues of a magazine entitled "Voices of the Future." They also participated in ROYM's six-week summer journalism camp, where they were able to meet local television and print reporters.

While grants from the Cleveland Foundation and the United Black Fund have helped to establish ROYM, the bulk of the scholarship money comes from a golf outing I instituted in the late '90s. With 96 participants (48 youth and 48 adults), we raised about $9,000 the first year and have watched that figure grow each year. At the 1999 outing, which was held at the Highland Hills Golf Course, Dave Rogers, the chief meteorologist at Cleveland's Channel 3, came out and did a remote broadcast from the event. Our proceeds should increase greatly in 2000 because the Cleveland Chapter of the National Football League Alumni is co-sponsoring the event. As many as 25 former Cleveland Browns could show up and play, and whatever money their presence generates will go toward scholarships for ROYM students. In honor of the Browns, we named two scholarships after the former players Marion Motley, the Hall of Fame running back, and Walter Johnson. Both men are deceased, and members of their families are helping to promote the golf outing.

As I was building ROYM into a vocational training program for others, I realized that I needed to advance my own education. Though I was intelligent, articulate and well read, I knew I had to enhance my academic background to be accepted within certain segments of the Black community. Beyond that, my own innate desire for self-improvement served as an impetus. I was not satisfied with where I was intellectually or monetarily and I needed to increase my marketability. I did not want merely to obtain credentials through a correspondence course. I wanted to work hard and earn whatever I achieved. So in 1992, I enrolled in a one-year certificate program in non-profit organization at Case Western Reserve University. The program was for people who were already employed as executives in non-profit organizations, and as the church administrator at Full Gospel, I qualified.

Returning to the classroom after 25 years away was quite an undertaking, particularly since I was doing it at the graduate level. Even though I had studied hundreds of books over the past 12 years, becoming a student again was an extreme adjustment because I had to work according to someone else's standard. When I studied on my own, I could go as fast or as slow as I liked, and of course, I did not force myself to write term papers on what I read. Adapting to what certain professors wanted in terms of the content of a report was a great challenge, but I was surprised at how quickly I grasped the necessary concepts. Naturally, my background in administration helped since I was doing many of the things that were being taught in the class, and with my experiential knowledge and the diligence I had always possessed working hand in hand, I completed the six-class program in 1994 with a 3.65 grade point average. I also developed solid working relationships with several members of the faculty, a fact that has since worked to my advantage on several occasions.

I would have finished the program in 1993, but I postponed my studies when a unique opportunity came my way at the beginning of that year. Out of the blue, a group of Christians who used to visit our fellowship at Lewisburg contacted me about pastoring an all-White church in Williamsport, Pennsylvania. The pastor had fallen into immorality and the church of about 450 people was on the verge of splitting up. In search of a leader who could bring healing to their fractured congregation, some of the members, remembering the knowledge and enthusiasm I displayed at Lewisburg, asked if I would consider taking the job. Knowing that Williamsport was not the place for me, I told them I would do it on an interim basis if they did not mind me commuting from Cleveland. They had no problem with that, so every Wednesday and Saturday night from January through September, I made the six-hour trek to the home of my first significant congregation, the Covenant Evangelistic Center.

I will admit that I initially found the thought of pastoring an all-White congregation bizarre. Though I harbored no prejudice toward Whites, I had worked almost exclusively in the Black community since leaving Lewisburg. In fact, besides my time in prison practically every moment of my life had been spent around Black people. Since becoming a Christian, my passion had always been for the upliftment of African-Americans through the gospel of Jesus Christ, and a sizeable amount of the sermons I preached dealt with that subject. The congregations I ministered to could usually count on receiving a message rooted in the prophetic books of the Old Testament, related to the contemporary oppression of African-Americans and steeped in the doctrine of justice.

But, of course, my preaching at the Covenant Evangelistic Center would have to be different. While I did not hesitate to share my views on racial justice, I spent most of my time delivering spiritual messages that would comfort and inspire individuals of all races. The experience really forced me to get back to the basic truth of the gospel: that God had sent his son Jesus Christ to liberate us from the oppressions, depressions, angers, insecurities and fears that the devil seeks to place on each of us. My congregation at Covenant was made up of blue-collar families and it would have been unfair and unfulfilling to them if I had focused on sociopolitical messages. My time there taught me that people - Black, White or other - often go to church because they are hurting and in need of spiritual direction. They struggle with relationships, with decisions, and what they need is spiritual truth, not necessarily social truth. My members needed personal messages that spoke directly to their particular situation, and through my increased sensitivity to the Holy Spirit, I worked hard to give them that.

My assignment at Covenant turned out to be a wonderful experience, one that made me truly internalize the oneness of the body of Christ. It also was somewhat prophetic in that, ever since then, I have found great acceptance from White Christians. Though most of my ministry takes place among Blacks, White congregations, pastors and denominational bodies have always been supportive of my ministry, even as it relates to the cultural, educational and economic advancement of African-Americans.

After concluding my service at Covenant and finishing the certificate program in non-profit organization, I left the Full Gospel Evangelistic Center. My departure was not motivated by scandal or trouble; I decided to leave simply because my theology and sociology had begun to differ with those of Pastor Exum. I had always been more Afrocentric and socially-minded than Mike but I had suppressed those aspects of my ministry while working within the confines of Full Gospel. That is why I had to hold the "Redirection of Young Minds" program in other churches. While Mike agreed with the overall tenets of the program, he thought the emphasis on African and African-American history would disturb some members of his congregation, even though it was an all-Black church. Also, as I increased my education and learned more about running non-profit, social programs, I knew that having a pastor who did not fully support my endeavors in the community would become a hindrance.

I thought the split was amicable enough but unfortunately, leaving a Black church is often like getting a divorce: it is hard to maintain a productive or even cordial relationship after doing so. For the next few years, I had no contact with Mike or practically anyone else at Full Gospel. But eventually Mike and I renewed our friendship. Doing so meant a lot to me because he was the man responsible for my move to Cleveland, a move that vastly aided my spiritual and intellectual endeavors.

Rather than take on an administrative position at another church, I set out on my own again, founding the Covenant Gathering Christian Church with Linda in August of 1994. As had been the case in North Carolina four years earlier, I thought I had everything in place to prosper. A couple of people from Full Gospel decided to go with me, though I had in no way recruited them, and we started meeting at the Civic Center in Cleveland Heights. Our services were being broadcast on Channel 55, a local television station, and also in North Carolina, so we were being noticed. And unlike in North Carolina, I had established my ministry and developed a reputation as an honest, caring and committed man of God.

Linda and I received a tremendous blessing a few months later when the Ohio Conference of the Churches of God gave us a grant for $60,000 over two years. A mostly White denomination, the Churches of God was looking to plant churches in the inner city. The grant stabilized us financially and allowed me to develop the church without the burden of trying to support myself from the tithes and offerings of a dozen adults. Though Covenant Gathering was small, it provided me with a rewarding and memorable experience.

When I left Full Gospel, I was determined not to have a congregation full of people who had left other churches in a huff; so I worked tirelessly at recruiting the unchurched by establishing ministries that provided food and tutorial programs for residents of the projects. The transformations we saw in the lives of the few poor families that joined the church made all the time and effort we put into building Covenant Gathering worthwhile. People who were unemployed when they joined the church landed jobs. People who at one time did not have cars purchased vehicles. People who had never owned a home bought houses and folks who had been shacking up came and got married. Those are the types of changes - lifestyle changes like mine – I love to see.

In December of 1994, I received a startling phone call from the Reverend Dr. Otis Moss, pastor of Cleveland's renowned Olivet Institutional Baptist Church. Dr. Moss and I had a cordial relationship, having worked together on a few projects in the community. I had also taught classes at Olivet's Bible Institute. But none of that quelled the surprise I felt when he asked me to preach at his church on an upcoming Sunday morning. Since Covenant Gathering met in the afternoon, there was no time conflict, so I quickly accepted his invitation, viewing it as an excellent opportunity to minister in one of the city's most influential houses of worship. I assumed he would be out of town that day because he had asked me to fill in for him, but it turned out that he was in downtown Cleveland, preaching in honor of some special occasion at the historic Old Stone Church. After I delivered my sermon, Dr. Moss's wife, Edwina, asked me to wait for Dr. Moss because he had something he wanted to talk to me about. After a polite discussion, he proposed having lunch the next day.

At that point, it had never crossed my mind that Dr. Moss might offer me a job; I figured he wanted to collaborate on some type of outreach project in the community. So, when he asked the next day if I would consider becoming Olivet's assistant to the pastor, I was stunned. Much of my astonishment stemmed from the fact that I had become known throughout Cleveland as a Charismatic preacher, and Charismatics and Baptists, though both Bible-believing Christians, do not always mix. I did a good job of hiding my surprise - at least I think I did - and told him about the responsibility I had to my own church, Covenant Gathering. Though it would have been easy to disband the church right there, I told him that I wanted to continue building Covenant Gathering, I could not in good conscience walk out on the 40 some odd members that I had. He understood my feelings and did not have a problem with the situation. And since Covenant Gathering met in the afternoon, the services of the two churches did not conflict. Though I was flattered by the offer and excited about the possibilities it presented, I left lunch that day without giving Dr. Moss an answer.

After several months of praying extensively about the opportunity, I concluded that it was too good to pass up. Rev. Moss was an internationally known minister whom I respected as a community leader, and his church dealt with many of the social justice issues that concerned me. On top of that, he offered me a substantial salary that would give me some financial breathing room for the first time since I had been out of prison. So with equal amounts of enthusiasm and curiosity, Linda and I joined the Olivet family in April of 1995.

Since then, my affiliation with the church has placed me in the company of numerous dignitaries. In addition to my brief interaction with Hillary Rodham-Clinton, I have met the Reverend Jesse Jackson, the South African leader, Allan Boesak, and Bishop Desmond Tutu's daughter. That is not to mention the various academicians, congressman and other politicians I come across on a regular basis at Olivet.

For all of the prestige that ministering at Olivet brings, I am most thankful for the unconditional love and unwavering support that Rev. and Mrs. Moss, the church leadership, and the entire congregation displayed when I went through my toughest experience since incarceration: my divorce from Linda. Rather than act like a cold employer or a self-righteous Christian, Rev. Moss stood by me fully. He never gave up confidence in me, never diminished my role in the ministry and never doubted the truth of my story, as sketchy as it was.

Here are the details: one Friday in May of 1996, I went to North Carolina for an Unmasked Ministers meeting. The Unmasked Ministers is a group of about 50 preachers from North and South Carolina who get together to fellowship and talk about whatever problems might be plaguing their personal and/or church life. The purpose of the group is to give pastors a support system and a place to work through their struggles without the fear of their dilemmas being exposed to the public. Donald Fozard, the pastor of Mount Zion Christian Church in Durham, established the group and because of my administrative skills, asked me to serve as its vice president in 1995. When I met with the ministers that spring night in 1996, I had no idea that I would soon be in dire need of their support.

I flew back to Cleveland the next morning because I was slated as a guest lecturer for a class of graduate students studying social work at Case Western Reserve University. I had been asked to speak about cultural diversity and the impact of racism in America, and I intended to use my experiences as the son of a sharecropper for a major part of my speech. But when I stopped by my home before heading to the class, I was shocked to find a nearly empty house. Linda and all of her belongings were gone.

I was totally blindsided. I had no idea of any major problems in our marriage, so the thought of her leaving me was unfathomable. But there was no time to mourn, at least not immediately. Faced with the choices of sitting in my all but barren home or going to teach that class, I decided to teach. And thankfully, by the sheer grace of God, I was able to concentrate on my subject matter and draw complimentary reviews.

As soon as the class ended, I was faced with another tough decision. I was scheduled to give the commencement address at Mount Zion Christian Academy in North Carolina that Sunday afternoon. So, was I supposed to stay and try to track down Linda or go and meet my obligation? As I pondered my predicament, I came to the conclusion that if I bailed out on my commitment in Durham I might never be able to preach again. Not because Pastor Fozard would not understand, but because I would know that I lacked the fortitude and the faith to preach the gospel through the storm. The next morning, after spending the night in a cold and lonely house, I flew to North Carolina to preach without mentioning a word about my quandary to Pastor Fozard or anyone else.

When I returned to Cleveland, I did not know what to do first. I wanted to talk to Linda because I was completely clueless as to why she would leave, but I did not know where she was. I called her family members, and her brothers started talking rough, like I had done something wrong, so I realized that I was in this alone. After a few days, she finally called, but she refused to discuss our relationship or her reason for leaving. Her tone and speech was very matter of fact, and she already had the divorce resolution prepared. She said, "You can pay a little or you can pay a lot." So, I decided to pay a little and not fight the inevitable.

To this day I do not know why Linda left. There definitely was no sexual immorality or physical abuse on my part. It is possible that my traveling bothered her, though she never said anything to that effect. Except for the extensive traveling I did while pastoring in Williamsport, I was probably out of town only once or twice a month. The divorce has never been difficult for me to talk about: it's just that I have never known exactly what to say. Linda and I have had several conversations since we split up. I even served as a reference for her when she applied for a counselor's position at another church. But she has never given me an explanation as to why she left.

Naturally, the divorce was incredibly hard to handle at first. I had enrolled in Case Western Reserve's Masters Degree program in non-profit organization in the Fall of 1995, so I had the burden of doing schoolwork at the time of the breakup. Because I did not have a Bachelors Degree, I had to make an appeal to Darlyne Bailey, the Dean of Case Western Reserve's Mandel School of Applied Social Sciences, to get into the program. Though some faculty members were against letting me in, I was eventually accepted because of how well I performed in the certificate program. I was doing just as well in the Masters courses until Linda left. During the summer and fall of 1996, while our divorce was being finalized, I struggled terribly to get through my studies. My grades never dipped below a B, but I had been doing A work before our separation.

The situation also threatened to ruin me in ministry because people are not likely to book a divorced minister to preach at revivals. In that regard, I thought the way that Linda left was malicious; it was like she was trying to destroy my ministry. By offering no explanation, she left me to explain to people what happened without actually knowing what happened myself. It made me look like I was guilty of something wicked. People were asking me all sorts of questions and I could not give them a straight answer. I was stammering and stuttering in folks' faces because I did not know what to say. I can only imagine what people, particularly Christians, were thinking. If somebody had come into my office and told my story - "My wife is gone. I don't know why. I had no idea she was leaving. I'm a good guy. I didn't cheat on her, didn't beat on her, never cursed in the house." - I would have said, "Come back when you're ready to be honest and work on this thing." It really looked bad.

That is why I was so appreciative and touched by the way the leadership at Olivet responded. When it would have been easy and somewhat admissible to react adversely, they demonstrated sincere Christian love. It was the greatest act of agape I have ever seen from a congregation. Everyone, from the top to the bottom, stood by me and anchored me. When I needed true Christian love and understanding, the Olivet Institutional Baptist Church family delivered.

My own members at Covenant Gathering also stuck by me, though everyone eventually dispersed. We were just beginning to see real growth when Linda packed her bags. But when the divorce was finalized, I encouraged those who wanted to go to find another church. I could not ignore the fact that people were looking at me as their role model. Because the membership was so small - we had a maximum of 15 families - I knew all of the children in the congregation intimately. And having a wife that divorced me without explanation made it impossible for me to be held up as a leader and an example for the children to look at. We broke down the fellowship slowly and started having monthly Bible studies at my house until everyone found a new church home. I still keep in touch with many of the members, praying with and counseling them on occasion.

Six months after Linda left, I finally felt the pain go away. I was driving to class, listening to WJMO, Cleveland's Solid Gold Soul station, when I heard Teddy Pendergrass singing "It Don't Hurt Now." As I reflected on the words of the song, which seemed to speak directly to my situation, the grief disappeared. In what seemed like a flash, I came to accept that Linda did not want me anymore. I stopped trying to figure out why, stopped replaying in my mind every argument and dispute we had, and just accepted it. There was no longer any need for me to mope around and drive myself crazy: Linda was gone, we were divorced, and that was that.

My grades improved over the final semester of the Masters program and I received my degree in non-profit organization in the spring of 1997. When I clutched my diploma, I thought about how difficult that piece of paper had been to attain and how, through the great challenges I had faced, I persevered to reach my goal. I also thought about the folks in North Carolina who, years ago, wrote me off as an ignorant and unqualified ex-con despite the intelligence with which I spoke. I treasured the fact that my erudition could never be questioned again. Now I could speak with authority concerning non-profit matters, as someone who was not only experienced but also academically trained in my field. Today, I am putting my expertise in the non-profit sector to good use as the Executive Director of the Olivet Housing and Community Development Corporation and as a consultant to several faith-based organizations.

It is difficult to convey what it is like to earn a Masters degree after being out of school for 25 years, particularly when you spent many of those years filling your mind with all kinds of poison. I consider it amazing that my brain could function at that level after all of the abuse, drugs and otherwise, that I put it through. It was truly the strength of God that enabled me to discipline myself to learn graduate-level material.

The joy I received from educational achievement was immense and I was beginning to fall in love with academia. So, immediately after receiving my Masters degree, I attempted to enroll in Case Western Reserve's Ph.D. program in Social Policy - United States History. I liked the fact that I could do high-level work and was thinking seriously about pursuing a second career as a professor at a historically Black college. While my lack of a Bachelor's Degree and the fact that I had no background in History proved to be obstacles, my performance in the certificate and Masters programs demonstrated my ability to do the work. That, combined with my rapport with many of the faculty members and a book I wrote and published in 1995 entitled *African American Christian Nation* got me into the program; and with a scholarship to boot. The book served as evidence that I was serious about writing and convinced the Chairman of the Admissions Committee that I was capable of obtaining a Ph.D.

The concept of the African American Christian Nation grew out of a lecture tour I intended to conduct on African-American nationhood. I held my first and only lecture at the Sheraton Hotel in Greenville, North Carolina in 1994. My church services at Covenant Gathering were being shown on television in North Carolina at the time, and I advertised the tour on the broadcast. Jim Rouse also publicized the series on his radio station and in his newspaper. The ad campaign worked brilliantly because when I arrived at the Sheraton, to my pleasant surprise, a group of about 80 people, including approximately 30 college students from the surrounding schools, had gathered in anticipation.

The college students were the most fascinated and had a lot of questions, more in fact, than I was prepared to answer. They were so intrigued by the idea of Black nationhood, which in my teachings differed substantially from Black separatism, that they asked me to come back and meet with them again. So a few weeks later, a mother of one of the students opened her home to those 30 students and myself, and we talked from 7 p.m. to 2 a.m. about the African American Christian Nation. One fellow asked to see my notes, but they were not organized in a way that would have made sense to him. So I told him that when I returned to Cleveland, I would systematize my notes and send him a copy of them. The thought that others might want to see my views in writing led me to cancel the remainder of my scheduled engagements and begin putting my ideas on paper. Over time, it evolved into a book.

When the African American Christian Nation first came out in October of 1995, on the heels of the Million Man March, I held a symposium at Case Western Reserve University for members of the faculty, administration and the student body. I opened by explaining that, contrary to popular belief, land is not a prerequisite for building a nation. I said that culture, religion and economics are what unify people and determine what is a nation. If African-Americans were able to establish nationhood in that context, I stated, it would enable us to interact with others as equals and remove our subservient role because we would then have something tangible to bring to the table.

Blacks, Whites and Jews were represented in the crowd of about 30 people, and it was interesting how the different races responded. Many of the non-Blacks said the African-American Christian Nation is just what Black people need. Their view was that African-Americans need to do something independently because doing such creates a position of strength and allows a group to provide for itself without being dependent on others. None of the African-Americans, however, took that view. They were fearful that my idea was reverting to the 1960s. The mere mention of the title scared most of them.

Very few people read the book, but I do not consider it to have been a failure because it helped me get into the Ph.D. program. I have not yet earned my doctorate, but it is a goal I will continue to pursue. I struggled in the program at Case Western Reserve, largely because I had spread myself too thin. I was working full time at Olivet, running Community Resource Inc. and Redirection of Young Minds, working on social issues in the community, traveling and preaching with regularity. With so much on my plate, I realized shortly after the start of the Ph.D. program that I was in over my head. One course alone required me to read five books a week, a demand I could not come close to meeting with my schedule so overloaded. I was able to earn C grades, but As and Bs are the requisite marks for a Ph.D. When the school year mercifully came to its conclusion, I met with the faculty members, and we mutually agreed that now was not the time for me to seek my doctorate.

Though my desire to earn a Ph.D. has not changed, I have decided to stay focused on public policy and the non-profit sector. I learned from my experience at Case Western Reserve that it is extremely difficult to earn a doctorate in History when you have not studied the subject at the college or graduate level. My plan now is to enter the Union Institute in Cincinnati within the next year or two and study toward my Ph.D. in non-profit organization. Union's program features 5- and 10-day intensive seminars rather than courses throughout the week, allowing for the flexibility I need due to my other commitments.

After spending nearly one-third of my life in prison, it is somewhat natural that my passion for the rehabilitation of the incarcerated matches my appreciation for the academic world. Obviously, my life experiences have provided me with unique insight into the thinking of the convict, both before and after release, and I use that knowledge to embellish my work in prison ministry and reform.

I began preaching in prisons while working at the Full Gospel Evangelistic Center. I had attempted to minister at a prison in North Carolina before that, but the warden recognized me and kicked me off the premises. He was angry because I had escaped under his watch and probably would have locked me up right then and there if he had had his druthers. While I was tremendously blessed by the Christians who ministered to us at Lewisburg, I have come to believe that churches must do more than hold worship services with the inmates. Such services help the inmates spiritually, but do little to prepare them to transition from incarceration to freedom. That is why when I go into penitentiaries, I hold intensive seminars and workshops over an entire weekend. I arrive on Friday night and hold a Bible study, spend all day Saturday conducting interactive classes, and then conclude with a worship service on Sunday. In the workshops, male and female inmates are taught the importance of being equipped with marketable vocational skills upon release, how to improve their spiritual life while in prison, and how to develop and formulate a feasible plan for life on the outside.

My work in prison reform is just as extensive. I have held two prison forums at Olivet, drawing more than 1,000 people who have family members in the penitentiary. The forums have featured judges, senators and high-ranking officials from the Department of Corrections and have given those in attendance the opportunity to ask questions about the prison system. My dedication and concern for this issue led Ohio's Director of Rehabilitation and Corrections to appoint me to the Council on Restorative Justice in 1999.

Because family members are greatly impacted when a loved one is incarcerated and released, I have also established a support group that addresses issues related to this phenomenon. I have learned so much from our discussions that I have been inspired to try and add to the concept of the halfway house. Instead of simply providing a bed space and access to the traditional support systems such as Alcoholics and Narcotics Anonymous, I hope to eventually institute a component that would help members of the convict's immediate family adjust to their changing situation. Such instruction is necessary because while welcoming back a loved one may sound like a natural act, it often turns ugly.

I came across a situation in my support group that illustrates that point to the maximum. A boy's father had been in prison since he was nine years old, and the youngster had come to think of himself as the man of the house. His little brothers and sisters had become dependent on him, and he was doing much to take care of his mother. Rather than overwhelm him, his increased responsibility drove him to work harder, leading him to become a straight-A student in high school. But when the father was released from the penitentiary, everything changed. The father immediately took charge of the household, stripping the son of the leadership role he had come to cherish. The youngster rebelled against this relative stranger who had usurped his position in the home, got involved in gangs and ended up getting killed. That is obviously an extreme, but less tragic cases occur on a consistent basis.

Another prison-related aspiration I have is to develop a job-training program in which businessmen in the community would unite to create entrepreneurial opportunities for men and women coming out of prison; everything from landscaping to construction to plumbing. I also would like to work with a local lending institution to establish an 18-month program that provides financial, practical and spiritual training for ex-convicts. I, along with an appointed staff, would handle the practical and spiritual teaching, while the banks would help the ex-convicts move toward home ownership upon their completion of the program.

I am working with Cuyahoga County on the creation of a similar program entitled "Welfare to Work to Wholeness" that will allow people to move from the welfare roll to home ownership in 18 months. Participants will attend specialized classes and quarterly retreats with the banks and be subject to monthly evaluations of their credit and job situation. If this program is instituted, those who complete the training will be assured of receiving the financial assistance necessary to purchase a home.

While these aims are high indeed, they pale in comparison to my ultimate goal: the establishment of an inner-city development project that would provide services, educational opportunities and vocational training to young and old members of the surrounding community. In a campus setting, this complex would feature The Redirection of Young Minds Academy, an accredited school that would provide its students with hands-on training in print and broadcast journalism, as well as the standard core curriculum; an assisted living facility for senior citizens; a hotel that would encompass a management training program; and an amphitheater, indoor theater complex and gymnasium.

Through my work as a consultant, I met an investment broker who secured the funding necessary to move my inner-city development project from a dream to a reality. So, just months before the publication of this autobiography, I thought the ground for my project would be broken in East Cleveland, Ohio. Unfortunately, I did not receive the land on which I proposed to build the complex. Of course, perseverance is one of my greatest qualities, so I will press on.

Clearly, I have tremendous ambitions and I believe my propensity to think big is rooted in the miracles God has already wrought in my life. I could very easily be in prison right now and I am aware that it is only God's grace and deliverance that enables me to enjoy the freedom that most Americans take for granted. That being the case, I put nothing past the Lord, for He has shown me time and time again how He can turn perceived impossibilities into incredible realities. I also know that the Bible says "to whom much is given, much will be required," which is why I have dedicated my life to helping others. Each morning when I awake surrounded by a loving family instead of iron bars, I am reminded of the wonders the Lord has worked in my life, of the fact that the decision I made for Jesus Christ in 1979 has afforded me much more than I ever could have imagined. Everything I have lost - from freedom to financial prosperity to love – has been restored.

When I met Jacquelyn Ragin Olds in the Masters Degree program at Case Western Reserve in 1995, I did not know she would later become one of the greatest gifts God has given me. Though I was married at the time, Jacqui made an immediate impression on me by delivering an intriguing introductory statement to the class. Everyone had been asked to stand up and introduce themselves, and when Jacqui's turn arrived, she described herself as being "happily divorced." Years later after I was divorced, I thumbed through the class directory, found her phone number and called to ask, "How do you become happily divorced?" We began interacting from there, and with the help of her young daughters, Brittney and Drema, our relationship blossomed.

215

I first met the girls when Jacqui invited me to her house for dinner. After an enjoyable evening, I headed for the door only to be summoned back by Drema, who at the time was 6 years old. To Jacqui's embarrassment, Drema shouted with conviction, "No! Stay and marry Mama." Moments later, before the unease left Jacqui's face, Brittney, who was 8, said to her mother, "Kiss him or something." I always tease Jacqui about that night, saying, "How much did you pay them to say that?"

Jacqui and I dated for about a year before getting married on August 1, 1998. She had been divorced for roughly four years and like me, wanted to make sure this time. She is a Christian and serves as the associate director of planned giving for the United Church of Christ, which is headquartered in Cleveland. We obviously have a lot in common since we both work for churches and have worked and studied extensively in the non-profit arena. She and I are intellectually compatible, which is a nice trait to have in a spouse. Jacqui is fully aware of my past and thankfully, does not have a problem with it. She is amazed by how far God has brought me and views it as evidence of His power to transform the hearts and lives of individuals.

I am enjoying the adventure of living with children for the first time in my life, and a new twist was added in the year 2000 when, with a daughter nearing 30 and a granddaughter in elementary school, I became a father again. On April 11 at 1:15 a.m., Jacqui gave birth to our precious baby girl, Madison Marie Ida Olds. I cut the umbilical cord and found it to be one of the most powerful experiences of my life. As I was literally releasing my child into the world, I was reminded of the awesome responsibility that God has bestowed upon me. I considered the charge I have to prepare my daughter for the world and also the duty I have to try and make the world a better place for her to live in.

I am ready. Though I will always be a bit older than the average parent – I often joke that I'll be going to PTA meetings until I'm 65 - I can't wait to do the dad stuff that I missed out on with Lashon. It's as if God is giving those years back to me.

I actually feel that way about my entire life. Obviously, I regret the criminal acts I committed, feeling most sorry and indebted to the people and families that I victimized. But in regards to myself, I do not look back in anguish or feel like I blew the prime years of my life. I believe everything I have experienced has contributed to my becoming the husband, father, minister and community leader that I am. My past has prepared me to become the person God needs me to be. I have learned not to focus on what I failed to achieve in my earlier days because God has greater goals for me to attain in the future. So, at 50 years of age, I feel like a young go-getter who is on the brink of success. In fact, that is my prayer: "God, make a success out of my life. I made a mess, now You make a success."

ABOUT THE MAN

Over the past decade, the Reverend Mark C. Olds has evolved into a bright new voice of leadership in the African American community of Cleveland, Ohio. His emergence has been spurred by a unique and multifaceted approach to ministry that has gained him respect and influence in the church, the academic community and the prison industry.

One of Reverend Olds' most inspiring contributions is his Redirection of Young Minds Program, a project that complements the traditional education of high-school students by giving them hands-on experience in several facets of print and broadcast journalism. Under his guidance, students have produced a radio show, a newsletter entitled *Today's Youth - Tomorrow's Leadership* and a magazine called *Voices of the Future*. In addition to providing an invaluable experience its participants, Redirection of Young Minds presents young African Americans in a positive, educated and articulate light, repudiating the many negative images that often are presented in the mainstream media.

More than an exhorter, Reverend Olds is an example of the importance and benefits of educational achievement. Well after his 40th birthday, he returned to school to earn a Master's Degree in Nonprofit Organizations from Case Western Reserve University and has since studied toward his Doctorate. Reverend Olds has put his education to good use in presiding over Community Resource Inc., a nonprofit organization he created to enhance the spiritual, cultural and educational aspects of life in African American communities. He also serves as the Executive Director of the Olivet Housing and Community Development Corporation, which is affiliated with the historic Olivet Institutional Baptist Church, where Reverend Olds formerly assisted Pastor Otis Moss Jr. Moreover, Reverend Olds' expertise in nonprofit management enables him to work as a consultant in helping faith-based organizations develop the necessary infrastructure to carry out their vision for the New Millennium.

Finally, as an ex-convict who experienced a life-changing transformation in prison, Reverend Olds has a deep and sincere passion for the incarcerated. Led by his steadfast belief in the possibility of total rehabilitation, he has developed a comprehensive prison ministry that addresses the spiritual, emotional, practical and familial issues facing convicts. His dedication, progressiveness and success in this area recently led to his being appointed to Ohio Department of Rehabilitation and Correction's Council on Restorative Justice.

A devoted husband and father, Reverend Olds lives in University Heights, Ohio with his wife, Jacquelyn, and their daughters Brittney, Drema and Madison. His daughter Lashon and granddaughter, Jasmyne, reside in Raleigh, North Carolina.